POLITICAL ADVERTISING IN WESTERN DEMOCRACIES

Parties & Candidates on Television

Edited by
Lynda Lee Kaid
Christina Holtz-Bacha

SAGE Publications
International Educational and Professional Publisher
Thousand Oaks London New Delhi

For information address:

SAGE Publications, Inc.
2455 Teller Road
Thousand Oaks, California 91320

SAGE Publications Ltd.
6 Bonhill Street
London EC2A 4PU
United Kingdom

SAGE Publications India Pvt. Ltd.
M-32 Market
Greater Kailash I
New Delhi 110 048 India

Printed in the United States of America

Library of Congress Cataloging-in-Publication Data

Main entry under title:

Political advertising in Western democracies: parties and candidates on television / edited by Lynda Lee Kaid, Christina Holtz-Bacha
p. cm.
Includes bibliographical references and index.
ISBN 0-8039-5351-8 (cl). — ISBN 0-8039-5352-6 (pbk.)
1. Television in politics. 2. Advertising, Political. I. Kaid, Lynda Lee. II. Holtz-Bacha, Christina.
JF2112.T4P65 1995
659.14′3—dc20 94-34627

95 96 97 98 99 10 9 8 7 6 5 4 3 2 1

Sage Project Editor: Susan McElroy

POLITICAL ADVERTISING IN WESTERN DEMOCRACIES

Contents

List of Tables and Figures

Acknowledgments

The editors are especially indebted to the authors whose chapter contributions make up the heart of this volume. Without their prompt and thorough responses to every request, the work could not have been completed.

Support was provided by the Political Communication Center at the University of Oklahoma and by the Sektion für Publizistik und Kommunikation at the Ruhr Universität Bochum. Lynda Lee Kaid would also like to acknowledge the support of the University of Oklahoma Office of Research (Research Council) and the College of Arts and Sciences. Some of the early work on this volume started when she was a Fulbright Scholar, and she would also like to express appreciation to the Council for International Exchange of Scholars (CIES).

Finally, the editors owe a special thanks to their spouses, Cliff A. Jones and Salah Bacha, for their support and assistance. It was more than just carrying the bags, toting the laptop computers, and driving the cars.

1. An Introduction to Parties and Candidates on Television

LYNDA LEE KAID

CHRISTINA HOLTZ-BACHA

Television's dominance in the electoral process of the United States is well known and well documented (Diamond & Bates, 1984; Roper Organization, 1987). In recent presidential campaigns it has become apparent that the most significant part of a candidate's expenditures goes to produce and buy airtime for television commercials (see Pat Devlin's discussion in Chapter 11), and researchers have demonstrated that such ads have significant voter effects (Kaid, 1981).

Although television spots have been a dominant part of U.S. elections for several decades, "American-style" television advertising has only recently gained significance in the political processes of Western European democracies (Gurevitch & Blumler, 1990). Although most European systems are basically democratic systems, there are many differences in the institutional and political systems and in the media structures. For instance, France, Germany, Italy, and Great Britain are characterized by multiparty systems, shorter campaign periods, greater emphasis on the political parties themselves, parliamentary electoral systems, and public-controlled media systems. Despite these differences there are increasing similarities among the electoral processes.

Researchers have verified that television has become a dominant force in German politics (Holtz-Bacha, 1990; Noelle-Neumann, 1978; Schoenbach, 1987) and is a major electoral information medium in France (Cayrol, 1988; Blumler, Cayrol, & Thoveron, 1978). As the role of television has increased in these and other democracies, there has been increasing interest in analyzing the role that party- or candidate-controlled television messages have in political campaigns.

The chapters in this book provide information on the political television advertising process and effects in several major Western democratic systems. In addition to focusing on the history, relevant media structures, content, and effects of such advertising, the book also provides a comparative overview and analysis of similarities and differences among the countries included.

Before examining the contributions of the individual chapters, it is important to understand the conceptualization of *political television advertising* used in the book. The term is used here to encompass all moving image programming that is designed to promote the interests of a given party or candidate. Basically, then, the term would incorporate any programming format under the control of the party or candidate and for which time is given or purchased on a broadcast (or narrowcast) outlet. In other words, the restrictive interpretation of the word *advertising* as often used in the United States to indicate the "buying" of commercial time or space is expanded here to encompass a broader concept.

This broadened concept of advertising is necessary to understand the inclusion and discussion of so many systems in which television time is basically given or provided to parties in an election year, rather than bought by candidates, as is the case in the United States. It would also include the distribution of moving image programming on new formats and through new systems, as they become available. For instance, in the United States political "spots" are now being distributed directly to voter homes on videocassettes; such political advertising is never "broadcast" at all. Computer video is also a new distribution environment.

The Impact of Media Privatization

Many of the chapters in this book make it clear that the pervasive political advertising system that is taken for granted in the United States has never been "taken to" at all by political systems in other democracies. The greatest barrier to such pervasiveness in other countries has been in the development of public, rather than private, commercial media systems. Among the countries discussed in this book, the United States stands alone in the dominance of private media outlets, allowing commercial advertising principles to be applied to the purchase of political advertising time.

However, many chapters in the book point to the growth of private media outlets throughout Western democracies. Karen Siune observes in Chapter 8 that the expansion of private television in Denmark has provided many new options for candidates/parties to buy time for local election campaigns. Such changes have affected Germany, France, Italy, and others. In Chapter 2, the editors attempt to provide an overview of these differences in both the media systems and the political systems as they relate to the types, amount, formats, and content of political advertising in each of the countries considered here. More details on each of the countries and the historical development of media system characteristics are included in individual country chapters.

Implications for Voter Exposure to Messages

Perhaps more interesting than the factual descriptions of the similarities and differences in media and political systems are the implications of these characteristics. For instance, how does the difference in the public/private media system translate to promotional opportunities and voter message exposure for candidates and parties?

In the United States it is no longer of much interest to scholars to assess whether many voters are exposed to political spot advertising; the pervasiveness is so great that in major campaigns (and not just for president) the messages probably do reach the voters, although how the messages are processed and interpreted is another matter. In other countries, the number of messages and the regularity of their broadcast is much less likely to result in complete penetration of the voting audience. In fact, until recently, little importance has been attached to the party-controlled broadcasts in many other countries. It is clear from all of the chapters in this book that very little scholarly research has addressed these advertisements in other countries, partly because their significance and effects were not taken very seriously. It is also clear that this situation is changing; more and more attention is being given to the party/candidate-controlled messages on television.

Research has begun to demonstrate that these spots reach substantial numbers of voters. For instance, Margaret Scammell and Holli Semetko indicate in Chapter 3 that Political Election Broadcasts (PEBs) in Britain have had exposure ratings of 13 million, exceeding the exposure of television evening news. One of the reasons for the increased credence given to spots and their penetration into voter consciousness is the greater coverage the spots achieve as a result of the news attention they are given. It has been well documented in the United States that news media have begun paying a great deal of attention to spots in their own coverage of campaigns (Kaid, Gobetz, Garner, Leland, & Scott, 1993). Scammell and Semetko note in Chapter 3 that this was also true for the 1992 British campaign. Akiba Cohen and Gadi Wolfsfeld in Chapter 7 observe that increased news attention is now given to party advertising in Israeli campaigns.

Consequently, one recurring theme throughout the chapters that follow is that the expansion of private media systems has generally led the way for an opening up of potential distribution of party/candidate messages to voters. There are a few exceptions. Italy, primarily as a result of new reforms in the aftermath of major political scandals, has recently taken a step back from this "opening-up" principle by barring political advertising during the month before an election campaign. Gianpietro Mazzoleni and Cynthia Roper point out in Chapter 6 that this rule was in effect for the 1994 Italian national elections. Whether such restrictions will continue in Italy or be revised is unknown at this time.

The Italian prohibition is an interesting contrast to the situation in Israel, where the news programs are forbidden to show candidates during the last weeks before an election (see Chapter 7). In Israel, then, the only voter exposure to the candidates is through party-controlled messages.

Contents and Styles of Political Advertising

One of the most interesting aspects of the comparison across countries relates to the content and style of advertising. These distinctions take many forms. Chapter 2 provides some overview of length and content restrictions that result from legal constraints in the various countries. The dictates of such regulations virtually guarantee, for instance, that French and British ads are much longer than American ads or Italian ads or even German spots.

More interesting than length differences, however, are the actual content characteristics discussed in Chapter 12. Comparisons across six countries (United States, Italy, France, Germany, Israel, and Britain) suggest some startling similarities across cultures. For instance, in all six countries broadcasts stress issues over images and concentrate more on positive than negative messages. The spots are also not particularly concerned with stressing the political party itself, lending some credence to the notion that increased "mediatization" has led to an increased emphasis on individual candidates and issues, rather than political parties.

These adaptations to modern media and political promotion, the importance of candidate image construction, have meant more difficult transitions for some political cultures than for others. The French in particular place great value on their logical/rational reasoning; issues and policy comparisons have great power for them, and they do not easily accept the notion that visual images can overshadow logical issue statements. The suspicion of visual imagery may be one reason for the detailed regulations the French place on the content of party broadcasts, as explained by Anne Johnston and Jacques Gerstlé in Chapter 4.

The broad descriptions, however, do not capture many of the individual differences among the actual contents of political broadcasts, and they say nothing about the ways in which political and social culture affect content. For instance, Americans are vociferously proud of their virtually uncensored, free expression system where restraints on political content of spots is almost unthinkable. Yet, one cringes to think of how American audiences would react to 1991 Finnish parliamentary candidates appearing in "discreetly nude" presentations, as Tom Moring describes in Chapter 10.

Effects of Political Advertising on Voters

Underlying all of the discussion of parties and candidates on television is, of course, the question of whether such broadcasts really influence voters. No one can claim an absolute answer to this question. Social scientists must always quickly qualify any answer—what kind of effects, on what types of voters, and so on? This book can offer no definitive answer either.

The evidence for effects of several kinds is strongest for American spots. Throughout the various chapters, however, it is clear that there has been relatively little research on effects questions in other countries. Kees Brants suggests that in the Netherlands (Chapter 9) no studies have been done at least partly because the parties themselves have not been particularly interested. In other countries, limited research has shown some effects for the spots among less interested, less attentive voters (see Israel, Chapter 7; Finland, Chapter 10).

In Chapter 12, the editors offer some indication that the broadcasts in Italy, France, Germany, and the United States can have similar effects on the images of political leaders. These results from experimental tests also indicate some relationship between candidate images and the emotional reactions evoked by spots.

Comparisons Across Cultures

Finally, the editors want to remind the readers of this book of the difficulties in looking at any political and media variables across cultures. Such undertakings are challenging and present many pitfalls. It is much easier to be discouraged by the differences in the trees and thus abandon all hope of seeing the big picture (the forest). Thus many researchers lament the differences in political systems and cultures, in media systems and regulations, and in television formats and productions, and conclude that it is not possible to make the kind of comparisons attempted here. In this research (particularly the efforts in Chapters 2 and 12), there is no intent to ignore these problems. They exist; they have important consequences. Neither are we content to allow these differences to crush opportunities for comparative work.

The significance of the comparative efforts here is perhaps all the more important because such efforts can point the way to new and expanding studies. The importance of such efforts on Western democratic systems is all the more important as other countries in Eastern and Central Europe, and around the world, begin their own journeys down the paths of democracy. They will look to older, established democracies as models. The descriptions and comparisons offered in this book may provide a start on the knowledge they will need.

References

Blumler, J. G., Cayrol, R., & Thoveron, G. (1978). *La télévision fait-elle l'élection? Une analyse comparative: France, Grande-Bretagne, Belgique* [Television: Does it make the election? A comparative analysis: France, Great Britain, Belgium]. Paris: Presses de la Fondation Nationale des Sciences Politique.

Cayrol, R. (1988). The electoral campaign and the decision-making process of French voters. In H. R. Penniman (Ed.), *France at the polls, 1981 and 1986* (pp. 130-154). Durham, NC: Duke University Press.

Diamond, E., & Bates, S. (1984). *The spot.* Cambridge: MIT Press.

Gurevitch, M., & Blumler, J. G. (1990). Comparative research: The extending frontier. In D. Swanson & D. Nimmo (Eds.), *New directions in political communication: A sourcebook* (pp. 305-325). Newbury Park, CA: Sage.

Holtz-Bacha, C. (1990). Videomalaise revisited: Media exposure and political alienation in West Germany. *European Journal of Communication, 5,* 73-85.

Kaid, L. L. (1981). Political advertising. In D. Nimmo & K. R. Sanders (Eds.), *The handbook of political communication* (pp. 249-271). Beverly Hills, CA: Sage.

Kaid, L. L., Gobetz, R., Garner, J., Leland, C., & Scott, D. (1993). Television news and presidential campaigns: The legitimization of televised political advertising. *Social Science Quarterly, 74,* 274-285.

Noelle-Neumann, E. (1978). The dual climate of opinion: The influence of television in the 1976 West German federal election. In M. Kaase & K. v. Beyme (Eds.), *Elections and parties.* Beverly Hills, CA: Sage.

Roper Organization. (1987). *America's watching: Public attitude toward television.* New York: Television Information Office.

Schoenbach, K. (1987). The role of mass media in West German election campaigns. *Legislative Studies Quarterly, 12,* 173-394.

2. A Comparative Perspective on Political Advertising

Media and Political System Characteristics

CHRISTINA HOLTZ-BACHA

LYNDA LEE KAID

It has often been argued that we observe a process of Americanization in the way election campaigns are conducted in Western democracies. For example, Gurevitch and Blumler (1990) in their plea for cross-nationally comparative research conclude: "The practices and ideologies of the American political communications industry are taking hold worldwide" (p. 311). Moreover, they say, "American-style 'video-politics' seems to have emerged as something of a role model for political communicators in other liberal democracies" (Gurevitch & Blumler, 1990, p. 311). Americanization of European election campaigns here stands for a gradual assimilation to the features of U.S. campaign communication practices. The central characteristics of American election campaigns are usually considered to be (1) the prevailing role of television among the different campaign channels, (2) the predomi-

AUTHORS' NOTE: Most of the information about national regulations used in this chapter was provided by the authors of the individual country chapters. The editors would like to thank the contributors for their help with this material.

nance of images instead of issues going hand in hand with a personalization in the presentation of the political process, and (3) as a consequence of increased media orientation, a professionalization of political actors in the development of their media strategies (cf. Gurevitch & Blumler, 1990). All of these factors are also thought to accompany or relate to a decline in the importance of political party structures.

The question is whether what is considered a process of Americanization may rather be a general trend of political systems in the Western world, a consequence of what Blumler has named the "modern publicity process," defined as "a competitive struggle to influence and control popular perceptions of key political events and issues through the major mass media" (Blumler, 1990, p. 103).

There are several global trends in the political systems of Western democracies that seem to speak for a general modernization of the publicity process. On the side of the electorate one can observe a decline in party identification. The voter dealignment as a decrease in long-term emotional attachment to a party is indicated by increased ticket-splitting and voter volatility. Although socio-demographic characteristics and sociocultural cleavages have traditionally been the best indicators for party preferences, new conflicts and value orientations have become influential for voting decisions. With the weakening of party ties, election campaigns have become even more important for politicians and parties hoping to win the volatile voter.

On the other side, with the restricted scope for political decisions, politicians seem less and less able to meet the expectations of the electorate. They therefore refrain from electoral promises they cannot keep and try to seek the support of voters without being limited in their own decisional autonomy. This is why political actors more and more tend to offer symbolic instead of material gratification of demands (Sarcinelli, 1986, p. 186; cf. also Edelman, 1976).

Symbolic or rhetorical politics are used to elicit the loyalty of voters and obtain legitimation for the political representatives. The important presupposition for such political success is active media management to secure the "power of definition" for the candidates and parties by determining the issue agenda and the features of candidate images themselves. The chances for getting media attention rise with the correspondance of messages to the formats of the media and the selection criteria of journalists. For this kind of active media management, political actors increasingly rely on professional consultants from the advertising and public relations industry.

One of the typical characteristics of symbolic politics is personalization, going hand in hand with the predominance of images over issues. Also widely discussed among the strategies of distraction from political problems and as a form of active agenda building are pseudo-events. Finally, slogans and value-laden rhetoric are used to distract from political problems.

Thus the Americanization of election campaigns as a "political export to 'sister democracies' " (Gurevitch & Blumler, 1990, p. 311) can also be regarded as an overarching tendency of political systems in the Western world, with the United States at the head of the trend. The temporal retardation of this development in Western Europe compared to the United States may be explained by different structures of the media systems. Although the United States has a long tradition of commercial broadcasting, most European countries did not introduce commercial stations before the 1980s. Commercial broadcasting with a multitude of stations—it is sometimes hypothesized—is more susceptible to the professionalized and image-oriented campaigns of parties and candidates. In addition, the more person-centered political system of the United States, particularly on the national level, may bring the characteristics of the modern publicity process to the forefront.

Among the different media channels, campaign political advertising, being produced by the parties or candidates themselves and thus not being "distorted" by journalistic selection, should best reflect the key features of this modern publicity process. Because television has developed as the most important medium of election campaigns—at least as far as the endeavors of politicians are concerned—this book concentrates on campaign advertising on television. In order to pursue the development of the modern publicity process, and supposing that the United States is ahead of a trend followed by other countries, an international perspective was chosen for this book.

However, even if there are similar trends in the countries represented here, any international comparison of political communication processes will have to take into consideration the differences in political structures and processes, in political culture, and in the media systems. These variables and their specific interrelations provide for a distinctive national background against which the regulations for political advertising, the role of television spots in communicator strategies, and findings about effects of political advertising have to be interpreted.

Political System Differences

The political system and the electoral system go hand in hand with the role of the parties. As far as the relevance of parties in the political system is concerned, there exists a homogenous situation in the European countries and Israel as opposed to the United States. In Europe and in Israel, parties are the dominant factors in the political process, with individual political careers being almost unthinkable without the support of a party, but the U.S. system more often allows concentration on single candidates. The different role played by the parties in the Western European countries and in Israel is mirrored in the fact that only in the United States are television ads sponsored by the candidates themselves.

However, the European countries and Israel differ to a great extent when comparing the party systems and the number of parties playing an influential role in the political process. One can distinguish countries with two-party systems (or two-party-block systems) and those with multiparty systems. As can the United States, the United Kingdom can be regarded as a two-party system (Labour/Conservative), with a third force only developing since the late 1980s but still standing very much in the shadow of the two big parties. The French political system has traditionally been dominated by two blocks, with the Socialist and Communist parties on the one side and the Gaullist party/parties on the other. The German party system until the 1970s was dominated by two big parties (Christian Democrats/Social Democrats), with a third, much smaller party (Free Democrats) helping one or the other into government through a coalition. With the establishment of the Greens and the recent success of radical parties on the Right, Germany has developed into a multiparty system. With several parties being represented in their parliaments, Italy, Finland, Denmark, and the Netherlands also can be characterized as multiparty systems. Israel, though also a multiparty system, is dominated by two big parties on the Left and on the Right (Labour/Likud).

The greater importance of the parties in the European and the Israeli political systems is clearly mirrored in the sponsorship of the television spots, as is shown in Table 2.1.

Only in the United States do the candidates themselves finance political advertising on television; in all other countries the spots are sponsored by the parties. In the Netherlands the government has subsidized party programs since the 1960s.

TABLE 2.1 Sponsorship of Spots

United States	candidate
Denmark	party
Finland	party
France	party
Germany	party
Italy	party
Netherlands	party + government
United Kingdom	party
Israel	party

The electoral systems of the countries presented in this book also differ considerably. Table 2.2 gives an overview of the electoral systems dominating in the respective countries.

The level of the race has proved to be an influential factor for the role and function of campaign ads on television. The importance of the election and the campaign itself is dependent on the role the institution voted for plays in the political process. All European states described here, as well as Israel, have parliamentary systems, with governments led by a prime minister. In contrast, in the United States the cabinet is less important. Although the U.S. president plays the decisive role in the American political process, the president in Finland, Germany, Israel, and Italy is—though the formal head of the state—confined to a representational function. The Netherlands, Denmark, and the United Kingdom are kingdoms, with queens being nominally the highest representatives of their respective countries.

Though in Israel and Germany the president is not directly elected by the people, France and the United States conduct direct elections (in the United States through the Electoral College). Early 1994 was the first time that a Finnish president was elected by the people.

Media System Differences

Besides the differences in the political systems, the specific features of the media systems should be of relevance for the formats and importance of political advertising in the different countries. This concerns the media system in general and more specifically the structure of the broadcasting system as well as the function/status of the different media for the audience. The countries represented in this book differ

TABLE 2.2 Electoral Systems

United States	majority vote
Israel	proportional representation
Denmark	proportional representation
Finland	proportional representation
France	majority vote
Germany	proportional representation
Italy	mixed
Netherlands	proportional representation
United Kingdom	majority vote

considerably in the historical development of their broadcasting systems, and this has consequences for current structures and finally for the regulations of political advertising. Although commercial broadcasting and competition among several television companies have a long tradition in the United States, such systems have only recently been introduced in most European countries. This has led to a comparably strong position of the public broadcasting sector, whereas in the United States broadcasting system public stations play rather a minor role.

Among the European countries presented here, the United Kingdom and Italy have the longest experience with commercial broadcasting. In the United Kingdom the monopoly of the public BBC was broken during the 1950s when commercial television was permitted, though left to public control. In Italy a multitude of private local broadcasting stations have sprouted since the 1970s, supplementing the public RAI. Germany opened the market for private broadcasting in the mid-1980s, which has led to a fierce competition between the public corporations ARD and ZDF on the one side and the commercial newcomers on the other. Almost simultaneously, considerable change took place in the French broadcasting system. The traditional influence of the government on broadcasting was taken back, one of the former public television channels was privatized, and commercial stations were licensed. Though Dutch television is only public, commercial programs in the Dutch language broadcast from outside the country have conquered the market. Until recently, Finnish television was exclusively public, though the TV corporation sold broadcasting time to a commercial company (Finnish MTV). Only since 1993 has this company been permitted to broadcast its own programming on Finland's third TV channel. The monopoly of Israel's public television also ended only recently, when the second channel was given to private companies. Among the coun-

TABLE 2.3 Where Spots Are Broadcast

United States	private
Denmark	public
Finland	private
France	public
Germany	public + private
Italy	private (until 1994)
Netherlands	public + private*
United Kingdom	public + private
Israel	public

* Private programs are broadcast from outside the country.

tries selected for this book, Denmark is the only one that has not yet allowed private broadcasting, though with the establishment of a second (public) TV channel in 1988, financing through advertising has been introduced.

Political Broadcasting Differences

The emergence of dual broadcasting systems and the commercialization process in the European countries and in Israel have on the whole led to an increase in media outlets for political advertising. Table 2.3 shows whether spots are carried on public and/or private TV channels in each country.

In the United States advertising of any kind was always confined to the commercial stations, and so was political advertising. Most European countries that have already opened the market for private broadcasting also permit political advertising on the new channels. Only France does not allow spots on the private programs. In Germany, in the Netherlands, and in the United Kingdom ads are broadcast on both the public and the private channels. In Israel, private television was only introduced recently, and it remains unclear whether it will carry political ads during the next parliamentary election campaign. Finnish public broadcasting did not have any advertising, except for the time sold to the commercial company (MTV), which moved to its own channel in 1993. In Italy campaign ads were broadcast by the private stations until a new law was passed in 1993, prohibiting TV spots during the last 4 weeks before the election date.

TABLE 2.4 Method of Political Broadcast Allocation

United States	free purchase
Denmark	equal time for all parties
Finland	free purchase
France	according to proportion of votes
Germany	according to proportion of votes
Italy	free purchase (until 1994)
Netherlands	equal time for all parties
United Kingdom	equal time for the two main parties; smaller parties according to certain criteria
Israel	according to proportion of vote; 10-minute minimum for new parties

However, commercialization of broadcasting in Europe and in Israel has not always led to open access for the parties to political advertising. Only Finland, where political ads are exclusively broadcast on the private television channel, has allowed free purchase of advertising time. This was also the situation in Italy until the new law banned spots from the "hot" campaign phase. The other countries keep allocation of broadcast time under control through regulations that either give all parties equal time or allot graded time according to proportion of votes. The private television channels in the Netherlands will probably make advertising time available through free purchase. Because they broadcast from Luxembourg, Dutch allocation rules are not effective for these private channels. Table 2.4 gives an overview of the different allocation methods for political advertising.

As a consequence of controlled allocation of broadcast time, the number of spots available for the parties is also limited in most countries. Only the United States and Finland, and Italy under the previous regulations, allow for an unlimited number of spots through free purchase, thus giving the bigger (richer) and already established parties an advantage over smaller competitors and newcomers. In the other countries, allocation rules limit the number of broadcasts per party.

There are considerable differences regarding the length of the party broadcasts. On the whole, free purchase of advertising time seems to lead to shorter spots. This trend is probably a consequence of the costs but might also be interpreted as an indicator of a commercialization of political advertising and an adaptation to economic advertising. In the United States and in Italy the most common length is 30 or 60 seconds; in Finland the mean spot length during the 1992 parliamentary election

TABLE 2.5 Number and Length of Political Broadcasts*

United States	unlimited	any length; mc: 30/60 seconds
Denmark	limited	10 minutes
Finland	unlimited	mc: 10-25 seconds
France	limited	mc: 1993: up to 4 minutes; 1988: 5-15 minutes
Germany	limited	2:30 minutes
Italy	unlimited (until 1992)	mc: 30/60 seconds
Netherlands	25 per year + 20 minutes extra during elections	public: 3 minutes
United Kingdom	5 per main party	5-10 minutes
Israel	limited	mc: 2-3 minutes

* Based on most common (mc) format in each country.

campaign amounted to 16 seconds. Party broadcasts in the countries with controlled allocation of time are usually longer. In Germany the length of election spots is fixed at 2.5 minutes. The most common spot length in Israel also is 2 to 3 minutes. During the French 1993 parliamentary election, campaign spots were up to 4 minutes, but broadcasts for candidates during the 1988 presidential election campaign were either 5 or 15 minutes. In the United Kingdom, broadcast time for the parties lies between 5 and 10 minutes. In Denmark, parties are also given 10 minutes each. Table 2.5 presents an overview of the regulations for amount of time available for spots, and the most common spot lengths.

The decision for or against restrictions on advertising content is a tightrope walked between a restriction of free expression of opinion and the endeavor for a moral and fair campaign. Table 2.6 gives an overview over the content restrictions in the single countries.

Most countries do not impose any restrictions on content of political advertising, thus avoiding a discussion about restricted expression of opinion. Among the countries presented here only Finland and France have limitations for the content of political advertising. In Israel, each ad is approved by the Election Commission prior to broadcasting, but only minimal restrictions on spot content are given.

In Finland the Administrative Council of the state-owned public service broadcasting company (Yle) sets the regulations for political ads. These do not allow for either negative ads attacking individuals or ads combining political advertising with other (product) advertising messages. In contrast to the other countries, France has introduced comparatively detailed restrictions for the production and contents of

TABLE 2.6 Restrictions on Content of Political Broadcasts

United States	none
Denmark	none
Finland	no attacks against individuals, no product advertising in political ads
France	detailed regulations for production and content
Germany	none
Italy	none
Netherlands	none
United Kingdom	none
Israel	ads approved by Election Commission prior to broadcasting

political broadcasts. For the 1988 presidential election campaign, spots could not use archival information without consent of those who appear in the films. Not more than 40% of a broadcast could be made up of film footage (video clips), and they were not allowed to use the flag, tricolors, or the national anthem on a soundtrack. Also, spots could not show places where candidates performed their official duties. Only one of the broadcasts could be shot outside a television studio. Moreover, film crews for the spots were required to come from a list of the French production society.

It seems as if free purchase of broadcast time is the crucial factor for the development of political advertising on television. Having to pay for advertising time obviously leads to shorter spots, which also might be seen as an indicator for commercialization in the sense of adopting the format of product advertising. In contrast, controlled allocation of time limits the variety of spot lengths and may also result in a greater conformity of the political broadcasts. Most countries represented here do not allow free purchase of broadcast time, which can be regarded as a consequence of the strong position of public broadcasting in the European countries as well as in Israel. Public control tries to limit the influence of the political system on the broadcasting system. Within publicly controlled institutions, restrictions on advertising and content are used in the different countries to more or less prevent unlimited commercialization of television and thus somehow carry on the public broadcasting tradition. This may be the greatest barrier to the adaptation of television political advertising to the features and necessities of the modern publicity process.

References

Blumler, J. G. (1990). Elections, the media and the modern publicity process. In M. Ferguson (Ed.), *Public communication. The new imperatives. Future directions for media research* (pp. 101-113). Newbury Park, CA: Sage.

Edelman, M. (1976). *Politik als Ritual. Die symbolische Funktion staatlicher Institutionen und politischen Handelns* [Politics as ritual. The symbolic function of state institutions and political actions]. Frankfurt am Main, Germany.

Gurevitch, M., & Blumler, J. G. (1990). Comparative research: The extending frontier. In D. L. Swanson & D. Nimmo (Eds.), *New directions in political communication: A resource book* (pp. 305-325). Newbury Park, CA: Sage.

Sarcinelli, U. (1986). Wahlkampfkommunikation als symbolische Politik. Überlegungen zu einer theoretischen Einordnung der Politikvermittlung im Wahlkampf [Campaign communication as symbolic politics: Thoughts on a theoretical classification of mediated politics in election campaigns]. In H-D. Klingemann & M. Kaase (Eds.), *Wahlen und politischer Prozeß. Analysen aus Anlaß der Bundestagwahl 1983* [Elections and the political process: Analyses from the 1983 German national elections] (pp. 180-200). Opladen: Westdeutscher Verlag.

3. Political Advertising on Television

The British Experience

MARGARET SCAMMELL

HOLLI A. SEMETKO

Conventional wisdom holds that television advertising plays a minor role in British general elections campaigns. Ironically, advertising was once *the* campaign on TV, in the early politics-shy days of British television. However, since the 1960s, its importance has been eclipsed by the growth in authority of TV news and current affairs and by the politicians' battle to influence the images and agenda of news programs.

Advertising's contribution is deliberately limited because paid political commercials are prohibited on television; instead, parties are rationed a small number (maximum five) of blocks of airtime for free advertising, party election broadcasts (PEBs), on all the main national channels. The PEBs are widely considered to have been in long-term decline (Harrison, 1992), partly because of the increasing independence of TV news and partly because the practice of simultaneous broadcasts on all channels was abandoned before the 1987 election. Once given a choice, viewers voted with their remote controls; on average one quarter to one third of the inherited audience turns off or switches over when a party broadcast comes on (Scammell, 1990).

Thus the main political significance of PEBs has come to be seen less in their content and more in their spin-off effect on the balance of TV news. British TV news is legally obliged to be balanced and, by convention, balance during general elections was measured by the stopwatch. Effectively, the amount of news time devoted to the three major parties was determined in proportion to the allocation of PEBs. "Stopwatch balance" has been important historically for the opposition, especially the third party.

The long-term decline of the system of PEBs is undeniable. In fact, the PEB's existing value will almost certainly diminish further as the TV audience fragments across the emerging satellite and cable channels, which are not required to broadcast PEBs. Clearly, the audience reach of each advertisement will dwindle. However, despite and rather against the long-term trend, advertising was unusually prominent in the 1992 general election. Arguably, PEBs raised a higher campaign profile than in any contest since the 1960s.

The explanation for this seeming paradox is primarily that the parties, deprived of their captive TV audience, have worked a great deal harder on their advertisements. After all, PEBs still command relatively large audiences, some 13 million in 1992, and are the *only* TV opportunities for parties to project their messages untrammelled by journalistic interference. Moreover, Labour's biopic on leader Neil Kinnock in 1987 seemed to demonstrate that a well-made PEB was capable of making an impact.[1] The major parties since 1979 have all enlivened their PEBs with the use of commercial techniques: actors, voice-overs, mood music, and more imaginative filmic techniques. The classic PEB format of the gray-suited politician speaking woodenly to a camera is still used but is less common. The influence of professional media advisers is more pronounced in both the direction and the scripts, and consequently the PEBs are moving closer to commercial-style advertising and, in the case of the Conservatives in particular, are more akin to U.S. political advertising.

A striking feature of the 1992 campaign was the way in which the parties pursued strategies to extract "news value" mileage from their ads. Labour and the Conservatives routinely held press previews of their PEBs, something pioneered by Labour in 1987 for their *Kinnock* broadcast, filmed by *Chariots of Fire* director Hugh Hudson. The involvement of big-name directors, Hudson and Mike Newell (*Four Weddings and a Funeral*) for Labour, and John Schlesinger (*Midnight Cowboy*) for the Tories, ensured both added news value and a more watchable product.

Another tactic, rare although not completely novel in Britain, came to be known as the "Benetton strategy"—the deliberate injection of close-to-the-bone emotive material, in the hope of provoking hostile reaction from rival politicians and thereby creating a news story. Most controversial was Labour's highly distinctive "Jennifer's Ear" PEB, directed by Newell, which excited a furor sufficient to dominate the TV news agenda for 3 days (Nossiter, Scammell, & Semetko, in press). Thus the parties have come to see the advertisements not merely as message vehicles but also as potential news stories and important tools for influencing the news agenda. Their efforts to draw attention to their advertising were amply assisted by the voluntary inclinations of the media, which to an unprecedented extent focused on the campaign strategies, tactics, and techniques. The unmistakably American political marketing lexicon, with its photoopportunities, sound bites, and spin doctors, became the common currency of media comment. TV news and current affairs seized upon the newfangled U.S. import of "people metering" to run special programs and features on voter reactions to the PEBs.[2] Media advisers to the politicians, almost completely anonymous before 1987, became minor celebrities on television, so frequently were they interviewed. Thus, by dint of party strategies, media interest, and the bizarre fallout from "Jennifer's Ear," advertising was far more than usually prominent in the 1992 campaign.

The general perception of a highly orchestrated, professional campaign fueled continuing concerns about the "Americanization" of British politics. Americanization, with respect to political conduct, is not a complimentary term in Britain, at least to judge by its common usage in the British press. The weekly news magazine *The Economist* captures well the popular view: "The influence of American politics is a touchy subject in Britain. A feeling has been gaining ground that British politics is being coarsened, even corrupted by the importation of American techniques."[3]

Rarely explicitly defined, Americanization is shorthand for a list of features deemed undesirable: The elevation of personality, glitz, glamour, and emotional, often negative, appeals over the promulgation of policy. Without overstating the case, examination of party advertising in 1992 lends some support to the Americanization thesis. Caution is necessary because it would be wrong to contrast the seedy present with an idealized past; there was no golden age when British campaigns were purely serious debates about policy differences. Many historical examples of "presidential" electioneering offer themselves, none more clear than the Conservatives' 1945 campaign, which was built entirely around Winston Churchill, under the slogan "Vote for *him*." Moreover, Parliament heard complaints as early as 1960 that British politics was descending into a battle between publicity agencies of Madison Avenue.[4]

Nevertheless, the evidence from 1992 suggests that the party advertisements have become increasingly hard hitting, more likely to be devoted to single themes, more personality focused, and more blatant in appeals to emotion, especially greed and fear. These general points were most clear in the victorious campaign of the Conservative party, which has moved furthest along the route to American-style political advertising and proved noticeably more willing than its rivals to wage a negative, scare campaign.

Our content analysis of the 1992 election campaign advertisements (below) reveals a pronounced contrast between the Tory PEBs and Labour's mainly positive, team-focused approach. In this, the ads faithfully reflect broader party electoral strategy. We concentrate here on the Tories, Labour, and the Liberal Democrats. Other parties also aired PEBs: the Scottish and Welsh nationalists, the Green party and, hilariously, the Natural Law party, which presented a demonstration of yogic flying. We do not attempt to offer any analysis of these.

Before moving on to an examination of advertising in the 1992 election, however, it is helpful to sketch a brief history of political advertising in the context of the British electoral and media systems.

Election Campaigns and Television: The New Monster

Until 1955, the state-owned BBC was the sole broadcaster in Britain, and at the behest of successive governments, it accepted what now seem astonishing restrictions on its political coverage. It avoided any analysis or comment on election campaigns, indeed any campaign coverage at all, except for a results program after the polling stations closed. Outside election times, the BBC was bound by the 14 Day Rule, which prohibited the reporting of any politically controversial matter in the 2 weeks preceding debate in Parliament. The rule, implemented during World War II, was carried into peacetime with virtually no dissent. "It would be a shocking thing to have the debates of Parliament forestalled on this new robot organization of television," commented Winston Churchill, expressing a sentiment shared alike by party leaders and BBC managers (Cockerell, 1988, p. 8).

Extreme caution and a high degree of deference characterized the BBC's attitude to politics in those early days. The BBC was acutely conscious of its role as a *national* broadcaster. It sought to avoid any taint of party bias or hint of interference in the parliamentary process, and as a result, noncoverage was the safest policy (Curran & Seaton, 1991).

However, BBC managers were keen to encourage politicians to make greater direct use of the airwaves. The first televised PEBs appeared during the 1951 general election, when the BBC persuaded skeptical parties to adapt long-standing radio practice to the screen. The three main parties agreed to one slot each of 15 minutes to address the national TV audience, then about 1 million households, or 5% of the population. The first broadcast demonstrated the reluctance of politicians to come to grips with the new monster. Octogenarian Liberal Lord Samuel read from a script, rarely looked at the camera, and was cut off midspeech when he inadvertently gestured the wrong signal to the producer (Cockerell, 1988, p. 10).

The period between 1955 and 1964 witnessed the flowering of the party broadcasts; they became established as a major political communications weapon and the main campaign tool on television. This was partly because the TV audience grew enormously, encouraged by the addition of a second national channel in 1955, the commercial Independent Television (ITV). By 1964, 90% of all households owned or rented a set. Party leaders also began to believe in the potential power of direct TV address to the electorate and were increasingly willing to listen to professional advice. One broadcast in particular, by Prime Minister Harold Macmillan in the 1959 election, was widely believed to have turned the campaign tide for the Tories (Cockerell, 1988, p. 74).

By 1964 (see Table 3.1) the number of PEBs had increased to five each for the Conservatives and Labour and three for the Liberals. It has been the custom ever since for both government and opposition parties each to receive five election broadcasts. The allocation for the minor parties (Liberals, nationalist Scottish and Welsh parties, Green, and others) is decided by broadcasters and parties represented on the Committee on Political Broadcasting, and has varied according to strength in Parliament, numbers of candidates, and standing in the opinion polls.

MODERNIZATION OF BRITISH CAMPAIGNS

The years 1959-1964 witnessed the general transformation of British electioneering and media along recognizably modern lines. Advertis-

TABLE 3.1 Allocation of Political Advertisements: Party Election Broadcasts 1951-1992

Year	*Party*	*No. of PEBs*
1951	Conservative	1 × 15′
BBC	Labour	1 × 15′
	Liberals	1 × 15′
1955	Conservative	1 × 30′
BBC	Labour	1 × 30′
	Liberals	1 × 15′
1959	Conservative	4 × 20′
BBC/ITV	Labour	4 × 20′
	Liberals	2 × 15′/10′
1964	Conservative	5 × 15′
BBC/ITV	Labour	5 × 15′
	Liberals	3 × 15′
1966	Conservative	5 × 15′/10′
BBC/ITV	Labour	5 × 15′/10′
	Liberals	3 × 15′/10′
1970	Conservative	5 × 10′
BBC/ITV	Labour	5 × 10′
	Liberals	3 × 10′
1974 (Feb.)	Conservative	5 × 10′
BBC/ITV	Labour	5 × 10′
	Liberals	3 × 10′
1974 (Oct.)	Conservative	5 × 10′
BBC/ITV	Labour	5 × 10′
	Liberals	4 × 10′
1979	Conservative	5 × 10′
BBC/ITV	Labour	5 × 10′
	Liberals	3 × 10′
1983	Conservative	5 × 10′
BBC/ITV	Labour	5 × 10′
	Liberals	4 × 10′
1987	Conservative	5 × 10′
BBC/ITV	Labour	5 × 10′
	Liberals	5 × 10′
1992	Conservative	5 × 10′
BBC/ITV/	Labour	5 × 10′
BSkyB	Liberals	4 × 10′

ing, the PEBs and increasingly press ads, became established parts of campaigning, along with opinion polls and daily press conferences. Campaigns became increasingly centralized and dominated by television coverage, where once they were concentrated in the constituencies, with land armies of agents and activists mobilizing voters.[5]

Television, meanwhile, had moved a long way from its self-denying ordinance of the early 1950s. The fledgling ITV deserves credit for breaking out of the straightjacket. From the moment it went on air in September, 1955, it introduced a less obsequious approach to political news: It rejected the BBC's custom of furnishing interviewees with an advance list of questions and pioneered the reporting of election campaigns, starting with a constituency by-election in 1958. Intense public interest in the Suez crisis of 1956 rendered the 14 Day Rule unsustainable and it disappeared, never to return. Under pressure of competition, the BBC began to extend its own political reporting, developed investigative current affairs programs, and by 1959 it, too, reported the election.

Despite these advances, prudence was the watchword as TV took its first tentative steps into election coverage, highly conscious of the need to report and reflect rather than interfere with the democratic process. The BBC, offered its first chance to cover a general election, "threw caution at the screen" (Cockerell, 1988, p. 68). It canceled a popular topical news program, kept politicians off its current affairs shows, and instead aired a series of hustings programs, with local audiences questioning party spokesmen. The parties were allowed to choose both the audience and the spokesmen. Because the audiences were composed entirely of party activists, the programs degenerated into such noisy clamor that it was 15 years before the parties agreed again to step into BBC studios in front of questioning voters.

The major event of contemporary campaigns, the in-depth leader interview, was totally absent from the screen. Indeed, in 1959 there were no TV interviews with either major party leader, in-depth or otherwise. However, campaign coverage gradually increased and by the next election, in 1964, studio interviews with party leaders were firmly part of the TV schedule. Yet Blumler and McQuail's (1968) seminal study of the 1964 election could still conclude that PEBs were *too* dominant in overall TV coverage. They called for abandonment of simultaneous transmissions, and they urged TV journalists to take a stronger stand in setting the political agenda, offering bolder and more challenging programs. Impartiality, they suggested, was guaranteed by the existing arrangements, but at the expense of increasing skepticism at party propaganda, boredom, and potential alienation of viewers.

TV reporting of elections continued to be corseted both by legal and conventional regulations and by its own self-censorship. Television was bound by law to be balanced and impartial, the "fairness rules." ITV also agreed voluntarily from the outset to run PEBs, and the annual series of free nonelection party advertisements (Party Political Broadcasts or PPBs), on exactly the same terms as the BBC. This both guaranteed PEBs a captive audience and had important consequences for election reporting, when the fairness rules were interpreted in a uniquely rigid way. By mutual agreement with the parties, the allocation of PEBs provided the working guidelines for appropriate balance during election campaigns. Hence both government and opposition parties had to be given equal news time and coverage in current affairs, while the Liberals could expect a share proportionate to their ration of PEBs, normally one third to four fifths. Both the news organizations and the parties monitored programs with a stopwatch to ensure that each party received its due.

This crude measure of balance was soon to become controversial, as was the allocation of PEBs to the minor parties. In practice, it meant that normal journalistic news selection criteria were sometimes superseded by the need to fill a party's time quota. Moreover, it gave parties effective power of veto; they could prevent an issue's being discussed simply by refusing to provide a spokesman for the program. Thus the interpretation of fairness, together with the practice of simultaneous transmission of PEBs, gave the parties a firm grip, if not stranglehold, over the TV agenda. Colin Seymour-Ure (1991) calls the period from 1960-1974 the "coming of age" of political broadcasting. The politicians held the whip hand, but by degrees TV broadened and emboldened its coverage, and some of the increasingly unworkable legal constraints were swept away.[6] The period from 1975 onward, Seymour-Ure labels as "TV ascendant"; the tables had turned. Where once TV adapted to the politicians and trod warily for fear of giving offense, now the politicians managed their campaigns for the cameras.

Although this is a broad-brush description of the development of political broadcasting in Britain, the politician's campaign day is now largely determined by TV news deadlines. Interviewers vie for the prize of grilling the party leaders, and it would be unthinkable for a leader to turn down such a confrontation. Television constantly attempts to find new formats to extract answers from the politicians, for example, live phone-in and studio audience programs and, occasionally, politicians questioning each other. Elements of disdain, characteristic of much American election reporting, are beginning to emerge in British reports from the campaign trail (Semetko, Nossiter, & Scammell, 1994).

However, by comparison with the unregulated broadcasters of the United States, British TV has remained relatively constrained, prudent, and deferent. The two main parties can rest assured of more or less equal treatment. The minor parties, especially the Liberals, are certain of coverage much greater than their normal nonelection helping. Normal news selection criteria have continued to be tempered with a sense of public service commitment, shared alike by the BBC and ITV (see, e.g., Blumler, Gurevitch, & Nossiter, 1989). The "tyranny of the stopwatch," as the time-based balance rule became known, survived, a little rough but still intact until the 1992 election, when ITV's national news organization, ITN, decided unilaterally to abandon it.

The Power of Advertising: Decline and Fall

It would seem that the only way was down for TV political advertising, given its initial monopoly on campaign coverage. However, the PEB's golden years were a little later, from 1959-1966, during which time the TV audience extended to nearly all the population, and television was still discovering the acceptable boundaries of election coverage.

Studies of TV and elections in this period tended to confirm an educational function, with exposure to TV associated with knowledge gain about party policies (e.g., Trenaman & McQuail, 1961). However, the studies were more concerned about exploding the prevailing myth of the power of televised persuasion, since they found no evidence to suggest that the party advertisements had altered either voters' behavior or attitudes. From this arose the new doctrine that TV may reinforce and inform but rarely converts (Harrison, 1965).

Blumler and McQuail (1968) pushed the pendulum back a little with their voter survey, which concluded that, while deep-seated attitudes remained impervious, the advertisements did affect some voters' opinions on important issues and influenced impressions of rival party competence to govern. Most significantly, they found that undecided voters relied more heavily on PEBs than on any other campaign source and that the standing of the Liberal Party improved among this group in proportion to the amount of campaign television watched.

It is significant that the viewing of party advertisements was absolutely central to these early studies, an accurate reflection of their perceived importance at the time. This soon ceased to be the case. By 1974 the PEBs amounted to no more than one tenth of the election output on any one of the by then three national channels (Harrison, 1974). News and current affairs soon usurped the educational function ascribed to PEBs. TV became universally recognized as the most important source of national political news for a large majority of the population (Gunter & Winstone, 1993; Seymour-Ure, 1991, p. 149). Increasingly, scholars of media and politics turned their attention to TV news, its production, agenda-setting, and influence on the audience (e.g., Blumler, Gurevitch, & Nossiter, 1986, 1989; Miller, 1991; Semetko, Blumler, Gurevitch, & Weaver, 1991). In general accounts of political communications at elections, the space devoted to PEBs dwindled noticeably. In 1974, Harrison thought that PEBs still had a "special place in campaign strategy" (p. 158); by 1992, he felt they were not sufficiently important to merit the summary table he had drawn up for every previous election (Harrison, 1992, p. 174).

Not surprisingly then, recent years have not furnished advertising research of the depth and quality of the 1960s. Research over the past 10 years has been dominated by the broadcasting authorities, which has added specific questions concerning PEB-appreciation to its regular nationwide survey sample (Wober & Svennevig, 1981; Wober, Svennevig, & Gunter, 1986). These surveys have tended to reach none too flattering conclusions about party advertisements: Watching PEBs is accidental and entirely determined by the slot in the schedule; a 1979 survey found that nearly half the viewer sample found them boring; party supporters appreciate most advertisements made by their preferred party; and a 1990 survey found that (nonelection) party ads were less believable than virtually any other media source—only the notorious tabloid, the *Sun,* was less credible (Bunker, 1992).

The 1992 General Election

THE NEW MEDIA ENVIRONMENT

The Thatcher era saw fundamental changes in the broadcasting system—the growth of cable and satellite, an inquiry into the future of BBC funding, and the 1990 Broadcasting Act, which eased the public service commitments of the terrestrial commercial broadcasters. The ITV network faced unprecedented pressures to emphasize ratings amid mounting financial strains, deepening recession, and the additional squeeze on advertising revenue from satellite and cable.

In the year before the election, ITV's national news organization, ITN, reduced its staff by more than 20%—one of a number of signals that prompted concern that the new forces of deregulation and competition might damage the range and quality of political programming on the mainstream channels (Blumler & Nossiter, 1991). Another alarm bell sounded in mid-1991, when ITN announced that it would no longer be bound by the stopwatch conception of balance; newsworthiness alone would determine its bulletins. This threatened to dispatch much of the value of the PEB system at a stroke. It was particularly worrying for Labour and Liberals, who rely on television for fair coverage; in April 1992, 6 of the 11 national daily papers supported the Tories (with a combined circulation of 8.7 million), 3 backed Labour (3.6 million), and none supported the Liberal Democrats (Harrop & Scammell, 1992).

The future of PEBs themselves was also in some doubt in the debates running up to the Broadcasting Act. The commercial TV companies made clear their dislike of what they saw as guaranteed audience losers and schedule disrupters (Scammell, 1990). In the end, the obligation to transmit party political broadcasts was written into the act, putting party advertisements on a legal footing for the first time. However, the requirement applied only to the main terrestrial channels; satellite and cable were exempt.

In the event, TV news coverage of the election changed rather less than critics feared (Nossiter et al., in press). There was no wholesale abandonment of the public service responsibility, even on ITV, with its decidedly marked horserace orientation by comparison with the BBC. Of course, the full effects of open competition had not yet hit home. Table 3.2 shows that ITV was still by a great margin the biggest commercial player in the broadcast market; Rupert Murdoch's BSkyB was potentially a serious threat but as yet too small to make much difference. In any case, Sky News gestured its own commitment to British traditions by volunteering to transmit the PEBs.

The allocation of the PEBs followed the usual pattern: five each for Conservative and Labour, four for the Liberal Democrats—one less than their unique moment of parity during the 1987 contest, but as much as they could expect, given their poor post-1987 showing in the polls. The broadcasters provoked a bout of party grumbling by moving the PEBs

TABLE 3.2 1992 General Election on TV: Channel Audience Shares

BBC1 (%)	*BBC2 (%)*	*ITV (%)*	*Channel 4 (%)*	*Satellite (%)*
34.9	8.9	40.5	10.9	4.8

SOURCE: BBC/Broadcasters' Audience Research Board.

from their usual slots, just before the main evening news to before 7 p.m. on ITV and about 9:50 p.m. on BBC1. The broadcasting authorities were "massively undermining" the whole process of democratic communication, exclaimed the Liberal's campaign director, Des Wilson.[7] Again, the concern seems exaggerated. The main national TV audience research body, BARB, found that the PEBs averaged 13 million viewers across BBC1 (4.7 million), ITV (7.7 million), and BBC2 (0.9 million). The combined total amounts to a sizable audience, given that the top-ranking soaps get around 19 million. It was less than in 1983, but slightly more than in 1987, when simultaneous transmission was scrapped on the main two channels.

THE CAMPAIGN: THE INCREASED PROMINENCE OF ADVERTISING

Political presentation in Britain reached a new milestone in the April 1992 General Election. This was the most professional campaign in British postwar history, in that all three main political parties adopted many of the techniques and disciplines associated with political marketing. Labour offered, after 1987, the most ostentatious example of a party remodeling its product in line with market research. The Tories ran a consciously marketing-inspired "branding" exercise to distance John Major's "caring Conservatives" from Kinnock's remarkably similar "moderate Labour." The Liberal Democrats also mounted a highly disciplined communications campaign, in total contrast to the muddled shambles of 1987 (Scammell, in press).

The trends and tactics associated with political marketing were much in evidence: Pre-campaigns (that is, before the official 4-week campaign period) were waged on all sides; advertising, especially on TV via the PEBs, became a more prominent weapon in the political communications arsenal; the corps of media experts—spin doctors, advertisers, pollsters, designers and so on—both swelled in number and seemed to increase in influence on party behavior.

However, the 1992 campaign represented an *intensification* of trends rather than a break with the past. The pattern of British electioneering had been fundamentally altered during Lady Thatcher's first campaign as Conservative leader (1979) when an advertising agency (Saatchi & Saatchi) was given overall responsibility for communications. This was a quantum leap because previously professional advertisers had been restricted to press and poster ads and slogans. PEBs, election addresses, and doorstep delivery leaflets had all been outside their remit. The Saatchi effect on TV advertising was immediate and dramatic: Politicians were used sparingly; and instead, actors, voice-overs, dramatic film footage, and mood-enhancing music became the stamp of political advertising.

Labour had caught up by 1987 with its highly-praised, although losing, communications campaign. Its novel contribution was Hugh Hudson's beautifully filmed biographical portrait of Neil Kinnock. It was the first "political bio" advertisement on British TV—Lady Thatcher had none during her 11-year reign. Labour made great, although unsubstantiated, claims for its impact upon viewers, but there was no doubt that it deeply affected Tory planning.

Shaun Woodward, the Conservative communications director, believed that Labour's presentation victory had deeply wounded the morale of Tory activists, and he was determined to avoid a repeat performance (Scammell, in press). He paid Labour the ultimate compliment of copying their 1987 formula. Film director John Schlesinger (*Midnight Cowboy*) was brought in to make two PEBs about John Major and, much as Labour with Hudson, this fact was announced with a fanfare. Harrison (1992) notes that Schlesinger's *John Major—The Journey* was previewed at the British Academy of Film and Television Arts with the pizzazz of a commercial launching. Conservative chairman Chris Patten fielded questions about artistic style and political rationale as "though he were at Cannes rather than Picadilly" (p. 174).

PARTY ADVERTISEMENTS: QUESTIONS OF STYLE

There were clear contrasts of style, both between the parties and between the advertisements made by the film directors and those made by the advertisers. Saatchi's trademark is the simple, uncluttered message, repeated often and heavily underscored with dramatic and filmic devices. This is reflected in the fact that there were fewer substantive policy issues in the Tory ads than in those of either the Liberals or Labour, and less time proportionately was devoted to them (below). Another consistent Saatchi characteristic is the limited use of politicians; in general, they prefer the documentary style with an actor's voice-over. The politician talking head is rare. Again, our content analysis demonstrates that the Tory ads were markedly less politician-dominated than the others, despite the fact that two 10-minute broadcasts were devoted entirely to John Major.

The style of some of Saatchi's ads seemed noticeably American compared to the other parties and to their own previous offerings. This was signaled early, some 2 months before the official start of the election campaign, in "Labour's tax bombshell," which was aired in January. The first 30 seconds were run almost exactly as a U.S.-type "polispot," and its use of sinister imagery and sound effects was highly reminiscent of George Bush's notorious anti-Dukakis advertisements. They repeated the dose, with different footage, during the campaign in another assault on Labour's tax plans. U.S. influence seemed confirmed in the billboard ad, "Labour's double whammy"—a piece of American slang that needed translation for British reporters.

It is far less easy to describe a Labour house style, probably because Labour used volunteer advertising experts (the Shadow Communications Agency) from a number of agencies. The most distinctive work has been carried out by the star directors. Hudson brought to PEBs, and Schlesinger and Newell followed his footsteps, the concept of the advertisement as a short film. Images meld seamlessly and artistically into one another and emerge as a whole picture, without the awkward changes of gear and style evident in most PEBs. Indeed, so aesthetically pleasing was Hudson's (and Labour's) first advertisement, that one party official grumbled, "It makes the country look so bloody marvelous, you'd think: why change the government?" (Harrison, 1992, p. 177). Commercial advertisers, even those as politically experienced as the Saatchis, are accustomed to making 30-second or 1-minute maximum pieces and seem to find the full 10-minute stretch of the PEB difficult to fill.

Thanks to another celebrity director, Mike Newell (*Four Weddings and a Funeral*), Labour produced the one genuinely groundbreaking political advertisement of the election, "Jennifer's Ear," as it became known. The shortest PEB of the campaign, at 4.5 minutes, it was a minidocumentary/drama, with child actors telling the story of two little girls requiring ear operations; one waiting in pain for nearly one year on the National Health Service, the other being treated immediately because her parents could afford to pay for private surgery. The story was told without dialogue, to a piano version of B. B. King's "Someone Really Loves You."

Clearly, the broadcast was intended to have powerful emotional appeal and shock value. Labour was reportedly delighted with Health Minister William Waldegrave's outraged reaction, which ensured that clips were repeated on national news bulletins. Matters took a bizarre turn, however, when the name of the girl, Jennifer Bennett, on whose case the fictional film was based, was leaked mysteriously to the press. Jennifer's father, a Labour supporter, claimed the advertisement was accurate; her mother and grandfather, both Tories, said it was a distortion. For 3 days TV news was dominated by the "battle of Jennifer's Ear," with claim and counterclaim from Jennifer's family, her surgeon, and the parties, while the press launched their own hunt for the mole who leaked her name.

Such shock tactics are relatively rare in Britain, although there are a few historical precedents.[8] Labour had signaled its intentions early; a full-page newspaper ad on the first day of the campaign pictured a baby girl who had died of a heart condition after her operation was canceled. The copyline contrasted cuts in the NHS with Tory tax cut "bribes" to the electorate.

The Liberal Democrats' advertisements looked like low-budget efforts, as indeed they were. The format was exactly the same for three of the four PEBs: politicians talking directly to camera intercut, with snippets of interviews with "ordinary" people in the street. The Liberals have used these formats so regularly that they are now almost distinctively Liberal style. The one exception was the final PEB, which was more of a mixture, part autobiography of the leader Paddy Ashdown, part usual formula.

PEBs: THEMES AND ISSUES

Table 3.3 shows the main subjects of the campaign advertisements and provides an accurate guide to the electoral strategies of the parties. The economy dominated the Tory broadcasts, followed by defense and security and the personal qualities of John Major. Labour's agenda was dominated by the social welfare issues, although the economy featured strongly. It was nearly equal first, trailing health by a matter of seconds.

TABLE 3.3 General Election 1992: Top Issues in Party Election Broadcasts

	Conservatives	*Labour*	*Liberal Democrats*
1	economy	health	education
2	defense	economy	hung Parliament
3	leader's qualities	education	economy
4	education	poverty/social justice	leader's qualities
5	health	welfare	constitutional reform
Total seconds	866	1,153	934
% of total PEB time	34.8	44.5	40.7

Within the broad category of the economy, tax was the single largest issue for both parties. This is not at all surprising for the Conservatives, but one might have expected Labour to make more of unemployment, which was perceived as a major national problem. The Liberals' agenda, with its strong emphasis on education, coalition government, and constitutional reform, was the most distinctive of the three.

The advertisements can be said to have performed an informative function, providing a fair guide to the programs of Labour and the Liberals, in particular. Both made clear their commitment to spending programs for health, education, industrial investment, training, and so on, and both admitted the need for some tax increase to pay for it. The Tories were less explicit about their own proposals. They tended to talk about their record in government rather than their future plans, or in generalities about the future, often framed in terms of Major's personal vision. A reasonably attentive viewer of the five Conservative PEBs would have learned that the Tories' priorities were to keep tax and inflation down, and national defense strong; Major also made clear his personal commitment to the continuance of the NHS. However, overall the Tories devoted significantly less time to the substantive issues than the other parties (Table 3.3). If one removes "leaders' personal qualities," then the contrast is starker still: just 29.8% of total Tory advertising time, compared to Labour's 44.5%.

FOCUS ON THE LEADERS

The Tories ran a consciously presidential campaign around John Major. The prime minister's visage beamed from the hoardings and the

TABLE 3.4 General Election 1992: Prominence of Leaders in PEBs

	Conservative (%)	*Labour (%)*	*Liberal Democrats (%)*
Leader	81.3	29.2	60.0
Other party spokesman	18.6	70.7	39.9
Leader (% of total PEB time)	35.3	14.8	44.1
All spokesmen (% of total PEB time)	43.4	50.7	73.6

party manifesto cover, and dominated the PEBs. This was a marked contrast to Lady Thatcher, who was never pictured in Tory press and poster advertisements, nor on the manifesto cover, and rarely appeared in PEBs. In 1983 she had vetoed a biopic PEB because she feared it would be too presidential (Scammell, in press). In 1992, two of the five TV advertisements were solely concerned with Major, his background, beliefs, and leadership qualities. Schlesinger's *Major—The Journey*, which featured Major returning to his childhood roots of working-class, multicultural Brixton, was only the second biographical political advertisement shown on British TV—Hudson's *Kinnock* was the first.

The Tories' personalization of the campaign is shown clearly in Table 3.4, which compares speaking appearances of the leaders and other party spokespersons. If anything, 81.3% underestimates Major's domination. The last ad of the campaign, for instance, was essentially an endorsement of Major and featured cabinet colleagues offering fulsome praise of his various statesmanlike and down-to-earth qualities. Two ads also provided a starring, nonspeaking role for Major, as he was shown in a series of successful scenarios, for example, greeting the troops in the Gulf and shaking hands with world leaders, to the tune of the Tory campaign theme, Purcell's Rondeau from *Abdelazer*, arranged by Andrew Lloyd-Webber.

By contrast, Labour's ads were much less leader-focused, the emphasis being on the team rather than Kinnock, who took less than one third of the total party spokesman speaking time. John Smith, Labour's future leader and then popular shadow chancellor, had almost as great a speaking part as Kinnock. Emphasis on Kinnock's personal qualities accounted for no more than 1 minute total, and this came in Hudson's final broadcast, essentially a celebrity endorsement of Labour and its leader, to music provided by the chart-topping Liverpool group, The Farm.

This represented a marked change of approach from the 1987 election, when the *Kinnock* biopic was shown twice and he took the lead role in other broadcasts. It reflected changed electoral circumstances: 1987 was Kinnock's first election as leader of the Labour party; he was the fresh-faced energetic newcomer. By 1992 Kinnock was recognized as an electoral liability; Harris's exit poll suggested that he was the main reason why voters *did not* vote Labour. Labour's approach, therefore, was to promote the cabinet-in-waiting and present Kinnock as the sober, statesmanlike chairman of a talented board. Some commentators criticized Labour's campaign because it overemphasized Kinnock in an "American-style" starring role.[9] Our analysis of the advertisements suggests precisely the opposite. However, outside the shelter of advertising, it proved more difficult to control party and leader images, because the media spotlight inevitably focused on the leaders (Nossiter et al., in press).

Labour's ads stood apart in this respect, because the Liberals also waged a highly presidential campaign, capitalizing on Paddy Ashdown's telegenic personality. Ashdown totaled more speaking appearance time than Major, even though the Liberal Democrats had one less PEB (10 minutes) to play with. His appearances were all straightforward to-camera pieces, apart from the hybrid final advertisement, which contained a 4-minute autobiographical sequence. To the strains of Vivaldi, Ashdown was shown wandering through fields and campaigning energetically amid crowds of people, overlaid with his own voice telling of his military service experience, his period of unemployment, and his personal political credo and aspirations for Britain.

Table 3.4 also confirms Liberals' far greater reliance on politicians. This almost certainly reflects the Liberals' limited campaign budget as much as deliberate intention. They attempted to make a virtue of necessity, by using street interviews with supposedly ordinary voters, partly to break up the monotony of politicians' talking heads, but mainly to demonstrate the "old parties' " alienation from real people. Unfortunately the same "ordinary people" were recycled several times throughout the course of the four PEBs. The Liberals made far more extensive use than the other parties of the vox pops device; although all parties used it to some degree, both as endorsements for their own side and also as a means of attacking rivals.

TABLE 3.5 Balance of Promotional and Attacking Content

	Conservative	*Labour* (*% of total advertising time*)	*Liberal Democrats*
Promote	57.5	64.7	65.8
Attack	23.3	12.8	17.2

ATTACK POLITICS: THE ADVERTISING CONTRIBUTION

Labour, as the party of opposition and with the campaigning slogan "time for a change," might have been expected to have run the most aggressive campaign of the three. In fact, Labour's was the least negative, as is shown in Table 3.5.

We regarded material as "attacking" only where it explicitly apportioned blame or criticized the policies, competence, and/or credibility of rival parties or politicians. Labour was noticeably reluctant to attack in such a plain way. Two PEBs dealt with the economy, which might be thought prime attacking territory. But even where images of recession, derelict landscapes, and closed factories filled the screens, the emphasis tended to be on Labour's program for recovery, rather than Tory blame for the mess. In "Jennifer's Ear," Labour's most aggressive ad, the Tories were attacked explicitly for only 18 seconds.

The Conservative campaign was far more combative, with 23% of total advertising time devoted to open assault on Labour. There was a marked difference in tone between the presentation of Major, gentlemanly, tolerant, and positive, and the ads in which he did not appear, which were overwhelmingly negative. All the hostile content was packed into three PEBs, two of which earned the description "video nasty" (Harrison, 1992, p. 176). The first, echoing the "tax bombshell" ad, featured a blacksmith laboring in a dank dungeon-like workshop, fashioning three iron balls to shackle voters: "taxes," "mortgages," and "prices." An anonymous doom-laden voice (actor Robert *Jesus of Nazareth* Powell) warned that a Labour government would mean higher prices, mortgages, and an extra £1,250 tax on the average taxpayer. The second, about defense, featured a little boy and girl playing a computer war game, intercut with a series of shots from real conflicts throughout Europe and the world. The unmistakable message was that Labour, with its plans to cut the defense budget, could not be trusted with Britain's security in a still-dangerous world.

The third broadcast assailed Kinnock's credibility directly, importing the American flip-flop device, to suggest a man desperate for power and willing to change any policy to get elected. This 52-second Kinnock sequence was the only directly personal attack of any television advertisement in the campaign.

The Liberal Democrats set out to contrast their own "commonsense" approach with the divisive, confrontational stance of Conservative and Labour. In fact, their ads contained rather more attacking material than Labour. This was partly achieved, as suggested, through the mouths of "ordinary" voters, but partly also by Liberal spokespeople who routinely referred to their opponents as the "old parties." While the Liberals criticized the "old parties," their opponents did not respond in kind, at least in their advertising. Effectively, there were two different election battles: the head-to-head confrontation between Conservative and Labour fighting on much the same terrain, and the Liberal campaign, which pursued its own distinctive agenda and went its own way, largely ignored by the other two.

The 1992 Election: The Impact of Advertising

British elections are generally believed to be decided in the 4 years, rather than in the formal 4-week campaign period, before polling day. The party system is considered too strong and the campaign period too short to make much impact (Rose, 1992). However, the 1992 election was easily the closest race since 1974 and probably not clearly decided until a last-week surge to the Tories. Conservative and Labour entered the race neck and neck at 40%. Labour led most of the polls until voting day; in the end the Tories won comfortably with a 42% share of the vote, compared to Labour's 34%. Thus the campaign was of greater than usual significance and may indeed have been crucial in swinging late votes.[10]

How important was advertising within this scenario? Of course, there is very little published opinion survey data to help answer the question. Even the parties themselves do not conduct any quantitative analysis, preferring to take soundings from focus groups. We rehearsed (above) the limitations of PEBs: not trusted, generally disliked, and unreliable

TABLE 3.6 General Election of April 9, 1992

	Conservative	*Labour*	*Liberal Democrat*	*Other*	*Total*
Seats					
dissolution	367	229	22	32	650
after GE	336	271	20	24	651
Votes					
% of total	41.9	34.4	17.8	5.8	100
change (1987)%	0.4	3.6	4.8	1.6	

NOTES: Conservative majority: 21 (84 at dissolution)
Swing (Conservative to Labour): 1.9% (1.7% in 1987)
Turnout: 77.7%

sources of information. However, it would be a mistake to underrate the significance of the PEBs. The average audience rating is relatively high—at about 13 million, much higher than the main evening news. During the course of the campaign most people will see at least one PEB. They remain the *only* opportunities for exclusive party control of the airwaves, and they achieve a greater national audience than any other direct party publicity, such as newspaper ads or billboard posters.

After the election, Labour's general secretary paid a compliment to the effectiveness of the Tory campaign by conceding that "the general unease about our economic competence or general distrust of the party and its leadership all took their toll" (Butler & Kavanagh, 1992, p. 5). Trust and economic competence were precisely the thrust of the Tories' negative campaign. The issue of tax also seems to have been a significant influence on voting behavior (Sanders, 1992; Scammell, in press), and here advertising supplied the graphic image, the "tax bombshell." Exit polls seem to confirm that the Tories' negative message—"Labour will cost you more"—was more believable than Labour's attempted reassurance—"eight out of ten families will be better off with Labour."

In the Labour postmortems, the "Jennifer's Ear" PEB was singled out as a serious campaign blunder, but there is no evidence that it did serious harm at the polls. In fact, Labour scored its highest poll leads in the week following the broadcast. The PEB itself was the single most impressive advertisement of the campaign, something recognized privately by Tory campaign managers and publicly by some Tory press. But the fallout over the leak of Jennifer's name was a serious blunder. It provided the Tories and their tabloid newspaper allies with the perfect ammunition to attack Labour's and Kinnock's trustworthiness. Most important, it clouded the health issue with questions of campaign ethics, and it failed to heighten voter dissatisfaction with Tory NHS policy (Scammell, in press).

Conclusion

The system of free party advertisements on television is in long-term decline, increasingly marginalized by the battle to influence the news agenda. However, by the standards of recent elections, advertising raised an unusually high profile in 1992; even Harrison, the arch-advocate of the decline thesis, was moved to note that the PEBs "received an exceptional degree of attention" (Harrison, 1992, p. 174). Without a doubt, this was partly due to the voluntary attentions of TV news and current affairs, which to an unprecedented extent focused on the strategies, tactics, and techniques of campaign persuasion. However, it was certainly also due to the efforts of the parties themselves, making more watchable programs and devising strategies to draw attention to their advertisements. It may well be that media interest will decline slightly at the next election; the "people metering" device will have lost its novelty value, as will the parties' engagement of star film directors. It is also true that there were certain specific campaign factors that encouraged party emphasis on the packaging rather than policy. It was widely commented by the press, and recognized by the parties, that since Thatcher's resignation, there was no real ideological difference between Major's "caring Conservatives" and Kinnock's "moderate Labour." As a marketing rule of thumb, the closer the products, the more important the packaging.

The marked personalization of the Tory campaign, in particular, was also due to specific circumstances that may not be repeated next time. Major was a new leader, unsullied by the extremist taint attached to Thatcher; his conciliatory approach offered a complete change of style with his predecessor; Thatcher tended to be blamed for many of the country's ills, not Major; and, most important, he had a large popularity advantage over Kinnock. In a situation in which there was no dramatic difference between the parties, but a clearly perceived difference in the leaders, the emphasis on Major was entirely rational. Equally, it was rational for Labour not to repeat their high-praised, leader-focused advertising of 1987. Thus one would expect the degree of emphasis on the party leader to change with circumstances. However, the personalization trend is certainly on an upward curve; the political biography ad, especially, is now clearly entrenched in the British communications arsenal.

It would be overstating the case at this stage to suggest that 1992 marked the turning of the long-term tide against advertising. As long as paid advertising is banned from TV, its impact will be limited and will most likely wane further as the new satellite and cable channels take a greater chunk of the market. However, the trend for parties to both pay greater attention to their advertising and professionalize their communications does not seem likely to abate. Indeed, the more competition chips away at the public service traditions of electoral broadcasting, the less protected the parties are in election news coverage and the more important advertising will become. Paid political advertising on television is still unthinkable in Britain, so one might expect more of the strategies employed in 1992 to attract media attention; perhaps more shock tactics and close-to-the-bone emotive material.

It is likely, too, that we will see more negative advertising in future elections. In the nature of political campaigning, success is copied, and the Conservatives' negative campaign was deemed to have worked. There are no rules governing the content of party advertisements (in contrast to commercial advertisements), apart from the length and number of broadcasts. Thus parties have carte blanche to launch hostilities, restricted only by their own tastes and the tolerance of the public. The last point will continue to be a restriction on personal attacks, which are used remarkably little in Britain, even in the Tory campaign, and if not handled with care, can backfire.[11]

Is this an indication that British advertising is becoming more Americanized? To some extent the answer is "yes." Some of the techniques, and even the language, in the Conservative advertising were clearly lessons from across the Atlantic. Labour's "Jennifer's Ear" was as blatant a tug at the heartstrings as ever seen in a British election campaign. It is becoming increasingly difficult to defend PEBs on the classical grounds laid out by Blumler and McQuail (1968): "Whatever their other faults may be, British party broadcasts have not yet abandoned all pretence of appealing to the reason of the voters" (p. 283).

American techniques have been imported into Britain at least since the 1960s, when Harold Wilson studied John Kennedy's television manner. By and large, new styles and techniques have been grafted on as and how it has suited the taste of British party leaders and campaign managers. However, if the Conservatives' victorious campaign and the notorious "Jennifer's Ear" supply the models, then Britons would certainly find themselves another step down the American route.

Notes

1. Labour claimed that Kinnock's personal popularity rating rose 16 points, according to a private poll conducted immediately after the broadcast. However, over the campaign as a whole his rating rose only a few points (see Scammell, in press).

2. Channel 4's main nightly news program ran a weekly feature on the impact of the PEBs, testing the advertisements on a viewers' panel. The BBC devoted an hour-length program on its main channel to weekly "people metering."

3. *The Economist,* March 14, 1992.

4. House of Commons Debates, *Hansard* Vol. 627, Col. 788, 21 July 1960.

5. The trend toward national campaigns is exposing anomalies in statutory campaign expenditure rules. Dating from the nineteenth century, the law imposes strict limits on candidates' expenses in the constituencies but puts no ceiling at all on the now far more costly national campaigns waged by the parties' central organizations.

6. The Representation of the People Act was changed in 1969 to ease the formal obligations for equal broadcast time for candidates. The law was exposed as nonsense after the 1964 election, when a defeated Communist in the constituency of Conservative leader Sir Alec Douglas-Home brought a legal action to invalidate the result because of unequal broadcast coverage.

7. "Parties to lose peak slots for election," the *Guardian*, February 18, 1992.

8. A Tory ad in 1974, which accused Labour of imperiling democracy, provoked similar reactions, although there is no comparable content analysis of its domination of TV news (Harrison, 1974, pp. 160-161).

9. Nicholas O'Shaughnessy, author of *The Phenomenon of Political Marketing*, made exactly this point in a review of the campaign, *Independent on Sunday*, April 12, 1992.

10. The result triggered a debate about the polls: Were they wrong all along or was there a late swing to the Tories? The consensus is that a late swing played an important role. See the Interim Report of the Market Research Society Inquiry into the Performance of the Opinion Polls in the 1992 General Election, June 12, 1992.

11. The Tories' onslaught against "synthetic" Harold Wilson in 1964 was widely believed to have backfired badly.

References

Blumler, J. G., Gurevitch, M., & Nossiter, T. J. (1986). Setting the television news agenda: Campaign observation at the BBC. In I. Crewe & M. Harrop (Eds.), *Political communications: The general election campaign of 1983* (pp. 104-124). Cambridge, UK: Cambridge University Press.

Blumler, J. G., Gurevitch, M., & Nossiter, T. J. (1989). The earnest versus the determined. In I. Crewe & M. Harrop (Eds.), *Political communications: The general election campaign of 1987* (pp. 157-174). Cambridge, UK: Cambridge University Press.

Blumler, J. G., & McQuail, D. (1968). *Television in politics*. London: Faber & Faber.

Blumler, J. G., & Nossiter, T. J. (Eds.). (1991). *Broadcasting finance in transition*. Oxford: Oxford University Press.

Bunker, D. (1992). *Party political and party election broadcasts*. BBC Broadcasting Research (Briefing Note).

Butler, D., & Kavanagh, D. (Eds.). (1992). *The British general election of 1992*. Basingstoke: Macmillan.

Cockerell, M. (1988). *Live from number 10*. London: Faber & Faber.

Curran, J., & Seaton, J. (1991). *Power without responsibility* (4th ed.). London: Routledge.

Gunter, B., & Winstone, P. (1993). *Television: The public's view*. London: John Libbey.

Harrison, M. (1965). Television and radio. In D. Butler & A. King (Eds.), *The British general election of 1964* (pp. 156-184). London: Macmillan.

Harrison, M. (1974). Television and radio. In D. Butler & D. Kavanagh (Eds.), *The British general election of February 1974* (pp. 146-169). London: Macmillan.

Harrison, M. (1992). Politics on the air. In D. Butler & D. Kavanagh (Eds.), *The British general election of 1992* (pp. 155-179). London: Macmillan.

Harrop, M., & Scammell, M. (1992). A tabloid war. In D. Butler & D. Kavanagh (Eds.), *The British general election of 1992* (pp. 180-210). London: Macmillan.

Miller, W. (1991). *Media and voters*. Oxford: Clarendon Press.

Nossiter, T. J., Scammell, M., & Semetko, H. A. (in press). Old values versus news values. In I. Crewe & B. Gosschalk (Eds.), *Political communications: The general election campaign of 1992*. Cambridge, UK: Cambridge University Press.

Rose, R. (1992). Structural change or cyclical fluctuation. *Political Quarterly, 45*(4), 45-65.

Sanders, D. (1992). Why the conservative party won—Again. In A. King (Ed.), *Britain at the polls 1992* (pp. 171-222). Chatham, NJ: Chatham House.

Scammell, M. (1990). Political advertising and the broadcasting bill. *Political Quarterly, 61*(2), 200-213.

Scammell, M. (in press). *Designer politics: How elections are won*. Basingstoke: Macmillan.

Semetko, H. A., Blumler, J. G., Gurevitch, M., & Weaver, D. (1991). *The formation of campaign agendas: A comparative analysis of party and media roles in recent American and British elections*. Hillsdale, NJ: Lawrence Erlbaum.

Semetko, H. A., Nossiter, T. J., & Scammell, M. (1994). The media's coverage of the campaign. In A. Hath, J. Curtice, R. Jowell, & B. Taylor (Eds.), *Labour's last chance? The 1992 election and beyond* (pp. 25-41). Aldershot, Hampshire: Dartmouth.

Seymour-Ure, C. (1991). *The British press and broadcasting since 1945*. Oxford: Blackwell.

Trenaman, J., & McQuail, D. (1961). *Television and the political image*. London: Methuen.

Wober, J. M., & Svennevig, M. (1981). *Party political broadcasts and their use for the viewing public* [Special report]. London: Independent Broadcasting Authority, Audience Research Department.

Wober, J. M., Svennevig, M., & Gunter, B. (1986). The television audience and the 1983 general election. In I. Crewe & M. Harrop (Eds.), *Political communications: The general election campaign of 1983* (pp. 95-103). Cambridge, UK: Cambridge University Press.

4. The Role of Television Broadcasts in Promoting French Presidential Candidates

ANNE JOHNSTON

JACQUES GERSTLÉ

De Gaulle's lament: "How can you govern a country where you have 40 varieties of cheese?" imparts the importance of understanding the diversity in political parties and politics in France. To understand the role of broadcasting to promote presidential candidates, it is also important to understand the diversity of factors and history that influence the state of affairs. This chapter will explore the history and development of regulation of presidential broadcasts and the influence of those factors on the past presidential broadcasts during the 1988 elections in France.

Numerous factors can influence how French candidates construct or discuss an image or issue in their political broadcasts. Certainly, one of the factors influencing the broadcasts in 1988 was the candidates' own personal styles. However, presidential broadcasts are also influenced by the governmental regulations and restrictions put on the broadcasts,

AUTHORS' NOTE: The authors would like to thank Arati Korwar, a doctoral student in the School of Journalism and Mass Communication at the University of North Carolina, for her assistance on this project.

the conventions of the television style available, the style associated with a particular political position that the candidate holds, and the context and climate of the campaign.

The French Political System

Like many European parliamentary systems, France has both a president and a prime minister. In the French system, the president is elected through direct national election, and the prime minister is chosen as a result of parliamentary composition. The president is more than a figurehead in France, serving as the official head of state.

The presidential election is conducted every 7 years and generally involves two ballots. After an initial 4-week campaign period, all major parties field a presidential candidate in the *first ballot*. Unless a majority is received by one candidate on this first ballot (unlikely, given the diversity and multiparty system), a *second ballot* is held 2 weeks later, between the top two candidates from the first ballot.

This system obviously allows for the possibility that the president and prime minister may be from different political parties. Such a situation is called "cohabitation" by the French and was, in fact, the case at the time of the 1988 election when François Mitterrand (Socialist party) was the incumbent president and Jacques Chirac (conservative RPR party) was prime minister.

French Election Broadcast Regulation

Prior to the 1988 presidential elections, the regulation of broadcasting had gone through several changes under the various governments, with tradition emphasizing the public service and cultural aspects of broadcasts. Before the deregulation of broadcasting, broadcast stations were owned and programmed by government institutions and were typically seen as being used by the government in power for their benefit. De Gaulle, in particular, had used television during the 1960s to "widen and continue the bases of his charismatic relationship with the masses" (Ehrmann, 1983, p. 144). Most observers considered De Gaulle very adept at using the medium to this end, to the point that his regime was sometimes spoken of in terms of a "telecracy" (Ehrmann, 1983).

In the 1970s, there was some attempt at broadcasting reform in France. The government, however, still maintained a role in the financial arrangements of stations by fixing the cost of licenses and, therefore, the revenue that the stations could bring in. Seventy percent of total income for stations was typically from the license revenue (Kuhn, 1980). For two television companies, TF1 and A2, the license revenue was not the principal source of income; these companies brought in commercial advertising. Also fixed by the government was the amount that program companies could give to broadcasting companies in return for their services (Kuhn, 1980). In addition to controlling financial aspects of broadcasting, government exercises control over broadcast services by making appointments to key posts in stations and companies.

This early public service model of broadcasting in France changed in the 1980s, with the adoption by Western European countries of guidelines that moved the countries toward an economic or a market model of broadcasting. The move toward the economic model was due primarily to the technological innovations made in broadcasting, as well as the desire to break the partisan hold on broadcasting (Dyson & Humphreys, 1986; Hoffmann-Riem, 1986). In the market model, the emphasis is on broadcasting's ability to provide a variety of programming for the audience, and state interference becomes less desirable and is seen as intrusive (Hoffmann-Riem, 1986).

During the 1980s Mitterrand's Socialist government in France continued the attempts to break with the tradition of political control of broadcasting. The government began to break up public service monopolies and move toward deregulation, but in a controlled fashion (Dyson & Humphreys, 1988, 1989; Hoffmann-Riem, 1986). The Socialists felt they had not benefitted and, in fact, had suffered from the Gaullist use of the broadcasts for partisan ends, because previous governments in power had used the broadcasts to denigrate their opposition and enhance their own political positions. The Mitterrand government in 1982 announced true decentralization of information and attempted to eliminate some of the government control in broadcasting (Ehrmann, 1983).

Before this push toward deregulation in France, freedom of communication was seen not as an emphasis on freedom to provide broadcast services but rather as "the political and cultural freedom of individuals to pursue self-fulfillment and truth" (Hoffmann-Riem, 1986, p. 129). The new concept of broadcasting freedom in France emphasized providing services and bringing in new programming. This new definition resulted in attempts to privatize radio and television stations in France, and in the passing of two significant laws to govern this freedom: the Law on Audiovisual Communication of 1982 and the Law of the Freedom of Communication of 1986 (Dyson & Humphreys, 1989).

As mentioned before, this decentralization and deregulation by the Socialist government was controlled. It was designed to liberate broadcasting from political pressures, introduce new technologies, increase consumer choice, support decentralization, and find programming for French broadcasts (Dyson & Humphreys, 1989), but it was sometimes considered contradictory. Although this liberalization was going on, there were still restrictions set up to preserve and promote French culture and cultural production, and the policies set by the government continued to encourage public service and cultural programs (Dyson & Humphreys, 1986). To this end, commissions were set up to regulate what was being done in the broadcasts. The CNCL, the National Commission for Communications and Liberties, was the central organization for this after 1988. Prior to January 1988, the CNCCP, or Commission Nationale de Controle de la Campagne Presidentielle, had regulated presidential broadcasts. According to Gerstlé (1991), some problems of jurisdiction arose when CNCL replaced CNCCP. In 1988 CNCL replaced the former commission for all election communication (television and radio) functions; however, CNCCP retained its power to regulate print communication and to protect the equal treatment of candidates (Gerstlé, 1991).

It was the CNCL, however, that regulated the French political broadcasts during the 1988 presidential elections, setting guidelines, making recommendations, and investigating and reporting on violations of these regulations. For the 1988 French presidential elections, French television was overwhelmingly privatized. Viewers had the choice of watching the broadcasts on public channels A2 or FR3 or watching other programs, such as entertainment or American programming, on the other channels.

This deregulation resulted in several differences in guidelines for the 1988 political broadcasts from guidelines for previous campaign broadcasts. In terms of their coverage of candidates, journalists were asked to be objective and impartial, and to treat the candidates equally in terms of their coverage; and the CNCL asked that stations not present information that disfavored one candidate over another. Also, commentaries and editing of statements were to be done in an impartial way, reflecting the initial declarations of the candidates and not distorting these declarations or the writings of the candidates (Textes et documents, 1988).

Since the 1981 presidential elections, all presidential candidates have received equal access to the broadcasts, with the order of programs determined by lot (Gerstlé, 1991). Before 1981 a candidate's airtime on state channels was proportional to the votes that the candidate had received during the last presidential election (Textes et documents, 1988). In addition, there were (and continue to be) regulations requiring public broadcast stations to carry the official radio and television broadcasts for the presidential and legislative elections, though private television was not required to offer airtime to candidates (Gerstlé, 1991).

In national elections since 1981, the actual amount of time given to presidential candidates has varied, sometimes depending upon the number of candidates in the race. Although a decree issued in March 1964 gave each candidate 2 hours of television and 2 hours of radio time, the allotment was reduced if there were numerous candidates running, such as in 1981 when the CNCCP restricted each of the 10 first-round candidates to 70 minutes of airtime (Gerstlé, 1991). Restrictions were also developed for the 1988 national candidates (see Gerstlé, 1991, for a detailed description of past time allotment for national candidates).

CNCL established rules for the production, programming, and broadcast of official programs for the 1988 presidential campaign. According to Gerstlé (1991), there was an attempt during this presidential election to modernize the broadcasts because of the competition the broadcasts would have from shows on private television.

In 1988 CNCL also provided candidates with specific guidelines and requirements for their television and radio broadcasts. For the two rounds of the elections, candidates were given slots of time of 5-minute and 15-minute duration. Broadcasts could not use archival information without the consent of those involved. This was intended to prevent candidates from denigrating their opponents and calling into question the earlier promises of opponents (Textes et documents, 1988).

CNCL suggested that candidates use their broadcast time in any way they wanted in terms of discussion of issues. During the broadcasts, the candidates could freely express all questions concerning the election and could raise issues of importance to the public. Broadcasts were asked not to use or discuss strange or new material, particularly during the final broadcasts. CNCL asked that during the weeks of the ballot vote, candidates not use their broadcasts to bring up things that had not been discussed previously.

In candidates' discussion of issues and concerns, the CNCL offered several methods of expression to be used in the broadcasts by candidates. As described by the CNCL, candidates could make declarations in their broadcasts in which the candidate appeared alone on camera and made some statement about an issue or a concern. Another method of discussing issues in the broadcasts was for candidates to be interviewed by journalists on camera, responding to questions about stands on issues. A third format for the broadcasts was to incorporate a debate format, in which the candidate debated some issue with several other persons on camera. A final format was for candidates to include videos or music in their broadcasts. The 1988 presidential campaign was the first campaign that had allowed the inclusion of music and videos in the broadcasts. These clips were done at the discretion and cost of the candidate, but not more than 40% of the broadcast could be made up of film footage (video clips). The broadcasts and clips could not use the flag or the tricolors in any way, they could not show places where candidates performed their official duties, and they could not use the national anthem on the soundtrack. In addition, only one of the spots could be shot outside the television studio. Film crews had to be chosen from a list of filmmakers from the French production society (Societé Française de Production) (Hayward, 1989). CNCL also encouraged making the broadcasts accessible for the deaf by including subtitles, written translation, or sign language with the broadcasts (Textes et documents, 1988).

CNCL also controlled and regulated the diffusion, production, and financing of the broadcasts. In terms of the production of the broadcasts, CNCL provided the candidates with regulations on the time given to produce the broadcasts; the type of equipment that could be used to produce the broadcasts in the studios; what could be shot inside and outside the studio; and the time, date, and order that the broadcasts would appear on the state channels. For example, on May 2, 1988, Mitterrand's and then Chirac's radio broadcasts were run between 8 p.m. and 8:11 p.m. on Radio France (Textes et documents, 1988).

After the election, CNCL also reported on letters they had received about violations of these guidelines. For example, Mitterrand's clip featuring a fast-paced montage of various world leaders and symbols of French culture was said to have included the French flag and several European flags and to have featured numerous political personalities in the clip with Mitterrand. In addition, the complaint also suggested that the fast-paced nature of the video used subliminal techniques to try to persuade French voters to vote for Mitterrand. There was also a letter accusing Chirac of having more than five persons appearing in the broadcast with him. (CNCL had restricted the use of persons on stage with the candidate to four others besides the candidate) (Textes et documents, 1988).

In the climate of these regulations, the French political broadcasts provided a structured format in which candidates could present issue as well as image information to voters. Regulation of the broadcasts and clips was not, however, the only contextual factor influencing the nature of the broadcasts. Traditionally, style in political broadcasts may be influenced by several factors, including political position as either the incumbent or challenger, the specific context and climate of the campaign, and the cultural context from which the candidates developed their ads.

One aspect of cultural context that may influence the types of communication strategies used in political broadcasts or advertising is the general functions that these forms of communication serve. In France, political broadcasts in 1988, as regulated by law, were either 5-minute or 15-minute broadcasts. There are strict rules about these broadcasts and the use of clips, which tend to result in the broadcasts featuring talking heads or interview formats with the candidates. French presidential candidates typically have used these broadcasts for the in-depth discussion of issues (Haiman, 1988). In the past, other campaign formats have been used for image construction. For example, in France, political posters are pervasive and generally construct images through the combination of the candidate's picture and a slogan (Haiman, 1988). One unique difference in the 1988 election was that French candidates were able to use clips in their broadcasts. The clips ranged from 4 seconds to 3 minutes in length and were fast-paced visual representations of the candidates' past, or comments on issues. (For a detailed discussion of the clips, see Gourevitch, 1989.) The use of clips to illustrate an issue position offered the opportunity for French candidates to do some visual construction of images along with their discussion of issues.

In addition to overall functions in campaigns, broadcasts may serve specific functions depending upon the candidates' political positions. Literature on American elections has identified advantages to incumbent and challenger positions, not only in terms of political resources but also in terms of communication posturing. Several studies have shown that candidates may assume a particular strategy in line with expectations of their positions or roles, and that certain strategies appear to be better suited for either incumbents or challengers than for the other (Bennett, 1977; Erickson & Schmidt, 1982; Polsby & Wildavsky, 1980; Trent & Friedenberg, 1983).

1988 Broadcasts for Mitterrand and Chirac

Given the political contexts of and governmental restrictions on official broadcasts, how have French presidential candidates used their broadcasts to communicate with voters? In 1988 a cohabitation government between Mitterrand's Socialist party and Chirac's conservative RPR had created a unique situation in which Mitterrand functioned as president and Chirac as the prime minister. Mitterrand had been president since 1981 and, as such, was given the head of state duties of overseeing foreign policy and security. Chirac, prime minister since 1986 and leader of the government, was responsible for the day-to-day operation of the government. This situation set up some similar political positions for these French candidates running for president. Mitterrand, as president, was distanced from the domestic duties that he normally would have had (Frears, 1988). According to Frears (1988), Chirac took over domestic affairs and controlled the policy decision making. Although Mitterrand was to have domain over foreign affairs and defense, Chirac also insisted on asserting his power here and frequently relegated Mitterrand to second in command. Frears argued, however, that Mitterrand continued to hold his own in summits and negotiations with foreign dignitaries. Because of the cohabitation situation and because Mitterrand was distanced somewhat from decision making, Frears (1988) argued this resulted in a position of strength for Mitterrand. In addition, as Eatwell (1988) observed, "The French came to love their President in a way Americans had loved Dwight Eisenhower during the late 1950s. He was a sage, elderly uncle rather than politician—almost a surrogate republican monarch" (p. 463).

To explore the ways in which the candidates presented themselves and their positions, and capitalized on the climate and context of the campaign in 1988, a content analysis was done on the political broadcasts and clips for Mitterrand and Chirac. The analysis was done primarily on the political broadcasts for the candidates, but the clips (which were shorter, more visually oriented broadcasts) were included because they contributed to the nature of the broadcasts. The final sample of broadcasts comprised 10 political broadcasts each for Chirac and Mitterrand. The broadcasts were also critiqued in how the overall ads for each candidate contributed to a particular pattern or image.[1]

Because of the previously discussed regulations on the broadcasts and clips, Mitterrand's and Chirac's broadcasts were very similar in terms of their structural style and the techniques used to highlight issues of importance to the candidates. During the 1988 presidential campaign, both Mitterrand's and Chirac's broadcasts were dominated by the introspection format or by an interview format (in which the candidates were featured with a journalist asking questions or fielding questions from audience members). Forty percent of Mitterrand's broadcasts and 50% of Chirac's used the introspective format, a format in which the candidate speaks for himself or herself, reflecting on issue positions or personal feelings in the broadcast. In 1988 Mitterrand and Chirac also used "confrontation" formats (30% of broadcasts for each candidate) and staged press conferences (20% and 30%, respectively) in their broadcasts. The clips used in both candidates' broadcasts were generally all either issue dramatizations or documentaries (highlighting the background of the candidate). Issue dramatization ads, which have become increasingly popular in American elections, are ads that present an issue or issue position by telling a story or dramatizing the problem. They are predominantly visual ads, and typically the candidate does not appear in the ad itself.

Mitterrand and Chirac both used an exhortive rhetorical style exclusively in their broadcasts. The exhortive style features language that urges voters to act on a particular issue or belief. The French presidential candidates used this style, as opposed to an informative or emotional style, in their broadcasts, which called upon voters to participate and take a stand on particular issues or beliefs.

For the French candidates, only Chirac's broadcasts contained any negative attacks, all made by the candidate and focused primarily on issue stands. In general, all of the French candidates' broadcasts were seen as being issue focused, because the 5-minute and 15-minute broadcasts allowed for lengthier discussion of issues, and CNCL had expressly called upon broadcasts to be used in this fashion. Chirac's broadcasts tended to focus on the economy, foreign policy, and release of prisoners; and Mitterrand's broadcasts addressed foreign policy, women's and family issues, economic unification, and the need to move France ahead.

In many ways it was the clips that did what 30-second spots do for American candidates: They provided an image framework within which a particular issue position might be viewed. They set up a story or sequence of events, hinting at the way in which that candidate viewed a particular issue position.

Both of the French candidates' broadcasts were dominated by appeals that used evidence and presented facts to persuade voters, although Mitterrand did appeal (in his broadcasts) to the voters' belief in him as the most credible and qualified candidate to be France's president. Twenty percent of Mitterrand's broadcasts were dominated by appeals to source credibility, and 10% by appeals to emotions. The presidential challenger, Chirac, used broadcasts in which 90% were dominated by evidence and logical appeals, with emotional appeals dominant in only 10%. The clips contained within the broadcasts of both Mitterrand and Chirac provided more appeals to source credibility, emphasizing in the visuals the ability, competency, and personality of the presidential candidates.

In terms of production techniques, the candidates were also similar, because of legal constraints, with both Mitterrand and Chirac using a formal indoors setting in almost all of their broadcasts (90% and 100%, respectively) and choosing live-sound instead of sound-over techniques. In their use of speakers other than themselves, the French incumbent and challenger differed slightly only in that Mitterrand appeared by himself in 40% of his broadcasts, and in combination with another speaker in 60%. This is reversed for the challenger, Chirac, who used himself as the dominant speaker in 60% of his broadcasts, and in combination with someone else in 40%.

Mitterrand used a combination of production techniques in 90% of his broadcasts—a combination that featured candidate head-on and slides with voice-over (broadcasts and clips combined)—and used candidate head-on in the remaining 10% of his broadcasts. Chirac used the combination technique in 60% of his broadcasts, appearing alone in a candidate head-on technique in 40% of his broadcasts.

As mentioned, in almost all of the categories such as production techniques, format, and style of the ads, Chirac and Mitterrand did not differ greatly in their use of these strategies to construct their image for voters. Primarily because of the constraints put on the political broadcasts by regulations, the challenger and incumbent in France used very similar structural components in their broadcasts. However, the style of the clips and the overall image construction were different for these candidates, as was their use of strategies in their broadcasts and clips. Mitterrand differed from Chirac in his use of the traditionally incumbent strategies, such as the legitimacy of the presidential office, competency in the office, and adopting an above-the-trenches posture; and Chirac employed the challenger strategies of calling for changes, taking the offensive position on issues, and attacking the record of his opponent.

The incumbent Mitterrand presented himself as the head of a harmonious family. In his broadcasts and clips, Mitterrand was a favorite uncle for La France Unie—a united France, one filled with harmony, peace, and brotherhood for French citizens. Mitterrand successfully set himself above the politics of governmental policy making, assuming an above-the-trenches approach in his broadcasts and clips. Mitterrand used his clips and broadcasts to illustrate and emphasize his place in France's history. One clip depicted him in the middle of world leaders and events. The clip presented slides of famous French citizens and events, with Mitterrand then put into the middle of these historical events. For Mitterrand's broadcasts, then, there was a consistency in the development of the image of the presidential candidate—one who was above dirty politics; one who had experience and a record of accomplishments in leading a nation; and one who could provide, as a head of a family might, the best for all family members. He could distance himself from the day-to-day operations of the government, because the majority party in the National Assembly was not his own, and the prime minister (head of government and the leader of this majority party) was the challenger.

In his use of strategies, Chirac used typical challenger techniques and called for changes, attacked the record of his opponent, and took the offensive on issues to a greater degree than did the incumbent. Chirac attempted to project voters into a future. His slogan "Nous irons plus loin ensemble" suggested that Chirac could take France to a farther point both defensively and economically. In his broadcasts he addressed his ambitions for the future. But Chirac was the prime minister and the government official who had enacted policies. He was accountable for his duties as premier and was forced to address and answer questions about these policies in his broadcasts.

For Chirac, the image of a challenger who could provide a better future for the nation was not as successful because of past accomplishments. In order to make attacks on the incumbent, a challenger needs to be free from having to defend his or her own position or record. Given the context and political position of his challenge, Chirac could not disassociate himself from his record and accountability in his past political office. In addition, the challenger strategy of projecting voters into a future was perhaps not as effective for this challenger, because he had a present and past that could be attacked or called into question by the incumbent.

Therefore, though there were structural and technical similarities between the two candidates' broadcasts during the French presidential election as regulated by law, the political positions of the candidates allowed them to present to voters dissimilar images of their campaigns.

Following is a summary of the strategies and structures used by Mitterrand and Chirac in their broadcasts and clips during the 1988 presidential campaign:

MITTERRAND

- used introspection format
- used an exhortive rhetorical style
- no negative attacks made
- all broadcasts judged to be issue-oriented
- broadcasts dominated by logical appeals (clips—source credibility appeals)
- broadcasts dominated by appeals to issue concerns
- used a formal indoors setting
- most popular production technique was a combination of candidate head-on and slides with voice-over
- used live sound in all broadcasts
- used a combination of himself with other speakers in most broadcasts
- emphasized his competency and legitimacy
- maintained an above-the-trenches posture in broadcasts

CHIRAC

- used introspection format
- used exhortive rhetorical style

- negative attacks made in one half of broadcasts
- all attacks made by candidate himself and all focused on issue stands of opponent
- all broadcasts judged to be issue-oriented
- broadcasts dominated by logical appeals (clips—source credibility)
- broadcasts dominated by appeals to issue concerns
- used a formal indoors setting
- most popular production technique was a combination of candidate head-on and slides with voice-over (used candidate head-on only more than incumbent)
- used live sound in all broadcasts
- spoke for himself in most broadcasts
- called for changes, attacked record of opponent, and took the offensive on issues

Given the structural constraints put on French candidates, it is not surprising to find that the 1988 incumbent and challenger in France were more alike in their use of communication strategies than they were different. Particularly, regulation of broadcasts required a strict adherence to production techniques and structures to be used. What may be surprising is how differently the candidates were able to mediate their images for voters in their broadcasts, and particularly in their clips, by capitalizing on the unique political position for each that cohabitation had created. In particular, in this campaign, Mitterrand used his position as the president to the same advantage that American incumbent presidents have, to distance himself from governmental policy, to force Chirac to answer policy questions while he elevated himself above politics. As Frears (1988) argued:

> Mitterrand . . . turned relative powerlessness into an advantage. He distanced himself from the government's actions, used the prestige of the presidency's 28 years of supremacy to intervene and to address the nation when he chose and place himself "above politics" to enunciate the "higher values" of fraternity and national unity. (p. 279)

Therefore, although government regulations ensured a similar structure to the political broadcasts during the 1988 French presidential election, the unique context of the campaign enabled Mitterrand and Chirac to run dissimilar campaigns in their construction of images for voters.

Looking to the 1995 French Presidential Elections

The next presidential election in France will be held in 1995. Several factors will certainly have an influence on the use of political broadcasts during this campaign and on the candidates' use of form and style. First, the role of television in politics (in general) certainly seems secure. Personality has increasingly become important in political elections, and television has increased its status in terms of helping set the agenda of political issues for campaigns (Ehrmann & Schain, 1992). During an interview with C-Span in 1993, the deputy director of news for France 2 (one of the public TV stations in France), Alain de Chalvron, suggested that it had been difficult for politicians to accept the new relationship between media and politics. In the past, politicians have been accustomed to media being more or less controlled by government; now, media is divided from government and free to report and follow the scandals, financial activities, and campaigns of politicians (C-Span, 1993). Political broadcasts in the 1995 elections may become increasingly important under these conditions in providing candidates a controlled means of structuring image and debate aside from the news coverage.

In March 1993 the political Left in France, specifically the Socialist party, suffered heavy losses in the National Assembly. The conservative alliance of two parties from the Right, the UDF and the RPR, won a total of 476 of the 577 seats in the National Assembly. Several observers of this change in status of the government suggested that Mitterrand's Socialist party had suffered a retrospective or negative vote from the French voters (C-Span, 1993). The result of the elections also sets into place a cohabitation government similar to the one preceding the 1988 elections, featuring a prime minister from the (majority) conservative party in the National Assembly, and a Socialist president, Mitterrand. In 1995 the conservatives will have a stronger position from which to run (as challengers), and the incumbent party of the president will be in a weaker and perhaps factionalized situation. The ability to use the strengths of one's political position as incumbent or challenger may be less concrete for the 1995 presidential candidates in France than it was for Mitterrand and Chirac in 1988.

Finally, there may be different restrictions and contexts for the use of political broadcasts in the 1995 presidential election. For the 1993 legislative elections, the Conseil Superieur de l'Audiovisuel (CSA) (which took the place of the CNCL) provided recommendations for the campaign. In general the CSA suggested that past broadcasts had not aroused the interest of citizens, and therefore the official broadcasts needed to be improved and modernized. The CSA recommended that two broadcast formats be available: larger blocks of 4 minutes and smaller blocks of 1 to 3 minutes. According to CSA, the general idea behind these changes was to offer viewers and listeners more variation and more interesting broadcasts. In addition, CSA recommended abandoning the traditional evening slot for the broadcasts and suggested that the campaign broadcasts during the legislative elections be made in the early and late evening and in the afternoon.

In terms of production techniques, CSA relaxed some of the formats and styles available. Production techniques could include outside footage, elaborate graphic images, and sequences shot on stage, as well as clips. The clips however, could comprise not more than 40% of a longer broadcast (4 minutes) or 50% of a shorter broadcast (1 to 3 minutes) ("Campagne Officielle Radiotelevisee," 1993).[2]

Because of some of these innovations for the legislative elections, the broadcasts for the presidential candidates in 1995 may be very different from those used in 1988. In addition, the expectations of what the broadcasts will do and how they will function in the political campaign may be different from expectations for the 1988 broadcasts. The 1995 presidential campaign in France may further define the role of political broadcasts in promoting presidential candidates because of some of the changes in the political context of the campaign, the evolution of media's role in political campaigns in France, and the innovations in the television style available.

Notes

1. For a detailed analysis of the 1988 French and U.S. presidential ads and broadcasts, please see Johnston (1991).

2. For a critique of the television coverage of the 1993 legislative campaigns in France, please see Gerstlé (1993).

References

Bennett, W. L. (1977). The ritualistic and pragmatic bases of political campaign discourse. *Quarterly Journal of Speech, 63*, 219-238.

Campagne officielle radiotelevisée pour les legislatives: Le CSA innove. [The official radio-television campaign for the legislative elections: CSA innovations] (1993, March). *Conseil Superieur de l'Audiovisuel.*

C-Span. (1993, March 28). *The French election.*

Dyson, K., & Humphreys, P. (1986). Policies for new media in Western Europe: Deregulation of broadcasting and multimedia diversification. *West European Politics, 9*, 98-124.

Dyson, K., & Humphreys, P. (1988). Regulating change in Western Europe: From national cultural regulation to international economic statecraft. In K. Dyson & P. Humphreys with R. Negrine & J. Simon (Eds.), *Broadcasting and new media policies in Western Europe* (pp. 92-160). New York: Routledge.

Dyson, K., & Humphreys, P. (1989). Deregulating broadcasting: The West European experience. *European Journal of Political Research, 17*, 137-154.

Eatwell, R. (1988). Plus ça change? The French presidential and national assembly elections, April-June 1988. *Political Quarterly, 59*, 462-472.

Ehrmann, H. W. (1983). *Politics in France* (4th ed.). Boston: Little, Brown.

Ehrmann, H. W., & Schain, M. A. (1992). *Politics in France* (5th ed.). New York: HarperCollins.

Erickson, K. V., & Schmidt, W. V. (1982). Presidential political silence: Rhetoric and the rose garden strategy. *Southern Speech Communication Journal, 47*, 402-421.

Frears, J. (1988). The 1988 French presidential election. *Government and Opposition, 23*(3), 276-289.

Gerstlé, J. (1991). Election communication in France. In F. J. Fletcher (Ed.), *Media, elections and democracy* (Vol. 19, Royal Commission on Electoral Reform and Party Financing). Montreal: Dundurn Press.

Gerstlé, J. (1993). La campagne électorale au prisme de l'information televisée [The election campaign through the prism of television information]. In P. Habert, C. Ysmal, & P. Perrineau (Eds.), *Le vote sanction* [Retaliatory voting]. Paris: Presses de la Fondation Nationale des Sciences Politiques.

Gourevitch, J. (1989). Le clip politique. *Revue française de science politique, 39*(1), 21-32.

Haiman, F. S. (1988). A tale of two countries: Media messages of the 1988 French and American campaigns. *Political Communication Review, 13*, 1-26.

Hayward, S. (1989). Television and the presidential elections: April-May 1988. In J. Gaffney (Ed.), *The French presidential elections of 1988* (pp. 58-80). Dartmouth, Brookfield, VT: Gower.

Hoffmann-Riem, W. (1986). Law, politics and the new media: Trends in broadcasting regulation. *West European Politics, 9*, 125-146.

Johnston, A. (1991). Political broadcasts: An analysis of form, content, and style in presidential communication. In L. L. Kaid, J. Gerstlé, & K. R. Sanders (Eds.), *Mediated politics in two cultures: Presidential campaigning in the United States and France* (pp. 59-72). New York: Praeger.

Kuhn, R. (1980). Government and broadcasting in France: The resumption of normal service? *West European Politics, 3*, 203-218.

Polsby, N. W., & Wildavsky, A. (1980). *Presidential elections: Strategies of electoral politics* (5th ed.). New York: Scribner.

Textes et documents relatifs a l'élection présidentielle des 24 avril et 8 mai 1988 [Texts and documents related to the presidential election of April 24 and May 8, 1988] (rassembles par Didier Maus). (1988). Paris: La Documentation française.

Trent, J. S., & Friedenberg, R. V. (1983). *Political campaign communication: Principles and practices*. New York: Praeger.

5. Television Spots in German National Elections

Content and Effects

CHRISTINA HOLTZ-BACHA

LYNDA LEE KAID

The design of election campaigns is influenced by the political system (the legal framework, role and number of parties, importance of the institution to be elected), the present political setting (political agenda, economic situation), and the structure of the media system. Before coming to the specific issue of political advertising on television, it is the aim of this chapter to describe the political structures according to these dimensions in order to illustrate the background against which political spots occur in Germany. A short description of the German media system is given afterward, followed by discussion of specific research related to political spots in the 1990 German national election.

The Political System Background

National elections are held every 4 years to determine the representatives for the Parliament (German Bundestag), which is one (and the more important) of two legislative bodies (chambers) on the national level. National elections follow the system of a modified proportional election also called *personalized proportional election.* Each voter has two votes: With the first vote a party candidate in the constituency is elected, and the second vote is given to a party list. Given that only the bigger parties have the chance to win the constituency, the second vote is more important, especially for the smaller parties. The first vote given to a small party can be regarded as a lost vote. Since the 1960s more and more people have split their ticket, giving their first vote to one of the big parties and their second vote to a smaller party. During the campaign all parties aim to solicit the second votes. As this electoral system, even for German voters, is somewhat complicated and the term *second vote* often leads to the association of being less important, political campaign advertising is also used to explain the meaning of the two votes. Thus the voting system itself becomes an issue during the electoral campaign, particularly in its "hot" phase shortly before election day, to remind people that the second vote is more important.

The party receiving the majority of votes, or a coalition of two or more parties, nominates the chancellor, who chooses the ministers for the government. Although the president is a representative and therefore comparatively powerless position, the chancellor is the most important position in the German political system. As neither the president nor the chancellor is elected directly by the people, the Bundestag is the only institution to be directly elected on the national level.

The parties play a central role in the German political system. Their task of "participating in the formation of political opinion and political will" is laid down in the constitution. In order to be represented in Parliament, parties have to get more than 5% of the votes. Until the 1980s the German political landscape was dominated by three parties: Christian Democrats (CDU, conservative), Social Democrats (SPD), and the Free Democrats (FDP, liberal). The CDU forms a permanent coalition with the Christian Social Union (CSU), which is only represented in the southern state of Bavaria, and the CDU is only represented in the other states. The largest parties by far have always been the CDU/CSU and the SPD. The German chancellor therefore always has been a member of either one or the other party. As usually neither the CDU/CSU nor the SPD gains the absolute majority of the votes, a coalition of at least two parties is necessary to push a candidate through as chancellor and to form a government. As a coalition of the two big parties is an exception and has only existed once, the Free Democrats have played a decisive role in helping one or the other party into government. During the 1980s the Greens, as an ecological party, became more and more influential and have developed as a fourth party to be available for a coalition. Since 1982 Germany has been governed by a coalition of the CDU/CSU and the Free Democrats, with Helmut Kohl (CDU) being the chancellor.

The 1990 political setting was dominated by the German unification of October 3. The election 2 months later thus was the first parliamentary election in a unified Germany. The unification and its economic consequences were therefore the main issues of the election campaign. The campaign was comparatively short because, due to the unification, the election date was set somewhat earlier than originally planned.

The German media system until the mid-eighties was characterized by a dual system of private press and public broadcasting. In 1984 the first private broadcasting stations were built up. Thus the broadcasting sector developed into a dual system in which different functions were designated to the public and the private stations (mainly through decisions of the Federal Constitutional Court; cf. Holtz-Bacha, 1991; Kleinsteuber & Wilke, 1992). In 1990 four channels dominated the television sector: the public ARD and ZDF, and the commercial RTLplus and SAT 1.

Electoral Spots and Their Regulation

As in many other countries, in Germany party spots on television are among the most important means of campaign advertising. The spots are produced by the parties themselves. Thus they can determine the topics that they want to place on the campaign agenda. The spots also allow the parties to create the image they want to have distributed.

The spots reach a considerable audience. The former campaign manager of the Christian Democrats (CDU) Peter Radunski (1983) expects 80% of the electorate altogether to be reached by the spots during a campaign. During the campaign of the 1990 national election, the highest rating of a single spot was 20%. The market share of the channel, that is, the reach calculated on the basis of all TV sets turned on, was 45.2%. This success was due to the preceding newscast, which was the most popular among German public affairs programs at that time.

This shows the spots' dependency on the program environment. The preceding or following program on the channel determines the size of the audience for the spots: Some spectators are still tuned in, and others are already waiting for the next program. It is thus a matter of chance whether a spot is watched at all. Moreover, people usually do not know in advance which party's turn it is for the spot. So, people are caught by the spots incidentally and sometimes watch the spots of parties of which they have never heard. Even the advertisements of the small and unknown groups and parties reach an audience and attention they would never get without television.

Voters themselves assign an important role to the party broadcasts. Before the European Parliament election in 1989, 55% of the German electorate named the spots when asked where they had heard, read, or watched something about the campaign. Compared to the other campaign channels like posters, newspaper ads, and the usual radio or television programs, spots thus ranked first (Holtz-Bacha, 1990). During the campaign of the national election in 1990, 67% of the electorate said that they had watched the commercials and often found something about the election in them (Schönbach, 1992, p. 18).

However, the German legal framework as well as conventions of the broadcasting stations limit the possibilities of spot advertising. In matters of broadcasting law the judicial responsibility lies with the German states (or Länder, i.e., the 16 federal parts of Germany). Nationally binding regulations exist only as treaties of the states (cf. Holtz-Bacha, 1991). Since the establishment of the dual broadcasting system during the 1980s, each state has different laws for its regional public and private stations. In August 1991 the prime ministers of the 16 states signed the latest "Interstate Treaty on Broadcasting in Unified Germany" regulating national public and commercial radio and television. The treaty was ratified by the Parliaments and thus became law for all states. A revision of the 1987 "Interstate Treaty on Broadcasting" had become necessary after the unification in order to integrate the five East German states into the existing treaties for the broadcasting system.

In its general regulations effective for public and national private stations, the 1991 Interstate Treaty prohibits political advertising and political sponsorship. This prohibition does not affect regulations allowing parties to be given broadcasting time during election campaigns. The limitation of advertising to economic purposes was a reaction to an uncertain legal situation, which was used during the 1989 European election campaign when party spots for the first time were bought and broadcast within the commercial blocks on private television.

Most state laws on public broadcasting contain a paragraph permitting airtime to be made available to parties and political groups participating in an election campaign. On public stations airtime for the parties is free, but on private stations airtime is made available on condition of reimbursement of the stations' prime cost. This means parties are given time without having to pay the usual spot prices. Thus party advertising is regarded more as serving an informational function for the electorate than as promoting the parties' interests. However, radio and television stations are not obliged to broadcast party commercials during election campaigns. If spots are broadcast, equal opportunity holds for all parties that are registered for the upcoming election. A limitation to the parties already represented in a Parliament is not allowed. However, the Federal Constitutional Court in several cases has approved a system of graded allocation of broadcasting time, with smaller parties getting less time (fewer spots) than the larger ones.

The party spots are not part of the commercial advertising blocks. The spots, one or two at a time, are generally included directly after the evening news programs. The amount of time allotted to the parties is not specified in the regulations but is usually set at 2.5 minutes.

The political parties produce the television spots themselves and are responsible for their contents. The broadcasting stations can refuse spots only if they obviously do not contain electoral advertising, or contravene criminal law. However, the stations do not have to judge whether a spot is in accordance with the Basic Law (constitution). Equal opportunity for the parties to present their programs is the supreme rule. During recent years the equal-opportunity rule has led to problems for the broadcasting stations: In some cases they refused spots of extreme Right parties containing xenophobic propaganda. The courts always obligated the stations to broadcast the controversial spots, stressing that equal opportunity has to be given to all parties as long as these are not prohibited. In order to avoid having to broadcast the spots of the extreme Right parties during the upcoming election campaigns in 1994, some public stations in summer 1993 initiated a discussion about the spots and proposed to change the broadcasting laws in order to eliminate electoral advertising. Politicians in their own interest are reluctant to do this. Moreover, a change of laws is a long process and the change of state broadcast treaties demands an agreement of all 16 states.

Research on German Political Spots

Although spots receive high viewer exposure, very little research has been done in Germany. Discussion of legal aspects has been prevalent in publications on party broadcasts (Becker, 1990; Bornemann, 1992; Franke, 1979; Gabriel-Bräutigam, 1991). Only a few German studies have addressed questions of creation, content, formal features, or effectiveness of party spots. Dröge, Lerg, and Weißenborn (1969) presented a description of content and styles of the commercials broadcast during the 1969 parliamentary election campaign. Martin Wachtel (1988) analyzed the argumentation content of the 1987 parliamentary election spots. He determined that communicating trustworthiness and competence is the major goal of the political parties in their television spots, and that visual qualities of the commercials played an important role in communicating these qualities. Holtz-Bacha (1990) analyzed survey data on the 1989 European Parliamentary election in West Germany. Results showed that attentiveness to the spots correlated with attentiveness to other campaign channels—that is, those who noticed political advertising in one medium also noticed advertising in another medium. These data also prove that watching party commercials correlates with a positive opinion about the campaign, and also with an improvement in the attitude toward the European Community, the German membership in the EC, and the attitude toward the European Parliament. As these attitudes influence the intention to cast a ballot, party spots can be judged as affecting voting intentions indirectly. In 1992, Klein presented a long-term analysis comparing the electoral spots of the most important German parties between 1972 and 1990.

Because so little research effort has been devoted to the role of television spots in Germany, the authors designed a study with two different aims: A content analysis of the party commercials broadcast during the 1990 parliamentary election and an experimental study to determine the effectiveness of the spots. Because this was the first national election in unified Germany, this also seemed to be an interesting setting for a comparison of the potential differential effects of the commercials on viewers from West German states with those from the former East Germany. Although Eastern Germans have seen party spots for many years, because West German television programs could be received in the former GDR, 1990 was the first time the spots had any significance for them in terms of voting decisions.

The Content of the 1990 Party Spots

During the 1990 campaign, 67 spots of 21 parties were broadcast per public channel, with the two largest parties, Christian Democrats (CDU) and Social Democrats (SPD), receiving 8 spots each. Six parties, among which were the smaller partners of the then-governing coalition—the Christian Social Union (CSU) and the Free Democrats (FDP)—were allotted 4 spots each. The 13 smaller parties received 2 or 3 spots. This arrangement was made for the two national public television stations, ARD and ZDF. The commercials were identical for both stations; only the order of the spots was different. Only the CDU produced one spot to be shown several times on commercial television. Because the parties did not produce different spots for each time slot, several spots were repeated. Thus 38 different spots could be seen during the 1990 campaign. All were 2.5 minutes in length. Commercials were broadcast starting 1 month before election day, on December 2. All 38 spots served as material for the content analysis.

The spots were coded on several dimensions. As far as possible, the categories were taken from an earlier study, which analyzed spots from earlier presidential elections in the United States and in France (Johnston, 1991; Kaid & Johnston, 1991). Although some national adaptations were necessary, the German results could be brought into an intercultural comparison of political broadcasts in three countries (Holtz-Bacha, Kaid, & Johnston, 1994).

Concerning the formal features, the spots were coded for the dominant format (e.g., documentary, issue presentation, testimonial, candidate statement), for the production format (e.g., studio presentation, testimonial, candidate statement), for the production technique (e.g., studio presentation, filmed outside, trick film), and for the presence of music and use of special effects, as well as for the overall impression of being more professional or more unprofessional. In order to allow a general classification of the spots as calm or hectic, coders counted the number of scenes. A *scene* was defined as a sequence, like change of place or film technique or a cut. Spots with no change of place were counted as one scene even if the camera angle changed.

The analysis of the contents differentiated between more image-oriented and more issue-oriented spots. Topics addressed in the spots were also coded for any evaluation. Moreover, the coding instrument attempted to assess the various types of appeals made in the ad, either in terms of ethical appeals (source credibility), emotional appeals, or logical appeals; the use of fear appeals; and the content of the appeal (Joslyn, 1980) in terms of partisanship appeals and personal appeals. Strategies identified by Trent and Friedenberg (1991) as appropriate for incumbents and challengers were also included.

Because the image of candidates is also influenced by nonverbal elements of their presentation in the ads, the candidates' overall eye contact, facial expression, body movement, fluency and rate of speech, pitch, and dress were ascertained. Coding based on a detailed written coding instrument, along with a corresponding codebook, was done by trained student coders. Intercoder reliability computed using the formula suggested by Holsti (North, Holsti, Zaninovich, & Zinnes, 1963) was +.87.

RESULTS OF THE CONTENT ANALYSIS

The most popular formats used for the party spots were candidate statements (32%) and a presentation of various issues (24%). These formats were particularly used by the small parties. The CDU chose a different format for each of its three spots, which were a documentary, a presentation of various issues, and a statement by Helmut Kohl. The SPD instead concentrated on testimonials, which were used for four of the five spots. This format was not utilized by any other party.

Corresponding to the most frequently chosen format of a candidate statement, the production technique used by most spots was the studio setting with one or more candidates. Almost 50% of the smaller parties' commercials were produced in a studio setting, with some candidates talking into the camera during the entire length of the spot. The most uncommon spots were presented by the alternative (ecological) parties, using special techniques. Eight spots were filmed outdoors. Other production techniques were exercised by only a few spots.

Table 5.1 presents an overview of the results for formats and production techniques. Data are shown for all parties and then split for the parties of the governing coalition and for the SPD as the biggest opposition party. Results for the smaller parties are summed up in the last column of the table.

According to an overall classification of professionality, 16 spots were perceived as not professional. All spots of the bigger parties were coded as professional productions. So, among 26 spots of the smaller

TABLE 5.1 Format of the Spots and Production Techniques

				Parties		
	All	*CDU*	*SPD*	*CSU*	*FDP*	*Others*
	n (%)	*n*	*n*	*n*	*n*	*n*
Format						
Candidate statement	12 (32)	1	1	–	–	10
Issue presentation	9 (24)	1	–	–	–	8
Documentary	4 (10)	1	–	1	2	–
Testimonial	4 (10)	–	4	–	–	–
Staging	3 (8)	–	–	1	–	2
Issue dramatization	3 (8)	–	–	–	–	3
Video clip	2 (5)	–	–	–	–	2
Question and answer	1 (3)	–	–	–	–	1
Production technique						
Candidate in studio	14 (37)	1	1	–	–	12
Outdoor production	8 (21)	2	–	–	–	6
Slides	4 (11)	–	–	–	1	3
Special technique	3 (8)	–	–	–	–	3
"Window on the world" (live)	2 (5)	–	1	1	–	–
Other studio production	2 (5)	–	1	1	–	–
Other	5 (13)	–	2	–	1	2
n =	38	3	5	2	2	26

parties, more than half were judged as being not professional. This was mainly due to the limitation to frequently dull statements, as well as the stiff and sometimes clumsy behavior of the candidates.

The number of scenes has to be seen in relation to a fixed spot length of 2.5 minutes. The minimum number of scenes was 1, the maximum 63. There were 18 spots with 10 or fewer scenes, classified as calm. Another 12 spots contained between 11 and 30 scenes. Eight commercials, having more than 30 scenes, were judged as rather hectic presentations.

ISSUES AND APPEALS

According to the general distinction only 10 of the 38 spots were coded as issue-oriented, compared to 22 dominated by images. Six spots could not be classified. The 10 issue-dominated broadcasts were exclusively produced by the smaller parties. All CDU spots and 4 of 5 SPD

TABLE 5.2 Issues in the Party Broadcasts

	Mentioned *n (%)*	*Not Mentioned* *n (%)*
Unification	21 (55)	17 (45)
Economy, finances, taxes	20 (53)	18 (47)
Environment, climate, nuclear power	17 (45)	21 (55)
Labor market	16 (42)	22 (58)
Family	12 (32)	26 (68)
Youth, young people	11 (29)	27 (71)
Peace, maintenance of peace	11 (29)	27 (71)
Elderly, old people	9 (24)	29 (76)
Abortion	9 (24)	29 (76)
Pensions	9 (24)	29 (76)
Foreign policy	9 (24)	29 (76)
Equality for women	8 (21)	30 (79)
Foreigners in Germany, asylum	7 (18)	31 (82)
Housing	7 (18)	31 (82)
European policy	7 (18)	31 (82)
Wages, prices	6 (16)	32 (84)

spots had an image emphasis. So the two big parties, being the only ones presenting chancellor candidates, relied completely on an image-oriented design for their broadcasts. Although the spots offered the parties a chance to deal with their own issues, the classification according to their dominant content shows that the opportunity was not used. Instead of describing the parties' stands on issues, the commercials were mainly used for image advertising. A long-term study of German electoral spots has shown that since 1972, the 1990 campaign was the only one with a prevalence of image spots among the broadcasts of the five most important parties (CDU, SPD, CSU, FDP, Greens). Only a small percentage of spots was coded as image-oriented during the earlier campaigns (Klein, 1992, p. 36).

Table 5.2 shows a detailed list of topics mentioned in the party broadcasts. Unification appears at the top of the agenda. Given that the 1990 election was held only 2 months after the unification, and especially because its economic costs were widely discussed in public, it seems important to note that almost half of the spots (45%) did not mention the unification at all. The topic instead appears as an issue of the CDU, which, as majority party of the then-incumbent West German government, had been responsible for the unification process. Thus it was no surprise that the unification is a topic of all CDU spots and was only referred to positively. The SPD mentioned the topic in two of its five different spots. During the negotiations preparing for German unity, the Social Democrats, and their top candidate Oskar Lafontaine in particular, had been opposed to a quick unification. The fact that the unification in the SPD spots was not treated in a critical manner reveals the party's advertising strategy of aiming at a broad public that included East German voters.

In addition to unification, the spots' agenda contained only another four issues also regarded as the most important by the West German electorate at that time: environmental policy, labor market, foreigners in Germany, and housing (Gibowski & Kaase, 1991). In November 1990 environmental questions ranked second on the West German public's agenda. The issue was mentioned by almost half of the party spots. It was also a topic of the big parties, CDU and SPD. Although two of three CDU spots stressed the success of the party's environmental policy, four of five SPD spots mentioned the issue, three of them referring critically to environmental questions. However, this issue proved to be the main focus of SPD's criticism; no other topic was referred to in an equally negative way.

The labor market as a long-term issue, because of the comparatively high unemployment rate in Germany, ranked high on the spots' agenda as well as on the public's agenda, where it ranked third. Ranking fourth, among the problems regarded as most important by the electorate in November 1990, was the issue of foreigners in Germany, relating to both the growing influx from East European countries and more and more people from Third World countries asking for asylum in Germany. However, the issue ranked low in the party spots, and the two big parties did not mention the topic at all. Seven spots of the smaller parties mentioned the issue, five of them critically.

Housing, including scarcity of apartments as well as rising rents, also was among the six most important issues on the public agenda. Only a few party broadcasts touched the topic. One CDU spot pointed out success in that realm; four of the five SPD spots did not mention housing at all; and one SPD spot referred to the topic but without any evaluation.

One issue that appeared on the public agenda in the last months of 1990, the Gulf crisis, was not addressed in the party spots at all. The spots concentrated on internal political matters; foreign politics in general, as well as European politics, did not receive much attention. Again, only the CDU described its successful role on the international political stage; the other parties rarely touched the topic.

Like the problem of foreigners in Germany, the abortion issue was totally avoided by the CDU and SPD. This is all the more interesting because abortion was one of the decisions put off during the negotiations for the unification treaty: Abortion was legal in the former GDR but was only allowed in West Germany under very limited conditions. The Unification Treaty of 1990 had left a new law on abortion to be decided within 2 years. The issue had always been controversial between the two big parties and was also controversial within the incumbent coalition of the CDU and FDP. So, although it was clear that the new government would have to decide about a new law on abortion, the big parties left the issue completely to the smaller ones. Six of nine spots that mentioned abortion referred to the topic critically, with one group being a single-issue party arguing against any legalization of abortion.

Altogether it can be summarized that issues, if mentioned at all in the spots, were rarely referred to in a clearly critical manner. Concerning the two big parties, it is not surprising to note that the incumbent CDU tended to point out success of their policy, and the opposing SPD tended to criticism, nevertheless restrained.

Unification as a success of its policies was the main topic of the spots of the incumbent CDU. This is also underlined by the use of national symbols: All CDU spots used German national symbols, but none of the SPD broadcasts showed the flag or German national colors.

Broadcasts were also coded according to the types of appeals used in the ads, categorized as logical, emotional, or ethical (source credibility) appeals. The spots were dominated by emotional appeals. More than half of the sample used emotional appeals ($n = 20$) followed by ethical appeals ($n = 9$). Only six spots used logical appeals. In regard to the appeals made in their spots, the big parties showed some difference. Two of the three CDU spots used emotional appeals, and the third relied on source credibility. Three SPD spots were dominated by ethical appeals, one by emotional appeals, and one by logical appeals.

Negative attacks were identified for almost one third of all spots. In most cases the attacks were made by the candidates themselves. The majority of the attacks were aimed at the opponents' issue positions; only a few were made on the personal qualities of other candidates. The long-term comparison of spots from six consecutive national election campaigns has shown that the 1990 campaign was the one with the lowest percentage of negative spots (Klein, 1992, p. 58).

STRATEGIES AND CHARACTERISTICS OF THE SPOTS

Table 5.3 presents the use of strategies in the spots. American research has identified these strategies in the analysis of political campaign communication and has judged them as either more appropriate for incumbents or more appropriate for challengers (Trent & Friedenberg, 1991; Wadsworth & Kaid, 1987). Strategies in Table 5.3 are classified as either incumbent or challenger strategies. The adoption of these categories raises some difficulties because German parliamentary elections are less person-centered, and in 1990 several spots did not even present a candidate.

A comparison of the spots of the big parties therefore comes closest to the dualistic situation of presidential elections in the United States, with the CDU as the party of the incumbent chancellor and the SPD as

TABLE 5.3 Incumbent and Challenger Strategies

		Parties				
	All *n (%)*	*CDU* *n*	*SPD* *n*	*CSU* *n*	*FDP* *n*	*Other* *n*
Incumbent strategies						
Charisma and the office	15 (54)	3	3	1	2	5
Competency and the office	9 (32)	3	2	1	2	1
Above-the-trenches posture	9 (32)	2	–	1	1	4
Position of chancellor mentioned	7 (25)	3	4	–	–	–
Emphasizing accomplishments	6 (21)	3	–	1	1	1
Consulting world leaders	4 (14)	1	–	1	2	–
Using endorsements by other parties	3 (11)	1	–	–	–	2
Using endorsements by others	3 (11)	–	3	–	–	–
Challenger strategies						
Call for changes	22 (79)	–	5	1	1	15
Taking the offensive on issues	9 (32)	–	4	–	–	5
Emphasizing optimism for the future	7 (25)	3	1	1	1	1
Speaking to traditional values	6 (21)	1	–	1	1	3
Attacking record of opponent	5 (18)	–	2	–	–	3
Representing center of party	3 (19)	–	2	1	–	1
$n =$	28	3	5	1	2	17

the biggest opposition party. In addition, Table 5.3 shows the findings for the FDP and CSU, which were the smaller partners of the CDU in the then-governing, Christian-liberal coalition. The strategies were coded as to their presence or absence in the spot. Data are based on those 28 spots in which candidates were shown.

In general, incumbent strategies can be found most often in the spots of the big parties and of the smaller coalition partners, FDP and CSU. Moreover, a comparison of the findings for the two big parties shows a division of incumbent and challenger roles. The CDU relied more on the strategies appropriate for incumbents, and the SPD used more challenger strategies. The smaller parties not yet represented in Parliament instead applied only few challenger strategies.

All CDU spots referred to the position of the chancellor, used symbolic trappings to transmit the importance of the office, focused on competency and the office, and emphasized the accomplishments of the candidate and his party. Two of three CDU spots created an above-the-trenches posture and emphasized charisma and the office. One strategy judged as more appropriate for an incumbent could not be found in the CDU broadcasts: No surrogates were used to speak for the party or the candidate. Among the six techniques regarded as challenger strategies, only two were used by the CDU. All three spots emphasized optimism for the future, and one spot spoke to traditional values.

The smaller coalition partners of the CDU in the incumbent government, FDP and CSU, also used several of the incumbent strategies. However, no reference to the position of the chancellor was made, which is due to the fact that both parties did not present candidates for the position of the chancellor. The FDP and CSU neither used endorsements by party nor other important leaders or surrogates to speak for the parties. Both parties also applied some challenger strategies: Two of their four spots called for changes, a strategy that might have been used to create a separate profile in contrast to the big coalition partner CDU. Two spots also emphasized optimism for the future and spoke to traditional values. One more CSU spot stressed the candidate as representing the center of the party.

The SPD spots, all concentrating on top candidate Oskar Lafontaine, also used those incumbent strategies referring to the office of the chancellor. One strategy was exclusively applied by the SPD: surrogates speaking for the candidate. Among the challenger strategies, only one was not used at all in the SPD ads: speaking to traditional values. This can be explained by the traditional role and ideological stand of the Social Democrats as a progressive party. Emphasizing traditional values instead would be more in accordance with a conservative party like the CDU.

All SPD spots made a call for changes, and four of five spots took the offensive on issues. This again corroborates the findings showing a trend toward taking a critical stand on issues for the SPD, but the CDU pointed to the success of its politics. Calling for changes was also the strategy used in most spots of the smaller parties.

All CDU ads, but only one SPD spot, emphasized optimism for the future, a strategy usually regarded as more appropriate for challengers. One reason for the CDU's demonstrating optimism may have been the historical situation of the first national election after German unification: The incumbent CDU, as the party responsible for a quick unification, had to show optimism in spite of economic problems coming up for West and East Germans with unification. Optimism for the future also seemed to legitimize decisions made by the CDU government.

Only five spots altogether, among them two SPD spots, used the strategy of attacking the record of the opponent. Two SPD spots emphasized their candidate as representing the center of the party. This strategy was probably chosen because the SPD top candidate Oskar Lafontaine and his stand on issues, particularly his attitude toward unification, were controversial in the SPD. The CDU, whose election campaign was very much concentrated on chancellor Helmut Kohl, did not use the strategy of presenting the candidate as the center of the party at all.

PRESENTATION OF CANDIDATE

More than half of the party broadcasts (58%) were judged as being more image-oriented than issue-oriented. One important element of the images is the characteristics being ascribed to the candidates in the spots. The analysis coded for whether seven characteristics were stressed in the presentation of the candidate. Table 5.4 shows the results for all parties in the first column, then compares CDU, SPD, and the smaller parties, again based on those 28 spots presenting a candidate.

Aggressiveness obviously is not regarded as an attitude appropriate for a political candidate. Only two spots show aggressiveness as a personal characteristic of the candidate; the two big parties do not emphasize aggressiveness at all. Among the characteristics attributed

TABLE 5.4 Characteristics of Candidates

		Parties				
	All *n (%)*	*CDU* *n*	*SPD* *n*	*CSU* *n*	*FDP* *n*	*Other* *n*
Toughness/strength	15 (54)	2	3	1	2	7
Honesty, integrity	12 (43)	1	4	1	1	5
Activeness	11 (39)	2	4	1	1	3
Performance, success	11 (39)	3	2	1	2	3
Competency	9 (32)	2	3	1	2	1
Warmth, compassion	6 (21)	1	3	1	–	1
Aggressiveness	2 (7)	–	–	–	–	2
n =	28	3	5	1	2	17

to the candidates positively are honesty/integrity, toughness/strength, performance/success, and activeness. Competency, warmth, and activeness are characteristics rarely used for the candidates of the smaller parties. Again, the CDU maintains its strategy, with all spots emphasizing success as a personal trait of its candidate. Honesty and warmth are the characteristics attributed to Helmut Kohl in only one spot. The main characteristics emphasized for Oskar Lafontaine are honesty and activeness, but also toughness, warmth, and competency.

For those candidates speaking into the camera, nonverbal elements as well as linguistic (verbal) characteristics could be analyzed. Almost all spots presented their candidates with a serious facial expression (13 of 15), and 10 spots showed candidates with little body movement. The serious appearance was further stressed by the formal dress of most politicians. Usually the speech is fluent, with a slow ($n = 5$) or moderate ($n = 8$) rate. A monotone pitch was coded for 8 spots, and pitch variety for 7. Music was present in 21 of 38 spots, in most cases with a moderate rate. Most used a modern style, 6 spots playing classical music. Music is mainly used as background: 2 spots were completely composed of instrumental music, and 1 spot played music with text.

Results of the Experiment

The experiment was designed to study the reception of the spots and the changes in the candidate images. Employing a pre-post research design, this study involved the administration of pretest questionnaires, the showing of television broadcasts, and the subsequent administration of a posttest questionnaire. The sample consisted of 171 voting-age students, representing a broad cross-section of university students enrolled in graduate courses in mass communication and journalism at two universities in West Germany and a major university in a former East German state. Among the students were 39% male and 61% female; the average age was 23.5 years. The experimental sessions were conducted between November 20 and November 29, 1990, shortly before the national election on December 2. Most students had already seen some party spots on TV, although 7% in the West and 10% in the East had not seen any spots before.

Between the pretest and posttest questionnaires, the respondents were shown four television spots, two from the CDU party and two from the SPD. Both spots not only emphasized the party's accomplishments but also placed considerable emphasis on the party's chancellor candidates, Kohl and Lafontaine.

The pretest questionnaire consisted of demographic information, political interest measures, media use variables, a thermometer scale to ascertain the general feelings toward each party's chancellor candidate, and a semantic differential scale, evaluating the candidates (Kohl and Lafontaine). The posttest questionnaire repeated the thermometer and the semantic differential scale on each candidate and also included several open-ended questions on issue, image, and visual recall, and other rating questions on emotional responses and learning.

The semantic differential scale used to evaluate candidate image consisted of 12 sets of bipolar adjectives (e.g., qualified-unqualified), each rated on a 7-point range. A list of all adjectives used can be seen in Table 5.5. This semantic differential scale was derived from earlier scales used to measure candidate image (Kaid, 1991; Kaid & Boydston, 1987; Kaid, Downs, & Ragan, 1990; Sanders & Pace, 1977).

Previous research has proved issue-oriented spots to have higher effectiveness but has also shown that candidate images are better remembered than issues (Geiger & Reeves, 1991; Kaid, 1991; Kaid & Sanders, 1978; Roddy & Garramone, 1988). To find out whether recall of images or issues is higher after presentation of the spots, the posttest questionnaire also contained several open-ended questions asking for issues and candidate images, as well as remarkable elements of the spots' format.

EFFECTS OF SPOTS ON CANDIDATE EVALUATION

Because the comparison of West and East German voters' reception was one of the key elements of the experimental study, all results presented here are split for respondents in West and East Germany. General feelings toward the candidates, as expressed on the thermometer scale, show the Social Democrat candidate Oskar Lafontaine to be rated more positively than the incumbent chancellor Helmut Kohl. This is not surprising, given that the respondents are university students. Before presentation of the spots Kohl is rated at 23.4 on the average, Lafontaine at 58.1. After watching the spots, evaluation of Kohl is somewhat lower (23.0), but Lafontaine is judged even better (58.7). The overall higher popularity of the SPD candidate among the sample is of no relevance to the study. Because the experiment was aimed at studying how the spots and the presented issues and candidates were perceived, and whether the spots led to changes in the candidate images, the initial good or not so good evaluation of the candidates is less important.

A multiple variance analysis was applied to ascertain the factors influencing the classification of the two politicians on the thermometer scale. In addition to the time (pretest vs. posttest) and the candidate (Kohl vs. Lafontaine) as dependent factors, the influence of respondents' gender as well as university (West vs. East) were included in the analysis.

As expected, the candidate variable proves to be the significant main effect ($F_{[1;166]} = 167.7$; $p = .001$). That means differences in the evaluation of the politicians are, independent of other variables, due to the candidates themselves. Moreover, the analysis provides another significant main effect for gender ($F_{[1;166]} = 3.57$; $p = .06$), showing that women and men differ in their evaluation of Kohl and Lafontaine. Watching the spots instead does not influence the evaluation of the candidates independently. However, there is a significant interdependence between the spots and the location of the university in East or West ($F_{[1;166]} = 6.16$; $p = .01$) showing that the spots are perceived differently and influence the rating of the candidates on the thermometer scale in a different way. There is also an interdependence for candidate and location ($F_{[1;166]} = 5.11$; $p = .03$), meaning that there is no correspondence between East and West Germans in their evaluation of Kohl and Lafontaine.

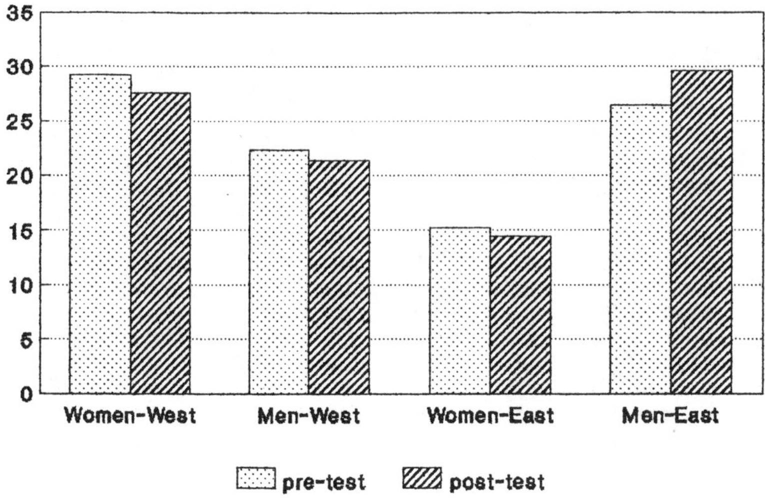

Figure 5.1. Ratings for Helmut Kohl
NOTE: Thermometer scale 0-100; means: pre 23.4 / post 23.0 (n = 171).

The presentation of results in Figures 5.1 and 5.2 takes these results of the variance analysis into consideration. The ratings for Kohl and Lafontaine are differentiated for gender, East and West, and pretest and posttest.

The evaluation of Helmut Kohl on the thermometer decreases in all groups with the presentation of the spots. Only East German men express better feelings after having watched the spots. For Oskar Lafontaine the pattern is different. Before viewing the spots East German women and men give a considerably better evaluation of the SPD candidate than West Germans. With the spots the evaluation of Lafontaine in the West decreases somewhat but is even more enhanced in the East. These results show that party spots can lead to immediate changes in the overall evaluation of candidates. However, these changes are dependent on the origin of the respondents, in the East or in the West.

A similar method was used for the analysis of the candidate evaluation on the semantic differential. As for the thermometer scale a multiple variance analysis with the 12 attribute scales was chosen. This produces significant main effects for the candidate ($F_{[12;145]} = 37.86$; $p = .001$), for the location of the university in the West or in the East

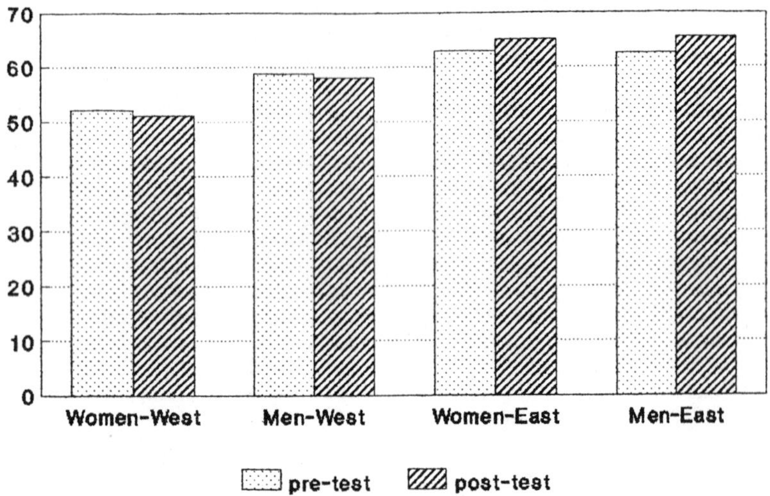

Figure 5.2. Ratings for Oskar Lafontaine
NOTE: Thermometer scale 0-100; means: pre 58.1 / post 58.7 (n = 171).

($F_{[12;145]} = 1.84$; $p = .05$) as well as for time (pretest vs. posttest; $F_{[12;145]} = 1.84$; $p = .05$). These three factors influence the evaluation of the candidates on the semantic differential independently. That means the evaluations of Kohl and Lafontaine not only are influenced by their personalities but also are different in East and West. The significant effect of the time of interview hints to an influence of the spots on the evaluation of the candidate.

Although the effect of gender is just below significance ($F_{[12;145]} = 1.77$; $p = .06$), it can be concluded that women and men again differ in their judgment of the candidates. Beside these influencing factors there are interdependencies for time and candidate ($F_{[12;145]} = 2.86$; $p = .001$). Another interdependence is indicated for time and geographic origin. So, it can be concluded that the presentation of the spots has different effects on the evaluation of Kohl and Lafontaine. Moreover, the spots lead to different consequences in the evaluation of the candidates in East and West.

Table 5.5 shows the results for Helmut Kohl and Oskar Lafontaine, before and after presentation of the spots, split for East and West German respondents. In the questionnaire the attributes were alternately given on the right or left side to prevent a uniform response behavior.

TABLE 5.5 Candidate Image Before and After Viewing of Spots

	Kohl			
	Pretest		*Posttest*	
	West	*East*	*West*	*East*
Qualified	3.3	3.5	3.5	3.8
Sophisticated	2.9	3.8	2.9	3.7
Honest	3.6	2.8	3.5	3.0
Believable	3.4	3.2	3.3	3.0
Successful	5.6	5.7	5.6	5.6
Attractive	2.5	2.6	2.3	2.6
Friendly	4.1	3.9	4.2	3.9
Sincere	4.8	4.9	4.7	5.2
Calm	4.5	4.4	4.6	4.0
Not aggressive	4.4	4.2	4.3	4.0
Strong	4.4	4.4	4.6	4.2
Active	4.2	4.6	4.3	4.9
	Lafontaine			
	Pretest		*Posttest*	
	West	*East*	*West*	*East*
Qualified	4.8	5.2	4.8	5.5
Sophisticated	4.9	5.0	5.0	5.3
Honest	4.9	5.2	4.8	5.4
Believable	4.7	5.0	4.6	5.1
Successful	3.7	3.9	3.9	4.1
Attractive	4.0	4.3	3.9	4.5
Friendly	4.8	5.1	4.8	5.4
Sincere	5.0	5.5	4.8	5.6
Calm	3.3	3.4	3.3	3.2
Not aggressive	3.5	4.1	3.5	4.1
Strong	4.7	4.7	4.6	5.1
Active	5.5	5.8	5.2	5.9

The table shows all attributes coded with a high value representing a more positive attitude. Because the scales ranged from 0 to 7, ratings above 4 stand for a positive and ratings below 4 for a negative attitude.

The results for Helmut Kohl are heterogenous. On some attributes ratings by East and West Germans differ considerably. Viewing the spots for some items leads to an enhancement, for others to a decrease of the evaluation. In East and West correspondingly, Kohl received his highest rating on the item *successful*, and the spots did not produce a remarkable change. The chancellor also got a high rating on *sincere*, even increased by East Germans in the posttest. The highest differences between East and West were established for *sophisticated*, *honest*, and *active*. East Germans found Kohl more *sophisticated* and *active* but rated him lower on *honest* than the West German counterparts. However, the East German rating on *honest* was better after viewing the spots.

Oskar Lafontaine received better ratings than Kohl on almost all attributes. Only the ratings for three characteristics were lower: Compared to Kohl, Lafontaine was seen as less *successful* and less *calm* but more *aggressive*. Lafontaine received the highest ratings for *active*, *sincere*, *honest*, *sophisticated*, and *qualified*. East Germans showed an image enhancement on most attributes after the presentation of the spots. The biggest changes are found for *strong*, *qualified*, and *friendly*. Ratings for Lafontaine in the West did not change much with the spots. After viewing the spots, West Germans found him somewhat more *successful*, less *active*, and less *sincere*.

Altogether the analysis shows that spots can change the image of candidates. However, change does not always stand for an image enhancement, but can also lead to a more negative view of the candidate.

RECALL FROM THE TELEVISION SPOTS

After viewing the spots, respondents were asked in open-ended questions to indicate what they particularly liked and disliked about Kohl and Lafontaine. These answers were categorized according to subject matter and were also classified as to whether each item mentioned was an image characteristic of the politician or a reference to an issue position or stance. The results are listed in Table 5.6. They clearly show a major difference between recall about Kohl and Lafontaine that is consistent across both geographic groups. After viewing the spots, recall about Kohl consistently focused on likes and dislikes related to his position on issues. The opposite was true for Lafontaine, whose recall mentions were overwhelmingly related to his image characteristics.

Although the content analysis has shown that the spots of the two big parties are mainly image-oriented, the reception is different: The spots lead to more image than issue recall for one candidate but not for the other. That recall for Lafontaine related more to images may be due to the fact that the SPD spots focused even more on the candidate than the CDU spots.

TABLE 5.6 Comparison of Likes and Dislikes From Party Spots

	West Germany		*East Germany*	
	Kohl %	*Lafontaine* %	*Kohl* %	*Lafontaine* %
Likes				
Image characteristics	25	89	37	90
Issues	75	11	63	10
Dislikes				
Image characteristics	37	82	37	92
Issues	63	18	63	8

NOTE: Respondents who gave no answer to this questions are excluded.

Respondents were also asked to specifically list the issues and personal characteristics of the politicians they felt had been stressed in the spots. Tables 5.7 and 5.8 demonstrate which attributes of the candidates' images were remembered. Answers are split for East and West German respondents. The tables include only those attributes that were mentioned by at least 10% of one group.

The recall patterns of image characteristics for Kohl and Lafontaine were very similar for respondents in the East and West. Nevertheless, there are some differences in the extent to which respondents identified individual characteristics with each politician. The heterogeneity of the perception of Kohl and Lafontaine is demonstrated even more by the choice of different attributes for their characterization. Moreover, among both regional groups, Lafontaine generated far more personal image mentions than Kohl in the open-ended questions. In the West, Kohl received an average of 2.2 image mentions per respondent, and Lafontaine received 2.7. This difference is even more dramatic in the East, where Lafontaine received 3.4 mentions per subject, compared to 2.4 for Kohl. This suggests a more differentiated image of the SPD candidate.

Lafontaine also received a much more favorable positive/negative image ratio than did Kohl in these open-ended responses. Of the image mentions elicited by the CDU spots, Kohl received 79% positive image mentions and 21% negative mentions in the West, and 64% positive versus 36% negative in the East. Lafontaine received only 6% negative (vs. 94% positive) mentions in the East, although he did less well in the West, where his negatives were 21% and his positives were 79%.

TABLE 5.7 Characteristics of Kohl After Viewing the Spots

	West %	*East* %
Physical appearance	25	12
Calm	24	47
Safe, secure	20	27
Self-satisfied	17	25
Successful	14	6
Perseverant	13	7
Takes credit for unification	13	3
Not eloquent	10	4
Energetic, active	8	16

TABLE 5.8 Characteristics of Lafontaine After Viewing the Spots

	West %	*East* %
Energetic, active	31	48
Honest, believable	24	29
Power hungry	24	4
Competent	20	33
Close to people	18	26
Social	18	10
Friendly	18	18
Eloquent	16	29
Ambitious	11	10
Likes children	9	15
Intelligent	7	19

Although these questions were related to image elements recalled after presentation of the spots, two other open-ended questions asked for the issues noticed in the party broadcasts. Results are shown in Table 5.9. Only those issues are listed that were mentioned by at least 10% of one group.

East and West Germans indicate economics as the dominant issue of the CDU spots. More than 90% of the respondents name this issue. Ranking second on the agenda is unification, though mentioned less by East Germans than by their West German counterparts. A similar difference is yielded for ecology, perceived more often in CDU spots by East Germans than by West Germans.

TABLE 5.9 Issues Recalled After Viewing the Spots

	CDU		*SPD*	
	West %	*East* %	*West* %	*East* %
Economy	93	97	62	71
Unification	85	71	–	–
Social security	51	58	55	70
Environment	40	52	77	81
Chancellor candidate	27	21	50	33
Family	22	16	–	–
Children	–	–	14	19
Reference to the government	–	–	8	11
Women	–	–	7	14

However, environment is regarded as the dominant issue of the SPD spots, mentioned by more than 75% of all respondents. Economy is also identified as an important issue. Ranking third is social security. The candidate as an issue of the spots was mentioned more often for the SPD than for the CDU. This result underlines once again the particular image-orientation of the SPD spots.

Other open-ended questions asked for formal elements that were recalled from the spots. Table 5.10 shows which elements were noticed for CDU and SPD.

TABLE 5.10 Formal Aspects Recalled After Viewing the Spots

	West %	*East* %
CDU		
Formal aspects	46	37
Patriotism	26	18
Safe world symbolism	20	25
Use of German symbols	24	4
Optimism	4	16
SPD		
Children	44	21
Statements of other politicians	32	26
Candidate	12	16
Appeals to emotion	8	10

Formal features such as quick and many cuts, hectic, or dynamic were mentioned most often for the CDU spots. More West than East Germans pointed to patriotism in the spots, the regional difference being even more distinct in the answers referring to the use of such German symbols as the national colors or the flag. East Germans instead more often mentioned the use of safe world symbolism.

Ranking first for the SPD spots is the use of kids, mentioned twice as often in the West than in the East. This is due to one spot that imitated a well-known TV show with children. The format of the second SPD spot, a countdown with politicians recommending Oskar Lafontaine as chancellor, was also mentioned. Pointing to the use of emotion in the spots—often negatively—refers to the use of children as well as to a remark on the attempted assassination of Lafontaine several months before the campaign.

Summary and Conclusion

Among the results presented here, two seem to merit further consideration. In several aspects, the experiment elicited differences between East and West. Multiple variance analysis showed that differences in the evaluation of candidates were also caused by a different reception of the spots among East and West Germans. This may be due to the differences in the political background of East and West Germany and to the fact that the spots concentrated completely on West German politicians. A repetition of the study during the next election campaign might show a convergence of evaluations in both parts of Germany.

The second result that should be subject to further research concerns the effects of image-oriented spots. Although the spots of the two big parties in the content analysis were judged as being more image-oriented than issue-oriented, the SPD spots elicited remarkably more image-related answers than the CDU spots. Thus a more detailed differentiation of image-related elements in the spots directly linked with audience reactions seems to offer a promising way to study the effectiveness of party spots.

References

Becker, J. (Ed.). (1990). *Wahlwerbung politischer Parteien im Rundfunk. Symposium zum 65. Geburtstag von Ernst W. Fuhr* [Broadcast election advertising by political parties: Symposium on the occasion of the 65th birthday of Ernst W. Fuhr] (pp. 31-40). Baden-Baden: Nomos.

Bornemann, R. (1992). Ideenwerbung im Rundfunk [Ideological broadcast advertising]. In Bayerische Landeszentrale für neue Medien (Ed.), *BLM Jahrbuch 92. Privater Rundfunk in Bayern* [BLM yearbook 1992. Private broadcasting in Bavaria] (pp. 127-138). München: R. Fischer.

Dröge, F., Lerg, W. B., & Weißenborn, R. (1969). Zur Technik politischer Propaganda in der Demokratie. Analyse der Fernseh-Wahlwerbesendungen der Parteien im Wahlkampf 1969 [The technique of political propaganda in a democracy: Analysis of electoral advertising of political parties on TV during the 1990 campaign]. In *Fernsehen in Deutschland. Die Bundestagswahl 1969 als journalistische Aufgabe* [Television in Germany. The national elections of 1969 from a journalistic perspective] (pp. 107-142). Mainz: v. Hase & Koehler.

Franke, E. (1979). *Wahlwerbung in Hörfunk und Fernsehen. Die juristische Problematik der Sendezeitvergabe an Parteien* [Electoral advertising on radio and TV: The judicial problem of time allocation to parties]. Bochum: Studienverlag Dr. N. Brockmeyer.

Gabriel-Bräutigam, K. (1991). Wahlkampf im Rundfunk. Ein Beitrag zur Problematik von Drittsendungsrechten [Broadcast election campaigns: A discussion of the problems of third party access to broadcasting]. *Zeitschrift für Urheber- und Medienrecht, 35*, 466-478.

Geiger, S. F., & Reeves, B. (1991). The effects of visual structure and content emphasis on the evaluation and memory for political candidates. In F. Biocca (Ed.), *Television and political advertising: Vol. 1. Psychological processes* (pp. 125-143). Hillsdale, NJ: Lawrence Erlbaum.

Gibowski, W., & Kaase, M. (1991). Auf dem Weg zum politischen Alltag. Eine Analyse der ersten gesamtdeutschen Bundestagswahl vom 2. Dezember 1990 [On the way to political normality: An analysis of the first all-German national election on December 2, 1990]. *Aus Politik und Zeitgeschichte, B11-12/91*, 3-20.

Holtz-Bacha, C. (1990). Nur bei den Wasserwerken Effekte? Eine Studie zur Parteipolitischen Spot-Werbung vor Europawahlen [Effects only at the waterworks? A study of political spot advertising by political parties before the European elections]. *Medium, 20*, 50-53.

Holtz-Bacha, C. (1991). The road to commercialization. From public monopoly to a dual broadcasting system in Germany. *European Journal of Communication, 6*, 223-233.

Holtz-Bacha, C., Kaid, L. L., & Johnston, A. (1994). Political television advertising in Western democracies: A comparison of campaign broadcasts in the U.S., Germany and France. *Political Communication, 11*, 67-80.

Johnston, A. (1991). Political broadcasts: An analysis of form, content, and style in presidential communication. In L. L. Kaid, J. Gerstlé, & K. R. Sanders (Eds.), *Mediated politics in two cultures: Presidential campaigning in the United States and France* (pp. 59-72). New York: Praeger.

Joslyn, R. (1980). The content of political spot ads. *Journalism Quarterly, 57*, 92-98.

Kaid, L. L. (1991). The effects of television broadcasts on perceptions of political candidates in the United States and France. In L. L. Kaid, J. Gerstlé, & K. R. Sanders (Eds.), *Mediated politics in two cultures: Presidential campaigning in the United States and France* (pp. 247-260). New York: Praeger.

Kaid, L. L., & Boydston, J. (1987). An experimental study of the effectiveness of negative political advertising. *Communication Quarterly, 35*, 193-201.

Kaid, L. L., Downs, V. C., & Ragan, S. (1990). Political argumentation and violations of audience expectations: An analysis of the Bush-Rather encounter. *Journal of Broadcasting and Electronic Media, 34*, 1-15.

Kaid, L. L., & Johnston, A. (1991). Negative versus positive television advertising in U.S. presidential campaigns, 1960-1988. *Journal of Communication, 41*, 53-64.

Kaid, L. L., & Sanders, K. R. (1978). Political television commercials: An experimental study of type and length. *Communication Research, 5*, 57-70.

Klein, T. (1992). *Zum Wandel des Kommunikationsstils in Wahlwerbespots von 1972 bis 1990* [The change of communication styles in electoral spots from 1972 through 1990]. Diplomarbeit Universität Erlangen-Nürnberg. Unpublished manuscript.

Kleinsteuber, H. J., & Wilke, P. (1992). Germany. In Euromedia Research Group (Ed.), *The media in Western Europe. The Euromedia handbook* (pp. 74-94). London: Sage.

North, R. C., Holsti, O., Zaninovich, M. G., & Zinnes, D. A. (1963). *Content analysis: A handbook with applications for the study of international crisis*. Evanston, IL: Northwestern University Press.

Radunski, P. (1983). Strategische Überlegungen zum Fernsehwahlkampf [Strategic thoughts on television electoral campaigns]. In W. Schulz & K. Schönbach (Eds.), *Massenmedien und Wahlen* [Mass media and elections] (pp. 131-145). München: Ölschläger.

Roddy, B. L., & Garramone, G. M. (1988). Appeals and strategies of negative political advertising. *Journal of Broadcasting and Electronic Media, 32*, 415-427.

Sanders, K. R., & Pace, T. J. (1977). The influence of speech communication on the image of a political candidate: "Limited Effects" revisited. In B. Ruben (Ed.), *Communication yearbook I* (pp. 465-474). New Brunswick, NJ: Transaction.

Schönbach, K. (1992, May). *Mass media and election campaigns in Germany: Recent developments*. Paper presented at the annual conference of the International Communication Association, Miami, FL.

Trent, J., & Friedenberg, R. V. (1991). *Political campaign communication: Principles and practices* (2nd ed.). New York: Praeger.

Wachtel, M. (1988). *Die Darstellung von Vertrauenswürdigkeit in Wahlwerbespots: Eine argumentationsanalytische und semiotische Untersuchung zum Bundestagswahlkampf 1987* [The presentation of trustworthiness in election advertising: An analysis of arguments and a semiotic study of the 1987 national campaign]. Tübingen: Max Niemeyer.

Wadsworth, A. J., & Kaid, L. L. (1987, May). *Incumbent and challenger styles in presidential advertising*. Paper presented at the annual conference of the International Communication Association, Montreal, Canada.

6. The Presentation of Italian Candidates and Parties in Television Advertising

GIANPIETRO MAZZOLENI

CYNTHIA S. ROPER

Although televised political advertising has been used in U.S. national campaigns since 1952, the advent of its usage in the Italian political arena is of relatively recent vintage. As in many other European countries, television in Italy has traditionally been viewed and organized as a public service. In keeping with this viewpoint, the Italian state-run broadcasting company (RAI) has never carried paid political advertising. During election campaigns, extensive airtime is made available to all competing parties. Some of these broadcasts are produced by the political parties themselves and are dominated by party propaganda consisting of speeches by leaders, interviews, discussions with intellectuals, and news events. Other broadcasts are produced by the networks and are conducted by journalists who question politicians, make comments, and report on campaign issues, thus ensuring the informative nature of such programs.

Despite televised political ads being banned on public channels, local commercial stations began airing some forms of these ads, mostly paid for by the candidates of a few parties, during the general election of 1979. From that moment on, each campaign that followed has witnessed a steady increase in the use of paid televised advertising, to the point that usage now closely resembles that of the United States.

The causal factor producing this change in the domestic campaign communication landscape was the rise of commercial television, at first (1976-1980) on a local basis, but soon after (in the 1980s) on a nationwide scale. Although the nature of public broadcasting was strictly regulated during general elections, for more than a decade commercial stations and networks enjoyed a tremendous amount of freedom. During the "pioneering" years, this freedom translated into a somewhat chaotic communication output in campaigns, including experimentation of daring formats and, in some cases, collusion of interests between candidates and station managers. The greatest effect, however, was seen in the bombardment of party broadcasts and spot ads on voters (Mazzoleni, 1987b). Because of a policy stalemate in Parliament and government, the neat rules of political and electoral marketing that were applied in neighboring countries (e.g., France, the United Kingdom) went largely unheeded in Italian election campaigns as far as media planning was concerned. Commentators spoke of the mad dash by political candidates to commercial television.

In the 1987 campaign, a more restrained approach to televised advertising was observed (Mazzoleni, 1991). Two possible explanations for this change are the increased costs of purchasing airtime and signs of audience boomerang effects registered in previous experiences. A particular modification in the organization of the 1987 campaign was the implementation of media planning and the engagement of television production experts and advertising agencies.

Regulatory Systems Related to Political Advertising in Italy

A law passed in 1975 imposed some restrictions on campaign advertising. These restrictions, however, applied only to street banners, fireworks, and such things as the use of loudspeakers in public places. This law did not mention televised propaganda, for the simple reason that commercial television had not yet been born. Because no new laws have been issued since that time, the inauguration and growth of televised political advertising on local and national commercial networks remained unregulated until the 1992 general election.

In the absence of regulations, parties and candidates were absolutely free to purchase as much airtime as they could afford and to abuse the viewing public in both quantity and quality of televised political spots. In addition, no restrictions could be enforced with regard to such issues as negative advertising. Following the rush of the early years, political actors began to implement a type of self-regulation, but mostly to avoid negative reactions from voters who, also being television viewers, at times made clear their annoyance with the intrusive advertising brought to their television viewing. Although still banned on public channels at the time of the 1992 general election, political ads had become a common and familiar feature in Italian election campaigns.

POLITICAL AND MEDIA SYSTEM STRUCTURES AND REGULATIONS

In prior studies, researchers (Mancini, 1992; Mazzoleni, 1992) have observed a number of distinctive characteristics regarding the Italian political and media systems and the interaction between the two. The political system has been primarily based on the centrality of the party. Traditionally, each party represented the organized expression of a given ideology: to its tenets that party action aspired, its leaders acted as guarantors of its orthodoxy, and voters identified fairly consistently with the subculture in which the ideological and political action of a particular party was rooted. Italian political scientists (Parisi & Pasquino, 1977) have theorized three distinct behaviors in voting patterns: (a) the *belonging vote* (*voto di appartenenza*), in which voters are influenced by their feelings of belonging to a specific subculture (i.e., Catholic, Communist, Socialist, and others); (b) the *exchange vote* (*voto di scambio*), which relates to the patron-client scheme and identifies with the phenomenon of clientelism, particularly prevalent in the southern regions of the country; and (c) the *opinion vote,* based on the voters' assessment of the public performance of a party and often influenced by the news media.

From the early 1950s until the late 1980s, these three patterns remained substantially unchanged and fostered stability in the political system. The belonging vote and the exchange vote represented the forces influencing the majority of voters, though a small minority cast their ballots based on the opinion vote model. Only in the past few years, following the general decline of ideologies, has the influence of opinion votes begun to increase in election outcomes.

Nevertheless, the centrality of the party and its ideology long overshadowed the political influence and stature of the party representatives, both in campaigns and in Parliament. During this time, Italian politics was identified with the parties and their top leaders, but everyone else remained an obscure majority known by the Hispanic nickname "peons." With the gradual process of de-ideologization of the parties, an increasing importance has been gained by single leaders, deputies, senators, and candidates.

Traditionally, the media system has been subservient to the political establishment. The press almost always supported either the government or one of the opposition parties, rarely acting independently. Political forces dominated practically every aspect of the public broadcasting domain, where the three public channels (RAI1, RAI2, and RAI3) were controlled, respectively, by the Christian Democrats (DC), the Socialists (PSI) and other minor allied parties, and the influence of the Left.

This flattening of the news media by political arrangement hampered its potential role as watchdog for the Italian people. Yet, an indirect effect of the media system on the political system must be pointed out. The commercial outlook of modern mass media (media logic) managed to some extent to force "political logic" to come to terms with it. The consequence of this effect has been a process of mediatization of party communication, first within the organization of the political system (e.g., leaders addressing other leaders via the printed pages of newspapers rather than in institutional settings), and second in the party leaders' communication with voters (e.g., accepting and creating spectacular public images through television, magazines, and other media sources) (Mazzoleni, 1987a). The employment of massive televised advertising by parties and candidates in the campaigns of the past decade is a reflection of this process of mediatization of politics.

THE POLITICAL ATMOSPHERE OF THE 1992 CAMPAIGN

Beginning in February 1992, a series of scandals involving key political figures of the governing parties sent shockwaves through the traditional party system and forced the nation to look for new rules by which the political game should be governed. Italian public opinion, supported by an unprecedented aggressiveness on the part of the media, demonstrated the general discontent with the established system on two separate occasions: the general election of 1992 and the referendum of 1993. It is true that the political scandal (known as "bribesville") had not yet reached its climax in early 1992 when the election was called, Bettino Craxi (former prime minister) had not yet been investigated following the explosive charges of the District Attorney of Milan, and Giulio Andreotti was still prime minister. Nonetheless, the general mood of the country had already been shaken by the initial disclosures about the deeply corrupt practices of the parties.

In addition, a referendum in 1991 had introduced a reform to the election process for the Chamber of Deputies, a reform that played an important role in the 1992 campaign. According to this reform, voters now would indicate only one "preference" on the ballot, instead of the five they were allowed in previous elections. This reform, intended to impose lucidity in the relations between candidates and voters, ultimately served to increase the power of the person-candidate vis-à-vis the formerly strong power of the party machine. Given this, the election campaign arena of 1992 was affected by both the mood of public opinion and the inauguration of new voting mechanisms.

Although a greater reform, introducing majoritarian rule into the political system previously dominated by proportional rule, was to be expected in the near future; thanks to the referenda, a more candidate-centered philosophy was a feature of the 1992 campaign. Accordingly, a campaign favoring personalization and spectacularization of communication events and output was expected. Yet the grave events undermining the prestige of almost all the parties and their most prominent leaders blew a ghostly wind over the campaign. Because of the sensitivity of the electorate to political corruption and the spending of public money, incumbent leaders carefully staged their public appearances, often dodging the scrutiny of the news media. Both old and new candidates spontaneously chose not to exaggerate their use of media outlets, including televised political advertising. One could conclude that a prudent, self-imposed austerity in communicating with voters characterized the 1992 campaign.

Immediately following the elections, almost all the old leaders who had been reelected to Parliament (e.g., Arnaldo Forlani for the Christian Democrats, Bettino Craxi for the Socialists, Ugo La Malfa for the Republicans, and many others) were forced to resign from their party offices because of accusations of corruption. The prosecutors had purposely held back these accusations so as not to influence the campaign.

Paradoxically, Italian voters had elected to Parliament dozens of politicians who rapidly disappeared from both the media and political scenes.

Analysis of Italian Ads

Unlike some other Western democracies, where voters cast their ballots for specific candidates, the focus in Italian general elections traditionally has been on the parties. Given the difference in emphasis, for this study parties and party leaders were used in lieu of candidates. Further, in order to gain a broader perspective of the effects and content of televised political advertising in the 1992 Italian general election, both a pretest-posttest experimental design and a content analysis of the ads were utilized.

PRETEST-POSTTEST EXPERIMENTAL DESIGN

A controlled experiment was conducted to examine the effects of political advertising on television viewers. Subjects completed a pretest questionnaire, viewed a series of televised political ads, and then completed a posttest questionnaire. To increase comparability with similar studies conducted in France, Germany, and the United States, only two of the many Italian political parties were used. In light of the recent scandals involving high-ranking Socialist (PSI) party officials, the decision was made to use ads from the Christian Democrats (DC), representing the incumbents, and the Democratic Party of the Left (PDS), representing the challengers.

The sample consisted of 100 voting-age students from the University of Salerno, 48 males and 52 females. The average age of the students was 19. Testing was conducted in two sessions, the first on March 25 and the second on March 26, 1993.

The purpose of the study was to investigate the effects of televised political spots from the 1992 Italian general election. Because this study was being conducted one year after the actual campaign period and election, and given the recent and prolific political scandals, several problems immediately became apparent. In an attempt to deal with these problems, the decision was made to divide the sample into two cells, which could then be examined separately.

The first cell consisted of 53 students who completed the pretest, viewed the six political commercials, and then completed the posttest.

The party representatives used in Cell 1 were Mino Martinazzoli (the current leader of the DC party) and Achille Occhetto (the leader of the PDS party).

The second cell consisted of 47 students who were instructed to think back to the political circumstances surrounding the 1992 campaign period. To facilitate this, the students were shown a video of news clips from the 1992 campaign period. The video consisted of political news coverage from the three public networks (RAI1, RAI2, and RAI3) that dealt with the two parties being used in the experiment. As has been mentioned, traditional ties exist between the parties and the public television stations. To control for any potential bias in news presentation, programming on both parties from all three RAI networks was included. After viewing the video, the students completed the pretest, viewed the six political ads, and finally completed the posttest questionnaire. The party representatives on the questionnaire administered to Cell 2 respondents were Arnaldo Forlani (the leader of the DC party during the 1992 campaign) and, again, Achille Occhetto (PDS).

The experimental treatment for the study consisted of six political spots that had been prepared by the parties. Three of the spots were from the DC campaign and three were from the PDS campaign. None of these spots contained either the appearance of or reference to any specific party representative, but rather called upon voters to support the party in the general election.

The questionnaire content for the two cells was identical, except for the DC party representative. The pretest questionnaire consisted of demographic variables, a semantic differential scale evaluating each party representative, and questions regarding media usage. The posttest questionnaire first repeated the semantic differential scales on each party representative, then included several open-ended questions regarding recall of issue, image, and visual and audio aspects of the ads. Finally, subjects were asked to respond to questions regarding learning and emotional responses elicited by the ads.

The semantic differential scale consisted of 12 sets of bipolar adjectives (see Tables 6.4 and 6.5). Utilizing a 7-point Likert scale, respondents rated the image of each party representative on each of the bipolar sets. This semantic differential scale was identical to those used in similar studies in France, the United States, and Germany (Kaid, 1991; Kaid & Holtz-Bacha, 1993). Given the translation problems already cited, reliability scores on the semantic differential scale were acceptable. The Cronbach's alpha on the pretest/posttest was .67/.76 for the

DC and .77/.84 for the PDS for the combined groups; .77/.80 for the DC and .76/.81 for the PDS in Cell 1; and .49/.68 for the DC and .76/.86 for the PDS in Cell 2.

CONTENT ANALYSIS

Content analysis was used to discover the makeup and elements of Italian political advertising. The sample consisted of 41 televised ads from 11 different parties broadcast during the 30-day campaign period prior to the 1992 general election. For a number of years, Italy has been run by a coalition government created by the strongest parties. Given the nature of the political system, the decision was made to divide the ads into two groups representing political incumbents and challengers. At the time of the 1992 election, the coalition consisted of the Christian Democrats (DC), the Socialists (PSI), and the Communists (PCI). Ads from these three parties (n = 17) were grouped and identified as the incumbents. The ads from the remaining eight parties (PDS, PSDI, PRI, PLI, MSI, PR, Lega Nord, and the Federalismo Pensionati Uomini Vivi) made up the challenger group (n = 24).

The ads were coded by two trained coders, both fluent in Italian (one a native speaker). Intercoder reliability was computed using Holsti's (North, Holsti, Zaninovich, & Zinnes, 1963) formula, yielding an average reliability of +.89. The coding instrument for the ads was based on earlier studies of U.S., French, and German political commercials (Kaid & Holtz-Bacha, 1991; Johnston, 1991). Verbal dimensions on the code sheet consisted of appeals, issues, strategies, characteristics, style, and amount and type of negative advertising. In addition, several nonverbal characteristics and production technique components were included.

Results of the Experiment on Advertising Effects

The presentation of televised political spots in Italy produced rather mixed results regarding image enhancement. Image scores were measured by summing responses to each party representative on semantic differential scales in the pretest and posttest questionnaires. The combined sample image score for the DC party representative actually went down significantly from 42.64 on the pretest to 39.84 on the posttest [$t(87) = 4.41$, $p < .01$]. Although this trend was also present in the

TABLE 6.1 Comparison of Party Representatives Image Scores: Cell 1, Ads Only ($n = 53$)

	Pre-DC	*Post-DC*	*Pre-PDS*	*Post-PDS*
Qualified	3.69	3.57	3.60	3.60
Sophisticated	4.88	4.48**	4.65	4.41
Honest	3.94	3.78	4.19	4.13
Believable	3.46	3.44	3.45	3.53
Successful	4.20	3.78*	4.25	4.10
Attractive	1.91	2.11	2.70	2.57
Friendly	3.77	3.75	3.54	3.79*
Sincere	3.71	3.46	3.69	3.83
Calm	4.90	4.75	4.08	4.34
Aggressive	2.96	2.88	3.73	3.55
Strong	3.96	3.94	4.08	3.94
Active	3.98	3.73	4.06	4.17
Overall image	44.85	43.13*	46.33	46.33

* *t*-test between pretest and posttest is significant at .05 for a one-tail test.
** *t*-test between pretest and posttest is significant at .01 for a one-tail test.

combined sample image score for the PDS party representative, the drop from the pretest score, 49.15, to the posttest score, 48.87, was not significant [$t(91) = .45$, $p > .05$]. When changes in image scores were examined by cell, some differences in party representative became apparent. In Cell 1, respondents rated Mino Martinazzoli significantly lower after viewing the ads, with a pretest score of 44.85 and a posttest score of 43.13 [$t(45) = .2.04$, $p < .05$] (see Table 6.1). However, these same respondents exhibited no change in their image rating of Achille Occhetto, the PDS party representative. He received a 46.33 image score on both the pretest and the posttest [$t(47) = .00$, $p > .05$].

The results of Cell 2 (in which respondents saw reminder 1992 campaign news footage) were similar to the combined sample scores in that image evaluations for both parties went down. However, the Cell 2 image rating of Arnaldo Forlani, the DC representative in this cell, dropped even more dramatically than had Martinazzoli's, from 40.21 on the pretest to 36.24 on the posttest [$t(41) = 4.26$, $p < .001$] (see Table 6.2). Although Occhetto's image rating also dropped from 52.23 on the pretest to 51.64 on the posttest, this change was not significant [$t(43) = .60$, $p > .05$]. Rather than enhancing the image evaluations of the party representatives, televised spots instead left these images unchanged or, as in the case of the DC representatives, appear to have damaged them.

TABLE 6.2 Comparison of Party Representatives Image Scores: Cell 2, News and Ads ($n = 47$)

	Pre-DC	*Post-DC*	*Pre-PDS*	*Post-PDS*
Qualified	2.35	2.24	4.22	4.39
Sophisticated	4.95	4.43**	5.11	4.44**
Honest	2.74	2.50*	5.13	5.04
Believable	2.59	2.17*	4.36	4.20
Successful	3.85	3.76	4.89	4.70
Attractive	2.17	2.02	2.67	2.87
Friendly	3.35	3.20	4.74	4.63
Sincere	2.41	2.07*	4.54	4.52
Calm	5.57	5.39	3.42	3.82**
Aggressive	3.11	2.89	4.07	4.11
Strong	3.82	3.20**	4.22	4.30
Active	3.36	2.81**	4.87	4.70
Overall image	40.21	36.24**	52.23	51.64

* *t*-test between pretest and posttest is significant at .05 for a one-tail test.
** *t*-test between pretest and posttest is significant at .01 for a one-tail test.

Some interesting results regarding image evaluations became evident when changes in semantic differential scores from pretest to posttest were examined for individual items. Both DC party representatives were rated significantly lower in *sophistication.* However, although Martinazzoli was rated lower only in level of *success* (see Table 6.1), Forlani was viewed as less *honest*, less *believable*, less *sincere*, *weaker*, and less *active* (see Table 6.2).

In contrast, although the posttest image scores of the PDS party representative, Achille Occhetto, did not change significantly, on individual factors he was perceived in a more positive light. In Cell 1, respondents evaluated Occhetto as significantly more *friendly* (see Table 6.1), but respondents in Cell 2 perceived him as significantly *calmer* though less *sophisticated* (see Table 6.2).

In order to explore the relationship between emotional reactions of viewers to the spots and their evaluation of party representatives, Pearson correlations were run between how much viewing the spots evoked specific feelings or emotions, and posttest image scores of party representatives. Correlations for the combined cells revealed significant relationships for eight out of nine emotions for the DC party representatives and for six out of nine emotions for the PDS party representative. The more optimistic, more confident, less anxious, more

TABLE 6.3 Correlations of Emotional Feelings With Posttest Image Scores

	DC		*PDS*	
Feelings	*Cell 1*	*Cell 2*	*Cell 1*	*Cell 2*
Optimistic	.28	.47**	.54**	.53**
Confident	.24	.33	.54**	.59**
Anxious	−.45**	−.26	−.21	−.12
Excited	.19	.29	.41**	.49**
Secure	.12	.33*	.60**	.54**
Fearful	−.27	−.40**	−.13	−.19
Bored	−.37**	−.43**	−.55**	−.53**
Patriotic	.02	.43**	.16	.36*
Concerned	−.24	−.07	.10	−.18

* indicates Pearson correlation is significant at $p < .05$.
** indicates Pearson correlation is significant at $p < .01$.

excited, more secure, less fearful, less bored, and more patriotic viewers felt, the higher they rated the DC party representatives. The PDS party representative received higher image ratings when viewers felt more optimistic, more confident, more excited, more secure, less bored, and more patriotic.

When results were examined by cells, some interesting differences became apparent, particularly for the DC party representatives. As Table 6.3 illustrates, Forlani's (Cell 2) posttest image score was significantly correlated with five out of the nine emotional reactions. In contrast, Martinazzoli's (Cell 1) posttest image was significantly correlated only with anxiety and boredom. The relationship between posttest image scores and emotional reactions for Occhetto (PDS) were much more consistent between the two cells, differing only for patriotism in Cell 2.

The most consistent relationships for all party representatives across both cells were for optimism, which showed a strong positive relationship to posttest image scores except for Martinazzoli, and boredom, which showed a strong negative relationship with posttest image scores for all party representatives (see Table 6.3).

CONTENT ANALYSIS OF THE SPOTS

All ads were sponsored by individual parties and were aired on privately owned commercial networks. The majority of the ads (73%)

were 30 seconds in length. Regarding format, incumbents and challengers both preferred issue dramatization (59% and 58%, respectively), with introspection being the second most popular form (29% for both). Music was present in 36 of the 41 ads, representing 94% for the incumbents and 83% for the challengers. However, incumbents and challengers differed greatly in their choice of rhetorical style. Although incumbents used an exhortive style 71% of the time, challengers demonstrated a preference for an emotional style (50%), using the exhortive only one third of the time.

Although incumbents focused positively on their own parties in all of their spots, 25% of the challengers' ads focused primarily on negative aspects of opponent parties. Further, although incumbents never made negative attacks, challengers used this strategy in one third of their ads. The most common attack used was negative association (25%); humor/ridicule, the second most popular style, was used in 13% of the ads. Attacks were generally made by an anonymous announcer (21%) and were focused on the opponent's past performance in the political arena (29%).

The ads were also coded according to their primary emphasis and dominant appeal. As is seen in Table 6.4, both incumbents and challengers emphasized issues (77% and 67%, respectively) over images (23% and 33%). However, a considerable difference was revealed in the dominant types of appeals chosen. Although incumbents preferred appeals focused on creating source credibility (47%), challengers relied on emotional appeals two thirds of the time (67%). The dominant types of content used by incumbents were concern with issues (35%) and specific policy proposals (29%). Challengers were even more likely to rely on issue concerns (54%), followed by a tendency to link their party or party representative with specific demographic groups (29%). In addition, unlike incumbents, challengers occasionally made use of fear appeals (17%).

As Table 6.5 indicates, incumbents displayed a decided preference for the cinema verité production technique (59%) and a combination of settings (47%). Although challengers used cinema verité in 17% of their ads, they favored animation and special production (25%), or a combination of techniques (25%). When challenger broadcasts were coded for setting, it was found that this category was not applicable in 42% of their ads (see Table 6.5). Regarding the staging of the ads, incumbents overwhelmingly selected natural or live scenes (82%) over those that

TABLE 6.4 Appeals Made in Broadcasts

	Incumbents $n = 17$	*Challengers* $n = 24$
Emphasis of the ad		
issues	13 (77%)	16 (67%)
images	4 (23%)	8 (33%)
Dominant type of appeal		
logical	3 (18%)	3 (12%)
emotional	6 (35%)	16 (67%)
source credibility	8 (47%)	5 (21%)
Dominant type of content		
partisanship	2 (12%)	1 (4%)
issue concerns	6 (35%)	13 (54%)
policy preference	0	1 (4%)
policy proposals	5 (29%)	2 (8%)
personal characteristics	2 (12%)	0
group affiliations	2 (12%)	7 (29%)
Use of fear appeal	0	4 (17%)

were obviously staged (6%). Challengers used natural scenes in 46% of their ads but also made use of obvious staging in 29% of their ads.

Party leaders/representatives for both incumbents and challengers appeared in approximately half of the ads (53% and 54%, respectively). In these spots, the dominant facial expression was smiling for incumbents (35%) and attentive/serious (39%) for challengers. Sound characteristics for incumbents and challengers also differed. Incumbents opted to use sound-overs 94% of the time. Challengers chose to use sound-overs two thirds of the time but also employed live sound in one third of their ads (see Table 6.5). Both challengers and incumbents preferred using an anonymous announcer as the dominant speaker (54% and 71%, respectively).

Strategies seen in the ads were examined, using Trent and Friedenberg's (1983) breakdown between incumbent and challenger tactics. Although incumbents occasionally made use of incumbent strategies (see Table 6.6), both the incumbents and the challengers tended to adopt challenger strategies. However, the challenger strategies chosen differed significantly between challengers and incumbents. Challengers called for changes almost twice as often as incumbents (88% and 47%, respec-

TABLE 6.5 Production Components and Nonverbals

	Incumbents *n = 17*	*Challengers* *n = 24*
Setting		
formal indoors	0	4 (17%)
informal indoors	3 (17%)	4 (17%)
informal outdoors	5 (30%)	3 (12%)
combination	8 (47%)	3 (12%)
not applicable	1 (6%)	10 (42%)
Production technique		
cinema verité	10 (59%)	4 (17%)
slides w/print, movement, voice-over	0	3 (12%)
party leader head-on	1 (6%)	3 (12%)
other than party leader head-on	0	2 (9%)
animation and special production	1 (6%)	6 (25%)
combination	5 (29%)	6 (25%)
Staging of ad		
all obviously staged	1 (6%)	7 (29%)
natural appearing	14 (82%)	11 (46%)
other	1 (6%)	4 (17%)
not applicable	1 (6%)	2 (8%)
Sound characteristics		
live	1 (6%)	8 (33%)
sound-over	16 (94%)	16 (67%)
Party leader present	9 (53%)	13 (54%)
Dominant speaker		
party leader	5 (29%)	6 (25%)
anonymous announcer	12 (71%)	13 (54%)
combination	0	2 (8%)
other	0	3 (13%)
Dominant expression of party leader		
smiling	6 (35%)	2 (8%)
attentive/serious	2 (12%)	9 (38%)
not applicable	9 (53%)	13 (54%)

tively), yet emphasized optimism for the future only half as often (42% and 88%, respectively). In addition, challengers were twice as likely as incumbents to focus their advertising on representing the philosophical center of the party (79% and 41%, respectively). Challengers also chose

TABLE 6.6 Strategies Used and Characteristics Emphasized in Ads

	Incumbents *n = 17*	*Challengers* *n = 24*
Incumbent strategies		
use of symbolic trappings	0	0
prime ministry stands for legitimacy	1 (6%)	0
competency and the office	2 (11%)	0
charisma and the office	0	0
consulting with world leaders	1 (6%)	0
using endorsements by leaders	0	1 (4%)
emphasizing accomplishments	3 (18%)	1 (4%)
above-the-trenches posture	0	0
depending on surrogates to speak	1 (6%)	4 (16%)
Challenger strategies		
**calling for changes	8 (47%)	21 (88%)
**emphasizing optimism for future	15 (88%)	10 (42%)
speaking to traditional values	2 (12%)	3 (13%)
**representing philosophical center of party	7 (41%)	19 (79%)
**taking the offensive on issues	0	10 (42%)
*attacking record of opponent	0	6 (25%)
Characteristics		
**honesty/integrity	0	9 (38%)
toughness/strength	9 (53%)	12 (50%)
**warmth/compassion	9 (53%)	4 (17%)
**competency	13 (77%)	8 (33%)
*performance/success	3 (18%)	0
*aggressiveness	5 (29%)	15 (63%)
**activeness	14 (82%)	6 (25%)
qualifications	3 (18%)	2 (8%)

* χ^2 is significant at $p < .05$.
** χ^2 is significant at $p < .01$.

to take the offensive on issues (42%) and at times attacked their opponent's record (25%).

Regarding party or party representative characteristics communicated in the ads, significant differences were found between incumbents and challengers in almost all instances (see Table 6.6). Incumbents tended to emphasize their activeness (82%), competency (77%), and warmth/compassion (53%). In contrast, challengers stressed their aggressiveness (63%), toughness/strength (50%), and honesty/integrity (38%).

Analysis and Conclusion

Although the findings concerning impact of televised political spots on image evaluations were not in the predicted direction, the results do indicate that the spots influenced viewer opinions about the party representatives, at least for the DC party. However, in order to understand these results, they must first be interpreted in light of the dramatic and unusual circumstances encompassing the Italian political arena at the time the study was conducted. Second, given the strikingly different public images of the two DC party representatives, the findings can best be understood by addressing the results for each of the two cells separately.

In Cell 2, an attempt was made to re-create the political atmosphere that existed prior to the 1992 general election. Although the revelations concerning political corruption had not yet overtaken the heads of the major parties, the confidence of the Italian people in their political leaders had already been seriously undermined by the first disclosures regarding the unscrupulous practices of the parties. Given these circumstances, the Italian people expected honesty in politics to be a key issue in the campaign. When the televised political spots used by the DC in the 1992 election campaign failed to address this issue, viewers experienced a deep sense of frustration.

In characterizing the DC spots, many of the viewers in this study described them as banal and unrealistic—pretty words and pretty images with little substance. Two of the most common words used, in fact, were hypocrisy and falsity. As a long-time party representative, Arnaldo Forlani was the embodiment of these images. Viewed in this light, the extreme drop in his posttest image scores regarding sophistication, honesty, believability, sincerity, strength, and activeness is not surprising. Just as the DC party had failed to deal honestly and sincerely with the Italian people, he too was perceived as being less honest, believable, and sincere.

In a way, the DC's failure to respond to negative information regarding the issue of honesty and corruption in politics resembles the phenomenon of failing to respond to negative advertising in American campaigns. According to research in this area, in order to blunt negative information, a candidate must respond directly (Garramone, 1985). Instead, the DC chose to ignore the issue altogether.

Mino Martinazzoli, although also a representative of the DC party, is a relative newcomer to political prominence. His integrity has not been challenged by the numerous charges of corruption and bribery. Because of this, he enjoys a much more clean-cut political image. In line with this image, viewers in this study did not rate him lower in honesty, believability, or sincerity.

Given the tremendous differences in posttest ratings on the semantic differentials for the two DC party representatives, it seems possible that viewers in Cell 1 were responding more to the personal characteristics of Martinazzoli, and viewers in Cell 2 were responding more to the historic image of the DC party.

Regarding the PDS, one must ask why there were no apparent effects from viewing their ads. A possible explanation for this seeming lack of impact could be simply that the expectations of the viewers were fulfilled. From its inception, the PDS has presented itself as the "clean hands" party. During the 1992 campaign, it represented the party of opposition and, as such, took it upon itself to deal directly with problems surrounding the issue of honesty in government. If this interpretation is correct, the lack of significant effects may merely reflect the fulfillment of expectations on the part of the viewers.

The most significant findings in this study are those found in Cell 2. Although the influence was not in the predicted direction, the DC ads did result in image alteration. Further, the posttest image of the DC party representative in this cell was strongly correlated with the elicitation of a number of emotional feelings. Therefore, it can be concluded that these spots did act as a significant stimulus.

In looking at the ads themselves, particularly in light of the unstable political atmosphere during the 1992 general election, the results of the content analysis yield some tantalizing possibilities for interpretation. As has been mentioned, the nation was reeling from the initial revelations of corrupt political practices, the potential impact of which was especially problematic for the incumbent parties. This was especially true for the PSI and the DC. The Italian people expected the parties to deal with this issue in the campaign. The message they presented in their televised spots in many ways seemed to ignore reality as it was perceived by the voters.

Both incumbents and challengers emphasized issues over images, but the specific content and emphasis differed significantly. The incumbents were much more concerned with bolstering their credibility and trustworthiness than in presenting factual information in response to the breaking political scandals. Although the dominant content of their appeals was concerned with various issues, they also spent a great deal of time (53%) in their ads emphasizing partisanship. Their exhortive style of rhetoric seemed bent on preserving their past image, by encouraging the people with scenes of prosperity and family. Possibly in an effort to underscore this, a smiling Craxi appeared as the dominant speaker in several of the PSI ads.

Challengers, on the other hand, overwhelmingly utilized emotional appeals that cut to the heart of issues the Italian people saw as vitally important (e.g., corrupt government, unemployment, unpunished crime). Their style of delivery also was emotional. In an effort to keep these issues from being buried in a morass of political rhetoric, they were willing to employ fear appeals and negative advertising. Further, when challenger party representatives appeared in their ads, they always presented an attentive and serious countenance, one in keeping with the serious circumstances surrounding the campaign.

The manifestly confident demeanor presented by the incumbents notwithstanding, their failure to utilize incumbent strategies revealed a decided lack of confidence in their position as incumbents. They never took an above-the-trenches posture or made use of such incumbent strategies as symbolic trappings or charisma and the office. In fact, the most commonly used incumbent strategy, emphasizing accomplishments, was found in only three ads (see Table 6.6). Like the challengers, they predominantly opted for challenger types of strategies. Even here, it is interesting to note the dramatic differences between the strategies chosen by the incumbents and the challengers. Although the incumbents elected to emphasize optimism for the future (88%), challengers used their televised spots to call for changes (88%). In addition, the challengers sought to rank themselves with the common man by demonstrating their allegiance to the philosophical center of their party in 79% of their ads. The PDS, for example, continually identified with workers, students, and others who had been exploited by the existing powers, and never failed to remind voters that they were the party of opposition.

Differences in how the two groups approached the campaign is also reflected in the characteristics they chose to emphasize. In keeping with their efforts to create credibility and trustworthiness, the incumbents highlighted their competency and activeness but neglected to talk about specific qualifications (18%). They also failed to mention their performance in office or any successes they had experienced (18%). In view of the fact that these parties had been in power for a number of years, it would seem logical that the leaders of these parties would not only be able to stress how their years of experience had prepared them for service but would also be able to point out their role in particular successes as evidence of their qualifications.

The characteristics emphasized by the challengers reflect not only their challenger status but also their recognition of the atmosphere of the 1992 general election. They used their televised advertising to exhibit their aggressiveness, strength, and integrity to seek government reforms and to confront the many injustices and social problems currently existing in Italy.

Although the paid televised advertising of the 1992 general election exhibited many similarities to American political ads in style and usage, that election may be the last time this type of political campaigning is allowed in Italy. With the ongoing revelations in the "bribesville" political scandals, the people and the Parliament are ready to make some radical changes in the traditional political establishment. The policy stalemate, which once existed in Parliament regarding the role of paid political advertising, has melted away in the heat of political scandals. Parliament is currently discussing a proposal to reform the election process, a proposal that could disallow completely any form of paid televised political advertising. Whatever the final outcome, it is almost certain that new rules will be enforced in future campaigns. In the recent March 1994 election, for instance, traditional campaign spots were forbidden on television in the last month before the election. Italian political advertising may, in fact, be headed against the trend in other Western democracies; that is, to less advertising with more stringent controls.

References

Garramone, G. M. (1985). Effects of negative political advertising: The roles of sponsor and rebuttal. *Journal of Broadcasting and Electronic Media, 29*, 147-159.

Johnston, A. (1991). Political broadcasts: An analysis of form, content, and style in presidential communication. In L. L. Kaid, J. Gerstlé, & K. Sanders (Eds.), *Mediated politics in two cultures: Presidential campaigning in the United States and France* (pp. 59-72). New York: Praeger.

Kaid, L. L. (1991). The effects of television broadcasts on perceptions of presidential candidates in the United States and France. In L. L. Kaid, J. Gerstlé, & K. Sanders (Eds.), *Mediated politics in two cultures: Presidential campaigning in the United States and France* (pp. 247-260). New York: Praeger.

Kaid, L. L., & Holtz-Bacha, C. (1991, May). *Audience reactions to televised political programs: An experimental study of the 1990 German national election.* Paper presented at the International Communication Association, Chicago, IL.

Kaid, L. L., & Holtz-Bacha, C. (1993). Audience reactions to televised political programs: An experimental study of the 1990 German national election. *European Journal of Communication, 8*(1), 77-99.

Mancini, P. (1992). Old and new contradictions in Italian journalism. *Journal of Communication, 42*(3), 42-47.

Mazzoleni, G. (1987a). Media logic and party logic in campaign coverage: The Italian election of 1983. *European Journal of Communication, 2*(2), 81-103.

Mazzoleni, G. (1987b). The role of private television stations in Italian elections. In D. Paletz (Ed.), *Political communication research* (pp. 75-87). Norwood, NJ: Ablex.

Mazzoleni, G. (1991). Emergence of the candidate and political marketing: Television and election campaigns in Italy in the 1980s. *Political Communication and Persuasion, 8*, 201-212.

Mazzoleni, G. (1992). *Communicazione e potere* [Communication and power]. Napoli: Liguori.

North, R. C., Holsti, O., Zaninovich, M. G., & Zinnes, D. A. (1963). *Content analysis: A handbook with applications for the study of international crisis*. Evanston, IL: Northwestern University Press.

Parisi, A., & Pasquino, G. (1977). Relazioni partiti-elettori e tipi di voto [Party-electorate relations and types of voting]. In A. Parisi & G. Pasquino (Eds.), *Continuità e mutamento elettorale in Italia* [Electoral continuity and change in Italy] (pp. 215-250. Bologna: Il Mulino.

Trent, J., & Friedenberg, R. V. (1983). *Political campaign communication: Principles and practices*. New York: Praeger.

7. Overcoming Adversity and Diversity

The Utility of Television Political Advertising in Israel

AKIBA A. COHEN

GADI WOLFSFELD

Political System Background

In order to appreciate the complex relationship among Israel's political parties, its electorate, and Israeli media in the context of political advertising, it is necessary to delve back to the historical roots of the state and even to its pre-state days.

Israel was founded on the basis of Zionist ideology, which since the late nineteenh century sought to create in Palestine—the ancient biblical homeland of the Jewish people—a new and modern political entity. Since the destruction of the second temple and the exile of the Jews to all corners of the earth, there was a constant yearning to return to the land of Israel. For nearly two millennia this was mainly a religious aspiration, but with the growth of nationalism in nineteenth century Europe the roots of modern political Zionism were planted.

The early Zionist Congresses held in Europe at the beginning of the twentieth century were highly political, with representatives of Jewish communities and organizations from the extreme Left to the extreme political Right. So was the Jewish Agency for Palestine, which was created in 1929 and served as the external arm of the Zionist movement, seeking political and financial support and demanding from the British mandate the right for immigration to Palestine. Following the holocaust in Europe and the decision of the United Nations to partition Palestine between Arabs and Jews, the State of Israel was declared in May 1948.

Thus the pre-state years had already witnessed heated political debates and the establishment of political parties, which, despite splits and mergers, still form the basis of Israel's current political system. Moreover, the role of Israel's political parties was never limited to national and local politics in the conventional sense. Many aspects of life were organized by the parties. Thus, for example, labor unions are highly politicized; medical care is administered through sick funds run by the major parties; much of housing construction was for many years connected to party politics; sports associations are affiliated with parties; many educational and cultural activities, including youth movements, have been connected to parties; and finally, all of the parties had, and some still do maintain, their own daily newspapers.

To reflect this highly diverse political culture, Israel adopted an electoral system that perpetuated and magnified the great variability of political forces.[1] Israel's parliament, the Knesset, has 120 members and is elected every 4 years in a system of proportional representation, with the entire country as one precinct. Each party can present up to 120 candidates in its "list" and gets seats in parliament based on its share of the total vote.[2]

From the first to the current 13th Knesset, there has been a range of 10 to 15 parties represented—though many did not pass the minimum threshold. Some of the parties had only one member; however, the largest win ever by a single party was 56 seats in 1969. For many years a party needed a minimum of 1% of the total vote to seat its first member, but prior to the election in 1992, this threshold was raised to 1.5% in an attempt to limit the number of tiny factions. Even this minimum is quite low compared to some other Western democracies.

As a result of the system, the government has always been based on a coalition of several parties. From 1948 until 1977 the Labor party (in its various forms) led the coalition; in 1977 the right-wing Likud took over with its coalition partners; and in 1992 Labor came back to rule with a coalition enjoying only a majority of one. For most of the years the religious parties, which won between 12% and 15% of the vote, formed the balance of power.

The prime minister has traditionally been the leader of the largest party forming the coalition and is selected by his or her party. In the past this selection was done by the party leadership, but in recent years there has been significant democratization within many of the parties, with various forms of primary elections. Also, according to a recent change in the law, to take effect in the next election scheduled for 1996, the prime minister will be elected directly by the people. This may have an impact on future election campaigning.

The Israeli society is heavily politicized not only because of its history but also due to the many issues that make its situation rather precarious. Ever since its establishment Israel has had severe security problems; it has fought five major wars with its neighboring Arab countries, and with the exception of a peace accord with Egypt in 1979, it has so far failed to make peace with the others. The country is also clearly divided on how to go about the peace process begun in Madrid in 1991 and what, if anything, must be given up in return for peace.[3]

Israel has absorbed approximately 2.5 million immigrants in its first 45 years (it had a population of only 600,000 Jews in 1948), which, in addition to the enormous financial burden, also created many social problems between newcomers and old-timers, between Jews from Western and Eastern backgrounds, and between religious and secular Jews. So far Israel has failed to draft a constitution or a bill of human rights, mainly because of the intense debate on the role of religion in what is basically a secular society, and what rights its minority Arab citizens should enjoy. All these and other issues are fiercely debated not only at election time, but between campaigns as well. It is not surprising then that Israel has been shown to have an extremely high level of political interest and discussion (Wolfsfeld, 1988) and that the voting turnout has often been above 80%.

Israel's election campaigns are very long. In Israel, as in many other parliamentary systems, parliament can be dissolved before its term is up and early elections can be called for. Although in most European countries the time from the dissolution of parliament to election day is about 1 month, in Israel—where the Knesset has been dissolved several times and early elections held—the law requires a period of at least 150 days before new elections can be held. This makes for very long, heated, and arduous campaigns.[4]

Legal Regulations and Restrictions[5]

The roots of Israel Radio go back to the pre-state days, and from 1948 to 1965 it was actually run as a department of the prime minister's office. In 1965 the semiautonomous Israel Broadcasting Authority

(IBA) was created. When television entered the scene in 1968, following much debate as to whether it should be established at all, it became part of the IBA.

With no television in the early years—hence no TV news—the only visual presentations of current affairs were cinema newsreels, produced weekly by two companies and shown in movie theaters across the country, which were frequented by Israel's avid moviegoers. Therefore, during the preelection periods, government officials and politicians attempted to utilize the newsreels to present their achievements, though members of the opposition had a much more difficult time gaining access to the big screen.

The main set of restrictions on election campaigning is contained in the Knesset Elections Campaigning Bill, passed in 1959 and amended several times since then. In addition, there is a general framework for the amount of money that each party can spend during the campaign, as well as the amount of money it can solicit and obtain as contributions from various sources, both domestic and foreign. Following are some of its major points that pertain specifically to campaigning in the broadcast media.

Except where otherwise noted, the time frame for the various restrictions is 150 days before election day. This is the case whether elections are held at their regularly scheduled time or if early elections are called for. In fact, as noted above, this is one of the reasons that the minimum time required for unscheduled elections is 150 days.

RESTRICTIONS ON THE VISUAL APPEARANCE OF CANDIDATES

During the 30 days before the election no election campaigning is permitted in movie theaters or on television, except during the special times allocated for this (see below). This means that during those 30 days no events can be reported in which candidates for the Knesset appear on the screen fulfilling any role. In the initial bill this limitation only applied to the cinema, but as soon as television became available, the law was amended to include the new medium. It should be noted that no such limitations were placed on radio broadcasts. The underlying logic for this was that those in power tend to have significant advantages in making news, thus these restrictions create a more equal playing field. In the debate in the Knesset in 1959 the ruling Labor party was the only voice against this section.

Although the law speaks only of the 30-day period, the IBA has interpreted this section in a strict manner. Accordingly, during the last few election campaigns the IBA canceled its main talk shows and discussion programs dealing with political and social issues about 10 weeks before election day—despite much indignation from the public. It is hard to decide who is more frustrated by this arrangement: the journalists or the politicians. The journalists must try to cover the election campaign without ever showing the candidate, and the candidates must sacrifice what many see as the most powerful weapon in their arsenal. It is also hard to believe that the citizens are well served by this policy: At a time when they have the greatest need for political information they are provided with only secondary sources.

Three examples illustrate this rather bizarre situation. In the 1973 election, which was postponed for several weeks because of the Yom Kippur War, Abba Eban, then Israel's foreign minister, was once again a candidate. Shortly before the election a conference for peace in the Middle East was convened in Geneva. Eban represented Israel at the conference, and only following intense debate among the various parties did the Election Commission[6] permit his speech to be broadcast on Israeli television, along with the speeches of the Arab foreign ministers. Years later, during the final 30 days of the 1981 campaign, Anwar Sadat, then president of Egypt, met with Israel Prime Minister Menachem Begin. Israel Television's news program could not show Begin's face, so it appeared that Sadat was meeting with an empty chair, but Begin's Likud party was able to show the meeting in a more photogenic way during its campaign broadcast that night. Finally, former Israeli president Ephraim Katzir—himself an eminent scientist—was given the honorary position of closing the Labor party's list of candidates (in the 120th slot). During the campaign he happened to be in the former Soviet Union for an important scientific convention. Because he was officially a candidate for the Knesset, Israeli television viewers could see only his feet when the conference and Israel's participation in it were reported on the nightly news.

SPECIAL TELEVISION CAMPAIGN BROADCASTS

Despite the severe restrictions on the appearance of candidates in regular broadcasts, their access to television and radio is not completely blocked. In fact, they get free broadcast time—on radio and television—

during the 21 days prior to the election, in what has cynically been called "election propaganda."

Each party and list of candidates is allocated broadcast time, based on its size in the outgoing Knesset. Each party—regardless of whether it is represented in the outgoing Knesset—is given a basic allocation of 10 minutes, and each party represented in the outgoing Knesset receives an additional 3 minutes per outgoing member. The time frame and precise scheduling for these broadcasts are determined by the Election Commission before the election, based on the number of lists running for the Knesset. In the past these broadcasts took place each evening immediately following the main news bulletin, although in 1992 they were shown directly before the news.

The material to be aired is prepared by the parties, at their expense, but their content must be approved each evening by the Election Commission, subject to certain restrictions. For example, a party is not permitted to use any footage previously shown on Israel Television. Each party can divide its total time allotment into segments, usually as small as 2 minutes. In several recent elections the major parties pooled part of their time, to facilitate a debate between the heads of their respective parties, who are the only viable candidates for prime minister.

The fact that broadcast time as well as campaign funds are distributed according to the number of Knesset members in the outgoing Knesset leads to a very uneven set of broadcasts. Although the major parties can afford the highest level of professional and technical production for two or three relatively long ads per night, the newly created parties present but a few short ads, which look very much like home videos. On the other hand, the fact that every party gets free broadcast time does allow for a much broader set of viewpoints to be aired. Indeed, many interest groups who have no hope of getting elected to the Knesset register as parties and "run" for election simply to gain access to this valuable political platform.

SPECIAL RADIO CAMPAIGN BROADCASTS

As with television, each list of candidates is given free radio broadcast time during the period prior to election day, based on the size of the party in the outgoing Knesset. Each list of candidates, regardless of whether represented in the outgoing Knesset, is allocated an initial 25 minutes; and each party represented in the outgoing Knesset receives an additional 6 minutes per outgoing member. As in the case of television, the entire time frame for these radio broadcasts is determined by the Election Commission before the election, based on the number of lists running for the Knesset. In recent campaigns these broadcasts took place during the last 3 to 4 weeks before the election and lasted about 90 minutes a day, in three 30-minute installments.

OTHER RESTRICTIONS

As noted, some of Israel's daily newspapers are still published by political parties and were naturally used for election campaigning. The political as well as the nonpolitical newspapers are also subject to limitations of campaign advertising, but only within the general restriction on the total amount of money that each party is permitted to spend during the campaign. In recent years the state controller's office has been quite strict in enforcing the restrictions on election expenditures, and heavy fines have been imposed on parties who spent more than they were allowed.

Finally, some restrictions also apply to the use of loudspeakers in public places, the use of neon signs, and the size of posters that may be displayed in public places.

The Utility of Televised Ads for Voters

Given the large number of parties competing for seats in the Knesset and the generous amount of free television allotted to each party, television campaigning is taken quite seriously by the parties. Months before election day the parties contract with consultants, advertising firms, and television studios. There are periodic surveys, and during the television campaign phase, there are nightly checks to study the impact of the messages and help plan for those the following night. Moreover, in recent years newspapers have tended to report in great detail about the television campaign, including cynical criticism and gossip on the behind-the-scene activities connected with the production of the messages.

A good deal of the research about the political ads has adopted a "uses and gratifications" approach. The question is not so much what effects the ads have on the Israeli public, but rather how Israelis use the ads for different purposes. In general, the research suggests that the

Israeli public does not take the ads very seriously, which is reflected in the relatively few people who claim to benefit from them in deciding how to vote. Moreover, entertainment has always been one of the leading reasons cited for watching the ads (Caspi, 1984; Caspi & Levinsohn, in press). The estimate of those who use the ads as a voting guide ranges anywhere from 2% to 24%, depending on the election year and how the question was asked.[7]

A similar survey of 504 adult Jewish voters in Jerusalem was conducted via telephone immediately following the 1992 campaign (Wolfsfeld, in press). Although some of its results tend to support the conclusions of previous studies, others suggest that the ads do offer some guidance for an important segment of the population.[8]

Despite the generally high level of political interest in Israel, the survey results show that the audience for the ads is growing smaller. Caspi (1984) reported that in 1981, 61% of the Israeli public watched all or almost all of the ads, but by 1992 the proportion had dropped to 25%. On the other hand, the proportion of the electorate watching at least some ads remained about the same, around 20%. It is not so much that fewer Israelis watch the ads, but rather that Israelis are watching fewer ads. Apparently, with the ads being broadcast 6 nights a week, an increasing number of voters have come to the conclusion that they can easily afford to tune in on a less regular basis.[9]

Most Israelis would also prefer to have fewer ads broadcast on Israeli television. When asked, 16% of the public said they would like to see the ads stopped altogether, 49% said they would like to see fewer ads, 27% wanted the situation to remain the same, and only 7% wanted even more ads. Most of the Israeli public is no doubt aware that the ads are funded by the taxpayers' money, and apparently many consider them a waste of resources.

The current survey results also suggest that most Israelis do not take the ads very seriously. As in previous research, the voters were provided with a list of motivations and asked to indicate the extent to which each was a reason for their viewing. Once again more people (63%) were willing to cite entertainment than any other motivation. Only 17% of the population stated that they were watching the ads in order to help them decide how to vote.

It is important, however, to draw a distinction between different types of voters. After all, not all voters need the information provided by the ads to make up their minds how to vote; in fact, many decide how to vote long before the campaign begins. The most relevant classification distinguishes between the decided and undecided voters. Caspi (1984) used this distinction and reached the surprising conclusion that undecided voters had even more negative opinions about the benefits of the broadcasts, compared with decided voters.

In the multiparty context of the Israeli political system, however, it is important to draw another distinction among voters. Three blocks (or in more recent years referred to as "camps") have typically characterized the Israeli political scene: the Left (primarily based on the Labor party), the Right (with the Likud and its affiliated parties), and the religious parties. The main difference between the Right and the Left concerns their respective positions with regard to whether Israel should give up territories for peace, but the religious parties are predominantly concerned with the extent of religious observance in Israel.

In recent years most of the religious parties have tended to side with the political Right, thus the major question in the 1992 elections was whether the left-wing parties would win back sufficient Knesset seats to block the creation of yet another government coalition between the right wing and the religious parties. The left-wing camp won the minimal margin—61 out of the 120 Knesset seats—thereby enabling Yitzhak Rabin to become prime minister, and the right wing and most of the religious parties were relegated to the opposition.

The importance of this division becomes clear when one examines the types of decisions confronting Israeli voters. For the sake of simplicity, we shall consider all of the religious parties as part of the right-wing camp.[10] Three types of voters can be distinguished: *committed voters*—those who are committed to voting for a particular party even before the election campaign begins; *internal floaters*—those who consider voting for one of the parties within a particular camp; and *external floaters*—those who deliberate between parties from opposing camps.

The current survey results show that 49% of the sample were committed voters, 34% were internal floaters, and 15% were external floaters. It is important to bear in mind that although those who vacillate between the two camps are the smallest group, they are also in many ways the most important one, for it is these voters who ultimately decide which of the two major parties will form the new government.

As might be expected, the demographic profiles of these three groups are different, which offers helpful insight about how each relates to the election broadcasts. A multiple classification analysis was performed in order to examine the differences in age, education, and political

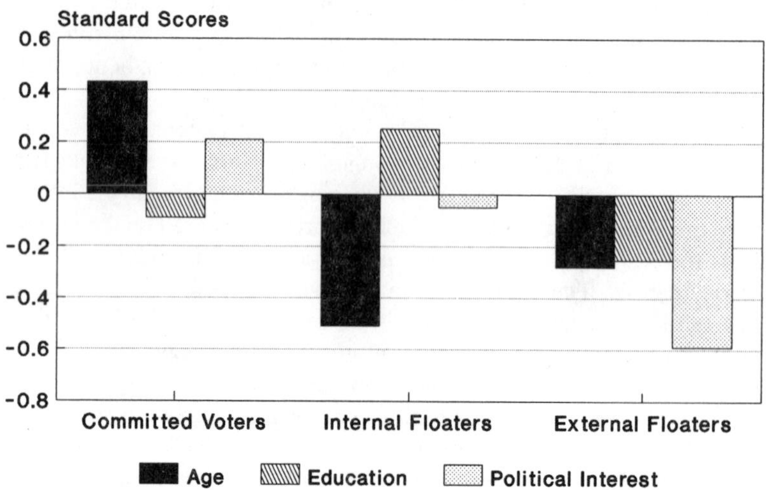

Figure 7.1. Demographic Profiles of Voting Types

interest[11] among the three groups. This procedure is based on an analysis of variance in which the means for all variables are converted to standard scores. This makes it possible to examine whether each group falls above or below the mean score of the population.[12]

As Figure 7.1 indicates, the committed voters tend to be older, have about an average level of education, and have an above-average interest in politics. The internal floaters tend to be the youngest and the most educated of the three groups, with an average level of political interest. Finally, the external floaters tend to be significantly below average on all three scales: They are younger, less educated, and the least interested in politics.

Given the demographic differences among the three voter groups, we now consider the extent to which each group is likely to depend on the television ads for political information. It is reasonable to assume that the committed voters would be least likely to rely on the ads for help. Not only have they already made their voting decision before the broadcasts begin, but their average level of education and especially their relatively high level of political interest combine to suggest that the ads are unlikely to teach them anything new.

The external floaters, on the other hand, are most likely to depend on the ads for help. They are relatively young and therefore politically inexperienced, they tend to be less educated than the other two groups, and they have the least amount of long-term political interest. Several studies (Barnes & Kaase, 1979; Converse, 1964; Neumann, 1986; Verba, Nie, & Kim, 1978; Wolfsfeld, 1988) have shown that education and political interest are among the most important determinants of political sophistication. Thus it is reasonable to assume that this critical set of voters would get the most help from the broadcasts.

Finally, the internal floaters would fall somewhere in between the other two types on this theoretical continuum. They are the youngest group and were still undecided at the time of the broadcasts, but it is also safe to assume that they have more political knowledge than the external floaters because of their relatively high educational level and their moderate level of political interest. It is noteworthy in this context that the small, more ideological parties in Israel obtain a good deal of their support from the better educated elements of the population. In the present sample, for example, 50% of the college-educated respondents said they ended up voting for small parties in the 1992 election, but only 34% of the least educated group did so. Although many educated voters consider the option of voting for small parties within a particular camp, very few contemplate the much more drastic step of voting for their political rival.

Finally, despite the differences in education and long-term political interest among the voting types, *no* significant differences were found among the groups in the extent of their interest in the political campaign, or their viewing of the broadcasts. This suggests that there is an important segment of the voting population that seems to suddenly become interested in politics during the campaign and that many of these people are understandably undecided about their vote. In theory, such voters should serve as an especially attractive target for televised election ads.

Our expectation, then, is that there would be a correlation between the voters' overall level of commitment to a particular party or camp and how they relate to the ads: External floaters should relate to the ads in the most serious manner, committed voters in the least serious way, and internal floaters to a moderate degree.

The findings confirm this supposition. When asked whether voting guidance was one of the reasons they watched the broadcasts, only 6% of the committed voters acknowledged this, but 23% of the internal floaters did so, and 42% of the external floaters responded affirmatively ($\chi^2 = 52.39$; $p < .001$). A similar trend was found with the motivation of "following the competition": Only 28% of the committed voters agreed that this was one of their reasons, but the percentages for internal and external floaters were 38% and 43%, respectively ($\chi^2 = 5.98$; $p < .05$).[13]

Further confirmation of the differences in dependency on the ads can be found by examining opinions within the three groups about the number of election ads being broadcast. As noted, most Israelis would like to see fewer ads, but there are also important disagreements among the three voting types. Although 70% of the committed voters wanted fewer broadcasts, 65% of the internal floaters felt this way, and only 51% of the external floaters would have preferred fewer ads ($\chi^2 = 12.12$; $p < .01$).

Perhaps the most important differences are those relating directly to the extent to which each group stated that the ads offered some type of help with voting decisions. Two questions were put to the respondents. The first was more general: "To what extent did the broadcasts help or hinder you in your decision about whom to vote for?" The second question related more specifically to the televised debate between Likud leader (and then prime minister) Yitzhak Shamir and Yitzhak Rabin. The 70% of the sample who reported watching the debate were also asked whether it (a) reinforced their previous decision, (b) helped them decide because they didn't have a prior opinion, (c) did not help them, or (d) didn't change anything for them. The last two categories were combined into a "no help" category, and those who said they either formed or changed an opinion because of the debate were placed into a "decision change" category.

The pattern of results presented in Figure 7.2 is now familiar: The external floaters consistently report the most amount of help from both the ads and the debate, and the differences between the two more sophisticated groups are very clear with regard to the question about the political ads, but less dramatic in reference to the debate.[14]

All these findings, though tentative and in need of further study, point in the same direction. The televised election ads in Israel appear to serve a useful purpose for an important—albeit small—segment of the population. Although the majority of Israelis do not take the ads very seriously, a significant number of undecided voters do find them helpful in making their final decision.

The fact that many in this group appear to come from the less educated and less politically interested can be viewed as either good news or bad news. The good news is that television can serve as an

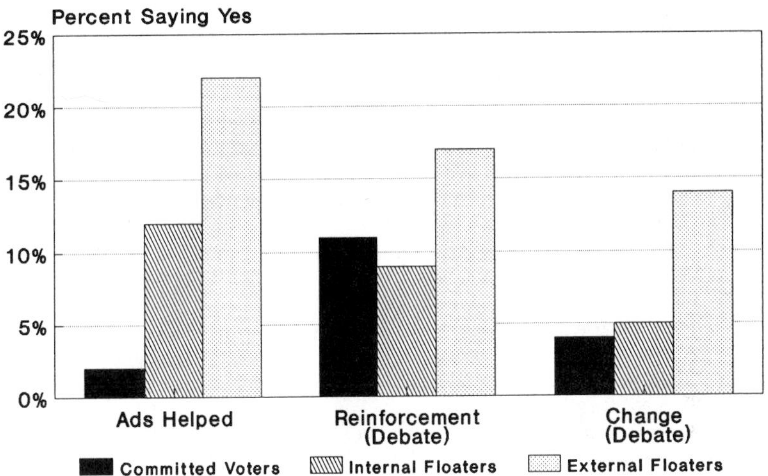

Figure 7.2. Help From Ads and Debate

important equalizing force, by allowing a convenient means for the less involved to catch up in time for election day. The bad news is that the format and content of these ads may leave a lot to be desired in the area of political education.

Notes

1. For a detailed description and analysis of Israel's electoral system, see Diskin (1991).

2. There have been several attempts over the years to modify the system, but so far the Knesset has not done so.

3. In September 1993 a Declaration of Principles was signed by representatives of Israel and the Palestine Liberation Organization, but so far it has not been implemented.

4. Along with several bills currently pending, this period may be shortened.

5. For a general review of the history and functioning of Israeli broadcasting, see Shinar and Cohen (1988) and Caspi and Limor (1992).

6. The Election Commission is chaired by a retired Supreme Court justice and consists of representatives of the parties, the Ministry of Interior which oversees the election, and other government agencies that fulfill some role in the election process.

7. The lowest percentages are recorded when subjects are asked the *most* important reason for viewing the ads, and the higher percentages are found when subjects are given the possibility of responding to a number of different motivations.

8. An earlier version of this analysis appears in an article by Wolfsfeld (in press). We would like to thank Asher Arian and Michael Shamir, the editors of that volume, for permission to cite some of these heretofore unpublished findings.

9. It should also be kept in mind that with the introduction of cable television, Israelis are being offered an increasing number of choices at election time. Although in previous campaigns Israeli television was essentially the only show in town, by the time the 1992 election ads were being broadcast, significant parts of the population had become cable subscribers. However, a comparison of those households with and without cable showed no significant difference in the extent of viewing the ads (Wolfsfeld, in press).

10. Prior to the election, all of the religious parties expressed a preference for a right-wing government. Following the election, however, one of these parties (Shas) joined the left-wing coalition but later pulled out. At this time of this writing, it is unclear whether that party will rejoin the coalition.

11. Political interest, both long-term and in the specific campaign, was measured by two questions, respectively: "How much do you follow and take interest in politics?" and "How much did you take an interest and follow the election campaign in the press, on radio, and on television?"

12. The results of the analysis of variance reveals that there are significant differences between the three groups with regard to age ($F = 22.33$, $p < .001$), education ($F = 6.13$, $p < .01$), and political interest ($F = 7.62$, $p < .001$).

13. There were also significant differences with regard to the motivation of entertainment, although in this case the internal floaters (71%) were somewhat more likely than the committed voters (62%) to also watch the ads for this purpose. The external voters were the least likely (49%) to watch for reasons of entertainment ($\chi^2 = 7.06$, $p < .05$). No significant differences were found with regard to two other suggested motivations: "For use in political arguments" and "For use in political discussions."

14. The notion of reinforcement is admittedly murky, because it is not clear how much either the internal or external floaters actually had previous opinions that could be reinforced.

References

Barnes, S. M., & Kaase, M. (Eds.). (1979). *Political action: Mass participation in five Western democracies*. Beverly Hills, CA: Sage.

Caspi, D. (1984). Following the race: Propaganda and electoral decision. In D. Caspi, A. Diskin, & E. Gutmann (Eds.), *The roots of Begin's success* (pp. 245-272). Kent, UK: Croom Helm.

Caspi, D., & Levinsohn, C. (in press). To influence and to be influenced: The election campaign to the 12th Knesset. In D. J. Elazar & S. Sandler (Eds.), *Who's the boss in Israel*. Detroit: Wayne State University Press.

Caspi, D., & Limor, Y. (1992). *The mediators: The mass media in Israel 1948-1990*. Tel Aviv: Am Oved Publishers (Hebrew).

Converse, P. (1964). The nature of belief systems in mass publics. In D. E. Apter (Ed.), *Ideology and discontent* (pp. 206-261). New York: Free Press.

Diskin, A. (1991). *Elections and voters in Israel*. New York: Praeger.

Neumann, W. R. (1986). *The paradox of mass politics.* Cambridge, MA: Harvard University Press.

Shinar, D., & Cohen, A. A. (1988). Israel. In P. R. Rosen (Ed.), *International handbook of broadcasting systems* (pp. 147-161). New York: Greenwood.

Verba, S., Nie, N., & Kim, J. (1978). *Participation and political equality.* London: Cambridge University Press.

Wolfsfeld, G. (1988). *The politics of provocation: Participation and protest in Israel.* Albany: State University of New York Press.

Wolfsfeld, G. (in press). Voters as consumers: Audience perspectives on the Israeli election broadcasts of 1992. In A. Arian & M. Shamir (Eds.), *The elections in Israel 1992.* Albany: State University of New York Press.

8. Political Advertising in Denmark

KAREN SIUNE

In Denmark, the smallest of the Scandinavian countries but the only one with membership in the European Community, the constitution secures for everyone the right to print, but the same right does not apply to broadcasting. In Denmark, as in Norway and Sweden, national television and radio have been, since their establishment, organized as public service organizations with written norms for balanced programming. One very important aspect of the dimension of balance in the electronic media has been political balance. For the old, formerly monopolistic stations, party access to broadcast election programs is regulated, not by the state as such, but by the broadcasting organization, obligated by its public service status and firm social and political responsibility. News programs are not regulated, but a fairness doctrine functions as the guiding norm.

None of the public television channels in Scandinavia allow the purchase of political party advertising. Political advertising is generally perceived as a threat to the principles of democracy. It means that all parties have equal right to communicate to the electorate via the medium perceived as the most powerful. The opportunity for purchased political campaigns on television is widely seen as a challenge to the political balance in the Scandinavian multiparty systems.

Political System Characteristics

PARTY STRUCTURE

Denmark is a multiparty system, with more than 10 parties running in every election. The parties can be arranged on a Left-Right continuum, but that is not the only way to look at the Danish parties. On some issues, for example, European integration, the extreme Right joins with the extreme Left. On this issue the extreme Right and Left are both against further integration, that is, against a European political union in the form of a political federation. On other issues, such as social welfare, most of the parties agree. Traditionally the bourgeois parties want to reduce the degree of public spending, because their general policy is to reduce taxes, which are, when viewed globally, extremely high in Denmark.

Coalition governments have become nearly a tradition in Denmark, because for decades no one party has had the majority. From 1982 to 1993 the government was based on conservatives and liberals, but since 1993 the government has been a coalition of Social Democrats together with the small Radical Liberals, The Christian Peoples Party, and Center Democrats; but these four parties together have a majority of only one seat in the Danish parliament, Folketinget.

POLITICAL PARTIES' ATTITUDES TOWARD CAMPAIGN COMMUNICATION

In Denmark, as in other Scandinavian countries, the mass media are perceived as very important to the political process, and all Danish politicians, eager for votes, want media access.

The interplay between political parties and mass media is an old, ongoing issue for debate. There are old traditional linkages between newspapers and political parties, because for many decades the party press has been considered a basic element in the Scandinavian democracies. Today television is seen as playing a much greater role for politicians, so they want access to it at the national, regional, and local levels. Representatives of all Danish political parties have expressed an interest in access to national television. They especially want to be interviewed on news programs, because they are very much aware of the psychological barriers in audiences who perceive that they are being exposed to party propaganda. Even in a country where party propaganda in the form of commercial advertising is not possible on national television channels, but where political parties have the opportunity to present their ideas in so-called presentation programs, news programs are still considered the most attractive. The parties view access to special programs during an election campaign a necessity, and television is considered the best medium for reaching those who are less interested in politics.

DIFFERENT TYPES OF ELECTIONS

In Denmark, as elsewhere, there are different types of elections. National elections must be held every fourth year, but they can be called when the government is in need of an election or is forced to take one, and in reality elections have been held far more often than every fourth year. Ten national elections were held in the period from 1971 to 1990, including every second year the 1970s. Traditionally the election campaign period is very short, and in relation to television it is defined as 3 weeks.

Besides the national elections there are municipal and county elections, which are held regularly every fourth year and cannot be called between fixed dates. Local media play a much greater role in local elections than national elections and, because there are few large social, political, and economic differences in the local areas in Denmark, local media also play a greater role for local candidates and local issues than do the national channels. Denmark has many local television stations, and candidates find these stations, especially the small, neighborhood ones, offer certain options. The small stations are not regulated as much as the national channels, and some of them let parties or individual politicians buy time.

Besides the above-mentioned national, regional, and local elections, Denmark, so far the only Scandinavian member of the European Community, also has elections for the European Parliament. The first of these so-called European Elections, which directly elect members to the European Parliament, was held in 1979, the second in 1984, and the third in 1989. A series of studies have been made of these elections, and the results from these studies will be referred to below.

In Denmark, as in the rest of Scandinavia, elections to the national parliament are generally of greater interest to both voters and social scientists than elections to the local and county boards. Elections to the

European Parliament are of less significance among voters than national elections, a situation also common throughout the EC. In terms of turnout, the European Elections attract even less attention among the Danes than local elections.

Structure of Mass Media

In this century the Scandinavian mass media have developed in three phases relevant to political communication (Siune, 1987). In the first phase, partisan newspapers grew expansively. In the second, consolidating phase, papers grew in size and decreased in number at the same time as professional news criteria began to dominate partisan political communication. Radio, and later television, became the most significant sources of information. In the third phase, the influence of electronic mass media has grown, with satellites, cable, video, and local broadcasting breaking the former monopolies. Television is still considered the prime medium, but now there is more than one nationwide channel in each country.

Broadcasting in Denmark is regulated by broadcasting acts (Kleinsteuber, McQuail, & Siune, 1986), and the fundamental basis of Danish broadcasting has been public service broadcasting without commercials. In the 1980s broadcasting regulations have made possible private local radio and television channels, some of them financed by advertising; and in 1987 a new Danish nationwide television channel was begun, financed partly by license fees and partly by income from advertising.

In Scandinavia there is a long history of both national and local newspapers being private property, but with traditional party affiliation (Euromedia Research Group, 1991). These local newspapers have been the primary contact between a party and its supporters. Traditionally, all political parties had their own newspapers in each region of the country. However, this system has declined, in Denmark more than in the rest of Scandinavia, where a kind of economic state support has kept small party newspapers alive. The whole idea of economic support for the press is based on the general perception that newspapers are of great value to both democracy and the political system. Most newspapers have been supported by subscriptions, but newspaper reading, and subscription rates, have gone down dramatically in Denmark. Today newspapers are increasingly sold as ordinary goods and, because of economic problems, have to be more market-oriented than party-oriented. Political coverage in the newspapers these days is based on news criteria, and coverage of a party because of its newspaper affiliation hardly exists anymore. Although content analysis shows significant differences in party coverage (Siune, Svensson, & Tonsgaard, 1992), the analyses also show that at election time all major parties receive wide coverage in all newspapers. Small parties and new parties do not get any kind of special treatment in newspapers unless they are perceived as a real challenge to the established parties. If they are a challenge, new parties can obtain wide coverage in the papers, and it is possible—as shown by some of the new parties that have emerged in the past 20 years in Denmark—to use the media to gain wide coverage, especially if they satisfy the major news criteria: status, power, and the ability to challenge the establishment. Colorful party leaders can do a lot in this context, but a colorful personality is not enough; subsequent influence is necessary as well.

Differences in the way newspapers treat the parties are accepted by the system, the parties, and the voters. No one complains about bias, and voters from all parties write comments and letters for publication in the newspapers. Content analyses show that this way of communicating is widely used by all parties (Siune, Svensson, & Tonsgaard, 1993), not least by the small parties who in this way try to compensate for their "lack" of news value according to traditional journalistic criteria.

Freedom of the press has been the guiding principle behind the development of the newspaper industry, whereas social responsibility and political balance have been the guiding principles for national broadcasting. In contrast, the new local broadcasting outlets are not guided by principles of diversity and balance.

PUBLIC SERVICE BROADCASTING

Public service broadcasting institutions in Scandinavia are in principle independent public institutions with the purpose of broadcasting news, information, and entertainment to the entire population. For decades broadcasting belonged to national monopolies, and the responsibility for radio and later (in the 1950s) television was given to the former national radio stations, in Denmark to Danmarks Radio (DR). This institution's monopoly on broadcasting was broken during the 1980s, but a lot of normative expectations are still there in relation to the "old" broadcasting companies. Among these expectations is balance in politics.

One could say that public service broadcasting institutions are trapped in a triangle of influences: the political authorities, the audience, and the journalists, all three representing challenges to ideas like balance, relevance, quality, and independence. To rely heavily on only one of these bases would easily transform the broadcasting company into a political commissariat, a purely commercial company, or a paternalistic institution (Østbye, 1991). There is a lot of external pressure, especially in relation to political communication, and the principles laid down for party access to broadcasting can be seen as a kind of protection against such pressures.

PRINCIPLES FOR PARTY ACCESS TO BROADCASTING

There are special regulations for party access during election campaigns. The rules are made by the broadcasting organizations themselves, not regulation by law: Only political commercials are forbidden by law. Neither the government nor the state as such has direct influence on the rules for party access to broadcasting.

In Denmark all parties are treated equally by the old, formerly monopolistic Danmarks Radio (1989, 1990). The guiding principle has been equal access for all parties participating in an election. Independent of whether a party is new or old, small or large, represented in the national parliament or not, as soon as a political party is accepted by the Ministry of Internal Affairs as running at the announced election, the party is allocated free time on radio and television. Free time means access on an equal footing to special election programs in the format decided by the broadcasting company. To be accepted by the Ministry of Internal Affairs "a party has to collect signatures amounting to 1/175 of the valid votes cast in the previous election."[1] Danes are receptive to the formation of new parties, but they are not very concerned about their preelection support for new parties. Often parties able to collect the requisite number of signatures from the population go on to garner a much smaller number of votes on election day. Accepting new parties to challenge the established parties in the national elections is part of the Danish democracy and is also reflected in the attitude toward new parties' access to broadcasting. The principle of equal access in Denmark has been strengthened by a statement from the Ombudsman and by a Supreme Court decision.

For the broadcasting organization Danmarks Radio, equal access includes equal airtime on Danish national radio and television. This principle applies only to the old, formerly monopolistic channel, not to the new television channel, TV 2, but so far no parties have complained. On the DR channel all parties get a party platform in the form of a 10-minute program, followed by a 30-minute program during which journalists question the party that just presented its program. At the end of this questioning program, a party representative, usually the leader, has the opportunity to close the evening with a 3-minute statement. This format has been used since the end of the 1960s. The party presentations may either be produced by the parties themselves or be made in cooperation with the broadcasting company. If produced outside Danmarks Radio, which today is the most common, the political party receives a fixed amount of money to produce the program.[2] There is no limit to the amount of money a party can spend on the production of the party platform, and there are no limitations on what a party can say during its 10 minutes.

Danmarks Radio has for decades allocated each party its series of programs at peak time, all parties starting at 8 p.m. Days are allocated according to the size of the party. The largest party receives first choice and usually selects the latest possible day before the election. With respect to scheduling on radio, the parties choose in the opposite order to counterbalance. It has become a tradition that a panel debate is broadcast on radio as well as on television, with representatives from all parties, one from each party, based again on the principle of equal time, 2 days before election day. This program usually takes 3 hours.

The day before election day has been exempt from election programs since television started broadcasting party presentations. The idea behind this day—clean from political propaganda, at least on television—was that voters should be allowed time to digest the relatively heavy amount of political communication they had been exposed to on television and decide on which party to vote for.

When the DR broadcasting monopoly was broken, the major event of relevance to election communication was that the new TV 2 introduced a panel debate on the night before election day. Another break with tradition was that the panel debate did not include representatives of all parties, as had always been the tradition in DR's panel debates. Only parties expected to be significant were invited to participate on the new channel. News criteria dominated over traditions, as they will in general if there are no normative obligations.

A normative obligation is also found in DR with respect to nonelection time, when all parties are given special coverage of their traditional annual meetings. All parties, independent of size and power, receive the same amount of coverage broadcast on a late evening following their annual meeting.

Political party access to broadcasting has been labeled "minute democracy" in Norway as well as in Denmark. In contrast to the Danish situation, where the Ombudsman and a decision made by the High Court actually reinforced the principles of equal access, the Norwegian Ombudsman once concluded that decisions about "who, when and how" access to the Norwegian national television channel belonged exclusively to the Norwegian broadcasting institution, NRK. The principles applied in the two countries are a bit different, though seen from an American point of view, they seem very much the same.

To receive equal treatment in Norway, a party must meet three criteria: It must have been represented in the Norwegian parliament, Stortinget, during one of the last two election periods; have run candidates in a majority of the districts; and have a current national organization. One exception is that a minor party in a coalition that forms the government, or is a clear alternative to the government, can participate with more than one representative in the final debate. The principle is that equal time is allotted to all parties in order to allow them to participate in the broadcast debate. The government as such has its own representative in programs where all political parties are present. The Norwegian program's format also does not provide parties time for their own platform in the form of a presentation program like there is in Denmark. Instead, candidates only respond to questions from journalists or a panel of voters. Parties not qualified for equal treatment in Norwegian television, but acknowledged as running for the election, will be be covered by short programs combining information and questioning.

The comparison with Norway illustrates the special equity of the Danish system, in which all parties running at a given election, regardless of size, power, or position in parliament, have the same right to present their ideas, independent of the party's economic position. Thus Denmark has some kind of publicly financed political advertising. Nevertheless we formally deny it, because political advertising is forbidden by law. In Denmark the party access to television described above is considered public service to the electorate, but how do the voters perceive it?

Party Platform Presentations on Television

CHANGES IN CONTENT OVER TIME

Over the years various types of party presentations have developed on Danish television. In the 1970s, and even today, some parties choose to let their leader use all 10 minutes to tell about the party, but such programs built totally around the party leader are not the dominant type on Danish television. Programs in which a series of candidates give their statements have been made over the years, and the type of programs in which a series of voters recommend "their" party have been very common. The most recent development in the structure of party presentations is a kind of story or dramatic format. Some presentations have been built around a young voter telling about the advantages perceivable if the party, in this case the Social Democrats, is strengthened. A new subtle style has emerged; for example, a program building upon a cartoon was used at the 1989 election by the major opposition party (the Social Democrats), and it was widely praised and generally accepted as an elegant way of presenting a party. It the latest EC Election, there was a new style introduced: a fixed, pretty picture of a Danish landscape, with swans swimming in a small lake in front of a beautiful old farmhouse, in which all the verbal messages from the party (the Progress Party) were presented on top of the "stillbild" like a poem.

Generally it is the party, not individual candidates, that is the focus in the party political programs. Naturally, it is the political leaders of the different parties, of which Denmark has a great number, who answer on behalf of their party when interviewed in news programs. Because news programs give candidates and political leaders the greatest opportunity to reach the audience, it is not without reason that Danish politicians most of all want access to news programs. But access cannot be bought, and access will be denied if any political leader, minister, or prime minister asks for time. Access will eventually be given, in the form of an interview if the man can present a news story, but no politicians can request access outside the above-described program types. Party press conferences are often held but seldom are shown on television. News criteria, not power of any other kind, prevails.

VOTERS' ASSESSMENT OF THE DANISH SYSTEM OF PARTY ACCESS

The equality principle, forming the basis for election campaigns on national television in Denmark, has been evaluated at several elections. In Table 8.1 we can see the great support of the principle that all parties, independent of the number of parties at an election, have the right to have their own presentation programs. With support from 85% of the population, the Danes indicate the democratic norm, prevailing so strongly that less than 10% dare to say "no." In a situation in which there is an alternative national channel, the Danes can always escape political communication, but they support very strongly the principle of equal access, not just access to programs run by journalists. Panel debates are supported as well. From the national election study in 1988, we know that 43% of the voters followed the panel debate; in 1987 it was 45%.

Elderly voters follow most of the presentation programs, but they are also closely watched by young voters. In 1988 there was a relative majority for dropping the presentation programs, but a sizable minority of 29% wanted to keep them (Table 8.2), and they have been kept so far. Young people especially wanted to keep this type of program.

When questioned about the "minute democracy" with equal time to all parties, even in debates, a strong majority favors keeping the principle of equal time for all (Table 8.3).

According to surveys, the population very strongly supports the principle of equal access for all parties. Although there are ongoing discussions of the quality of the programs, 15% or more of the population responded that election programs on Danish national television did help them make up their minds about which party to vote for. The

TABLE 8.1 Voters' Attitude to the Principle of All Parties' Right to Own Program on Television, Independent of Number of Parties Running at Elections*

	1987	*1988*	*1989*	*1990*
In favor of principle	82	85	75	85
Not in favor	9	6	9	11
Don't know	8	10	17	4

* Data from DR surveys at three national elections (1987, 1988, and 1990), and one European Election (1989).

TABLE 8.2 Voters' Attitudes to a Question Presenting the Idea of *Dropping* the Party Presentation Programs Made by the Party and *Keeping* the "Cross-Fire" Program, Where Journalists Question Party Representatives*

	All	*Socialists*	*Social Democrats*	*Bourgeois*
Idea accepted	45	37	45	51
Don't know	26	18	25	21
Idea not accepted	29	45	30	28
Number of responses	765	143	194	213

* Data from DR surveys, national election 1988.

TABLE 8.3 Attitudes Toward the Principles of Equal Time to All Parties in Panel Debates*

	Percentages	
In Favor of:	*All 1988*	*Watched the Debate the Night Before Election 1988*
All, equal time	66	75
All, free time	6	6
Some, free time	14	13
Other responses	2	2
Don't know	11	5
Sum	101	101
Total: All parties	72	81
Total: Free time	29	19
Number of responses	1,665	592

* Data from DR surveys, national election 1988, European Election 1989.

media's role with regard to educating the voters is less clear; and, according to surveys combined with content analyses of election campaigns, how much is learned varies, depending on the content of the campaigns. In general voters learn which issues are on the political agenda, and several examples indicate that voters learn basic facts from television programs during an election campaign (Siune, 1993). Readers of newspapers learn more about the election issues than those solely using television as a source of information, especially if the issues are

TABLE 8.4 Time of Decision When to Vote for a Specific Party in Denmark at Four National Elections*

	1981	*1984*	*1987*	*1988*
Before election campaign	72	77	76	69
During election campaign	13	12	10	10
During the last few days	15	11	13	17
Don't know	–	–	1	4
Number of responses	842	921	1,022	670

* Data from Danish Data Archive.

complicated. The most recent referenda on European integration confirm that it is difficult to learn about complicated matters, but television viewers did increase their level of information during the 1992 campaign (Siune et al., 1992).

Danish election surveys during the 1970s and the 1980s showed that although the majority of voters have decided how to vote before the election period or during the last few days before election day (see Table 8.4), a considerable proportion of the electorate makes up its mind during the campaign period or during the last few days before election day. Seen in this context, a heavy television campaign might influence the voters.

Voters' Use of Channels for Political Information

The Danish citizens use the information offered to them through the mass media rather heavily. Over the years a little more than half the population followed political campaigns on television, either for information or out of habit (Sauerberg, 1976). Data in Table 8.5 show the use of television at three recent national elections and the 1989 European Election. Television is the primary source of information, but it varies from election to election. The use of newspapers has remained relatively constant over two decades, whereas the use of radio has declined but is now relatively stable. In Denmark television is still the most used channel for political information, and the old DR channel is generally referred to as a source of information much more than the new TV 2 channel. This picture has been confirmed at the two most recent

TABLE 8.5 Most Important Source of Information in Four Danish Elections*

	1987	*1988*	*1989*	*1990*
Television	37	51	34	46
Newspapers	29	24	27	28
Radio	7	6	13	8
Conversation	8	9	8	5
Other sources	9	5	4	6
Don't know	9	5	15	7

* Data from DR surveys at three national elections (1987, 1988, and 1990), and one European Election (1989).

referenda, in 1992 and in 1993, about increased European integration, the so-called Maastricht Treaty.

The media's efficiency in educating and giving information to the voters may be discussed. Surveys show that there are differences between subjective perception and objective measures. A significant but varying proportion follows the national election campaigns on television to find out which party to vote for. In 1975, 23% did so, and in 1973, when Denmark had several new, potentially very powerful parties running for election, 35% did so. In 1987, it had fallen to 14%. In 1988, 16% responded that television had been a significant help for them in deciding which party to vote for. Although a minority in number, these voters nevertheless represent a sizable number of people open to influence. The most recent data about the gratification sought comes from the 1993 referendum study, in which a national survey indicated that 24% watched television to find out how to vote.[3] Among young people 22% indicate that television helped them. In this context it is important to note that it is especially the young in Denmark who strongly support the principle that all parties shall be treated equally and that the principle of equal time shall be followed. It appears that they need a kind of window to the parties, and television functions as such for them.

The question has been raised about how efficient the different media are in allowing parties to convert voters. This is not an easy question to answer. A summary statement would be that television has shown a stronger potential power to convert voters than any other medium. But whether it functions as such at a given election depends totally on those using the medium. High interest in politics and high degree of knowledge about political parties, often indicated by higher education, function as a kind of protection against conversion. Low interest, limited amount of knowledge, and high degree of exposure to television enhance the power of the medium, a conclusion that has been reached again and again.

There are several examples of incidents in which mass media have changed public opinion during the campaign period, either as a result of specific programs or due to the performance of a single politician. We are, however, not able to find any general percentage being persuaded during an election campaign. From surveys in Denmark we know that between 25% and 33% make up their minds about for whom to vote during the campaign period or during the very last day, so it is a sizable potential to influence. But how much citizens learn from politics on television is very limited. Recall of candidates' names has not been studied in Denmark for years, but recall of what it is "all about" has been studied. The more informed citizens believe they are, the more they know, but the general level of knowledge about such complicated matters as European issues, structures of decision making at a European level, and so on, is very low even after several informative campaigns on television. The recent EC referenda have shown that it is not so much the presentations prepared for the special platforms that influence voters; it is much more the conflict-oriented news stories that influence voters' attitudes. Fear of losing political freedom was one of the issues in the 1992 campaign, and during the campaign period there was an increased awareness of this fear (Siune et al., 1992).

During the 1993 campaign we found an intensified economic orientation that influenced the voters, and a majority turned out to vote "yes" to further European integration, an issue a majority of the same population, very small but nevertheless a majority, just 11 months before had turned down. In the meantime all the media in their coverage turned more and more positive toward the object of the referendum, the Maastricht Treaty (Siune et al., 1993).

New Media Channels

COMPETITION FROM COMMERCIAL CHANNELS

In Denmark the introduction of an alternative national television channel has been studied carefully. The expectation was that when the Danes got a chance to escape, not so many would follow the traditional election campaign as usual. At the European Election in 1989 we found fewer viewers of election programs than of the national election campaigns in 1987 and 1988. This was primarily explained by the minor interest in European Elections (Nordahl Svendsen, 1989). In 1990, at our most recent national election, we also found a reduction in the number of viewers of the traditional election programs, and this time it was a result of the competition from TV 2 (Nordahl Svendsen, 1991). A special Christmas program series did attract quite a number of voters, but when the program stopped, they turned back to watch election programs. The mean number of viewers was 13% for presentation and questioning. Compared to the usual figures this was only half the size of the normal audience for an election campaign in Denmark. But at the recent referenda, in 1992 and in 1993—which, in campaign structure, both followed the same pattern as described for national election campaigns—we found only a limited impact from that part of the campaign in which the parties had access to party presentations on television. The majority change, voters switching from voting "no" to voting "yes" to the Maastricht Treaty, took place in between the so-called campaign periods. On the other hand, one can argue that the whole year between June 1992 and May 1993 was one long campaign, and in this way the media and the party leaders from the government—which at a meeting in Edinburgh in December 1992 managed to get some promises through from the rest of the EC-member states—managed to persuade enough of the negative Danes to vote "yes" at the May 1993 election. The process was carefully studied, using content analysis and panel studies over a year-long period (Siune et al., 1993).

NEW LOCAL BROADCASTING

The Scandinavian countries experimented with local radio and television in the 1980s. Apart from their controversial financial arrangements—funding partly from public and partly from private money—the issue was the appropriate use of local broadcasting for politics. In the 1980s a lot of expectations were related to the decentralization of electronic mass media. The dream was that politics would become relevant to the local citizens, much more so than it had been as a result of centralizing via national television.

Today local radio and television have become permanent in Scandinavia, and they are organized according to a new set of regulations. Income from advertising is accepted in Norway and Denmark, but not in Sweden. Local media are used for political campaigning, and there is no regulation like the type described above for national radio and television.

Local media play a role in local politics, but the old dream of local media as the incentive for local political activity did not turn out as expected. In reality only very few channels serve the original purpose of decentralizing the political life. The majority of the local channels have become locally edited entertainment programs (playing music, bingo, and so on) much more than an instrument for local political activity.

Nevertheless, with the establishment of a large number of local channels, political parties have extra chances for access to local audiences. In Denmark the practice is that parties get access, sometimes free and sometimes paid for, to air their political messages to a local audience. At the Danish national election in January 1984, 70% of the local stations were asked by political parties to air election campaign material, and two thirds of them agreed. At the European Election later in 1984, fewer agreed to do so.[4] Most party requests were to air preproduced tapes, but some wanted transmission of press releases, arrangements of cross-party political debates, or interviews with candidates. Only 12 of 68 radio stations accepted the parties' prepared tapes, according to a survey made by the Ministry of Culture. The main reason for refusing their offer was the wish to remain unpolitical or neutral.

Due to the problematic economy of private radio stations today, they are more willing to sell airtime to political parties. In this way political communication depends on the party budget for campaigning. The budgets vary a lot, thus introducing an imbalance in favor of wealthy parties and candidates. So the new media structure, with privatized television channels, will in the future influence the campaign situation, but so far the old flag is still up for public service giving equal access to all for free.

Conclusion

In Denmark, as in the other Scandinavian countries, there is in principle no access for political advertising on national television channels. By law it is forbidden, but political parties in Scandinavian countries have the opportunity to broadcast their own ideas in special programs during election campaign periods. Political platforms on television therefore are also possible in Scandinavia, but the rules according to which the principle of free access is regulated are strict within the former monopolies, bound by their public service obligations. Access cannot be bought. Generally, the principle of fairness forms the basis for handling political parties in broadcasting in general, as well as during an election campaign. Apart from the fairness principle there are no special rules for presenting parties in news; ordinary news criteria prevail.

In Denmark the equal treatment of all parties has been discussed a number of times, but the principle has been strengthened by a statement from the Ombudsman and by a Supreme Court decision, dating back to the 1960s. The latest judicial confirmation of the rules was sought in 1986, when a minor party asked the Ombudsman for help in its fight for access to television on the same basis, that is, the same amount of time on the air and the same programming schedule as the parties represented in the Danish parliament, Folketinget, had received prior to the 1986 referendum about speeding up the European economic integration within the EEC.

Within Scandinavia, the Danish principle of equal access also to new parties is considered to be an element that could eventually create political instability. The break-up of Danish party structure in the 1970s can be taken as a result of weakening or disappearance of the party press, combined with easy access to television for new parties (Hadenius, 1983).

In general the Danish (and the Scandinavian) system meets the voters' needs, so far as it is in an accepted, balanced form of presenting political parties and a format that has been used for decades. In general, formally and socially it is not perceived as advertising. Danish voters have some knowledge about how political advertisements can be organized in other countries, but most Danes have a different perception of the role of political party television as it is aired in Denmark, and Danish voters refer to mass media and specifically to television as their prime source of information about the political parties.

Although in Scandinavia there are principles for access to broadcasting during an election period, access is not equal and access is not allocated according to the same principles in Norway, Sweden, and Denmark. Denmark has the most extreme system of equality. Equal time is given to all parties in special election programs, altogether approximately one hour to each party, including time in panel debates.

In a way, Denmark provides a full range of public-sponsored political advertisements.

Notes

1. The Danish Folketing has 175 seats, and the threshold is equivalent to one seat, presently approximately 20,000 votes. The limit to representation in Folketing is 2% of actual votes.

2. At the 1990 election, it was approximately $11,500 Canadian per party.

3. Data from Vilstrup Research for Danmarks Radio and Politiken, May, 1993.

4. Report from the Committee on Local Radio and Television, Ministry of Culture, Copenhagen, August, 1985.

References

Danmarks Radio. (1989, March). *Regler for udsendelse i radio og TV i forbindelse med valget til Europa-Parlamentet* [Rules for transmission in radio and television in connection with elections to the European parliament].

Danmarks Radio. (1990, November). *Regler for udsendelse i radio og TV i forbindelse med folketingsvalg* [Rules for transmission of radio and television in connection with general elections].

Euromedia Research Group. (Eds.). (1991). *Media systems in Western Europe, the Euromedia handbook.* London: Sage.

Hadenius, S. (1983). The rise and possible fall of the Swedish party press. *Communication Research, 10*, 287-310.

Kleinsteuber, H. J., McQuail, D., & Siune, K. (Eds.). (1986). *Electronic media and politics in Western Europe, Euromedia research group handbook of national systems.* Frankfurt/New York: Campus.

Nordahl Svendsen, E. (1989). EF-Valget 1989 i DR TV [The EC election in 1989 on Danmarks Radio's television]. In E. Nordahl Svendsen (Ed.), *Medieforskning i Danmarks Radio 1988/1989* [Media research in Danmarks Radio 1988/89]. Danmarks Radio Forskningsrapport nr. 2B/89.

Nordahl Svendsen, E. (1991). *Lighedsprincip i konkurrence: Folketingsvalget 1990 i Danmarks Radio* [The principle of equality in competition: The general election of 1990 on Danmarks Radio]. Paper from Medieforskningen, Danmarks Radio.

Østbye, H. (1991). Norway: Local orientation and internationalization. In Euromedia Research Group (Eds.), *Media systems in Western Europe, the Euromedia handbook.* London: Sage.

Sauerberg, S. (1976). Kommunikation til vælgere—og mellem vælgere [Communication to voters—and between voters]. In O. Borre et al. (Eds.), *Vælgere i 70'erne* [Voters in the 1970s]. Copenhagen: Akademisk Forlag.

Siune, K. (1987). The political role of mass media in Scandinavia. *Legislative Studies Quarterly, 12*(3), 395-414.

Siune, K. (1993). *EC på dagsdordenen* [EC on the political agenda]. Århus: Forlaget Politica.

Siune, K., Svensson, P, & Tonsgaard, O. (1992). *Det blev et nej* [The Danes said no]. Århus: Politica.

Siune, K., Svensson, P., & Tonsgaard, O. (1993). *Fra et nej til et ja* [From a no to a yes]. Århus: Politica.

9. The Blank Spot

Political Advertising in the Netherlands

KEES BRANTS

If the relationship between politics and mass media can best be described as Siamese twins, then political advertising in the Netherlands is the orphan, so to speak, of political communication. In the election campaigns of the main political parties, it has always been last on the priority list; for the television viewer it was often the "sanitary stop" between more worthwhile programs; and scientific researchers considered it a no-go area. No wonder longitudinal data on content, style, and effect of political television advertising in the Netherlands are conspicuously absent.

A meager excuse might be that in a country dominated by consensual, some might say dull, politics and a stable, if not docile, electorate, political spots are an unnecessary luxury. For years links between political parties and media have created a fairly closed political communication system; and, judging from the money spent (at election time usually not more than a small percentage of the total campaign budget), official party political broadcasts were considered neither help nor hindrance, just TV time to be filled out of necessity.

Things have changed. In the past few years, with traditional politics in a state of flux, a notable cynicism on the part of the electorate, and the public broadcasting system in turmoil with the arrival of commercial competitors, political advertising, as a means of addressing floating and even turned-off voters and restoring trust, has entered a sudden current.

The recent history of political communication in the Netherlands and the development of the political spot can best be told in three phases: the years of stability (1945-1965), of prudent change (1965-1989), and of uncertainty (the present). This chapter provides a sketch of the Netherlands and an illustration of the first 40 postwar years and the recent jump into what seems to be the Great Unknown of political advertising in the Lowlands.

The Political and Cultural Background

This small country by the North Sea, with 15 million people crammed into 41,000 square kilometers, has long been a typical example of what is known in political science as "segmented pluralism": a diversity of political parties, social movements, educational and media systems, and voluntary associations organized vertically (and often crosscutting social strata) along the lines of religious and ideological cleavages (cf. Brants, 1985; Lijphart, 1968). This "pillarized" structure consisted of four large social blocs: the Catholic and the Calvinist "pillars" (in the first years after the Second World War, encompassing more than 50% of the population); the Socialist movement (about 25%-35%); and, from a socioeconomic point of view as its mirror image, the secular conservatives (only 10%-15%).

At mass level society was divided, with the people of the different blocs living more or less separated from each other. Each pillar had its own world, where schools, clubs, media, and youth associations strengthened the feeling of belonging. At the present time, with individualism as the main social characteristic, it might be difficult to imagine that in the first 20 years after the war, one could be looked after from the cradle to the grave within the boundaries of one's own religious or ideological group, without ever really knowing how the other half lived. Within the Catholic pillar, for example, families not only attended Mass but would also read a Catholic newspaper, listen to the Catholic broadcasting organization KRO, and vote for the Catholic People's Party (KVP); the father would be a member of the Catholic union or employers association, the mother would be a member of the Catholic women's guild, and the children went to a Catholic school or university and enjoyed the close-knit familiarity of a Catholic soccer or gymnastics club.

The most important feature of what is also referred to as "the politics of accommodation" was that of bargaining and compromise among the elite at the top. The price that society paid for the relative peacefulness of this arrangement, in which the elite possessed an equal stake in continuation of the system, is that, of necessity, it entailed secrecy at the top and pacification of the lower levels of society; the elite consciously creating an "information gap" to keep its own rank and file both quiet and divided. The politics of accommodation were also the politics of acquiescence and paternalism, with, as a result, not only a relative absence of class conflict but also a relative immunity of the elite from criticism.

Media Systems and Party Organizations

The organization of the mass media was both a confirmation of this division and an instrument of its internal cohesion. Two thirds of the postwar daily newspapers were connected to the major pillars, with notable interlocking directorships within the Catholic and Socialist pillars. For example, the editor of the Labour paper *Het Vrije Volk*—for a while the largest Dutch daily—was appointed by the Labour party (PvdA) conference, though its lobby correspondent attended the internal meetings of the parliamentary party.

The same situation generally applied to radio. The connection with other organizations within the pillar was even stronger here than could be said of the press, because in the 1930s government—fearful of the intrusive nature of this new and supposedly powerful medium—had already ruled that only broadcasting organizations with strong ties to the different pillars should be allowed on the air. The Dutch broadcasting system is therefore a peculiar mix of private member-organizations, with traditional party political links and a clear religious or ideological message but at the same time public service aims. The only neutral organization, AVRO, had strong links with the liberal sphere, which is not surprising, considering its commercial (Philips) background.

Generally speaking, the broadcasting organizations became the mouthpieces of the party elites within the pillars. With the electorate forming a stable group that political parties could count on at election time, the media had a strongly integrating function within the pillars. They were the pulpit of pillarization, the "spreaders of the word," communicating the elites' message. The media both demonstrated and confirmed the correctness of a pillar's ideology. Prior to elections, the party leaders used "their" microphone to disseminate and explicate their views. Debate or confrontation scarcely existed; political communication formed an almost closed system.

Television was slow in coming to the Netherlands, and when it came the organization had the same pillarized structure as that of radio. Five years after the introduction of TV in 1951, there were still only 25,000 sets, but then the new medium took off. Two years later there were almost 400,000, and at the end of the decade "the Box" had established itself in the Dutch household.

History of Political Party Broadcasts

Party political broadcasts, based on a system of proportionality, had existed on radio since 1925. The 1959 elections saw the first experimental TV spots, 10 minutes freely allocated twice to each party regardless of electoral support. In 1962 political broadcasts were officially introduced when government claimed regular time for the political parties on what was then the only channel. The spot became part of the information function of public service broadcasting.

With television reasonably well established with 2 million sets, weekly political broadcasts were introduced, alternating so that each party would have about five 10-minute programs per year. Parties represented in Parliament had equal time as a matter of principle; and in the weeks prior to national elections, parties with candidates in all electoral districts (often amounting to 30 different parties) were also allowed a 10-minute slot twice. Studio and camera facilities were freely provided by the public broadcaster NTS (after 1967, NOS), and the government subsidized the 10-minute programs with Dfl 400 (now about $200) each; this was raised to Dfl 1000 at the end of the 1960s. Apart from a steady increase of government subsidy, this system remained virtually intact until 1989.

What little research there is on political broadcasts during the first 10 years stems more from scientific curiosity than party political interest (Boef, 1971; Manschot, Niemantsverdriet, & Noldus, 1968; and half-yearly ratings reports by the NOS research department). No empirical evaluation of content—issues raised, topics discussed, mode of address—exists, let alone effect studies, whether in an experimental setting or not. There are not enough spots left in party or other files to allow for scientific analysis and comparative longitudinal conclusions. However, there seems to be a general agreement among political scientists, political commentators, and party officials of the time that the spots were dull and more a form of visual radio: talking heads, nervously looking in and around the camera, unfamiliar and uncomfortable with the new medium.

Given that the main parties had a very accessible political communication system, a stable electorate that could be counted on at election time, and politics characterized by consensus and compromise, these broadcasts were scarcely necessary anyway. In spite of the fact that in principle the whole population was addressed, the talking heads talked more like Dutch uncles preaching to their own congregation, to use a typical Dutch metaphor. Whenever there was a reference to other noncoalition parties, the tone was critical but seldom attacking. Sometimes documentary film was used to convince the electorate about the seriousness of politics and the party's awareness of postwar issues like housing shortages and the Cold War, but in general one addressed one's own electorate. If other denominations watched, that was fine.

Available data of that time do not reveal whether one's own congregation indeed watched.[2] The composition of the audience was similar to that of other "heavily informative" programs: the old and the less educated, who watch more television than any other group anyway. As compared to present ratings, the novelty attracted a wide audience, although not for long, and right from the start there were grave doubts about the meaning of these viewing figures. With only one channel, high scores could usually be explained by previous or following popular programs, such as news broadcasts, feature films, or televised soccer matches. Whether people actually watched could not be detected by the rating technique at the time, but even the political parties themselves doubted the validity of the figures.

In 1963, 43% of householders and single adults in possession of a TV set watched the election spots (Algemeen Handelsblad, 7-13-1963). In 1965 the average rating (now of the entire population 15 years and older) was 41%, and in the first half of 1966, after the introduction of a second channel had lowered ratings of all programs, it was 32%.[3] The appreciation of these programs was just under 6, with a considerable standard deviation (on average 1.4) as these kinds of programs raise strong emotional reactions pro and con (Manschot et al., 1968, p. 89).

In 1968 the ratings had dropped to 26% (ranging from 13%-50%, depending on the proximity of a soccer match), a mere 2.3 million people aged 15 years and older. However, by then the shaky pillars of Dutch political culture had been seriously rocked.

The Changing Politics of the Netherlands

The foregoing sketch of the Netherlands as a closed system of subcultures and political communication is, to a certain degree, both ideal and typical. Although it is true for the most part, there must have been some chinks—otherwise, the abrupt changes that took place in the 1960s are inexplicable.

In the middle of that decade de-pillarization and a decline of religious feeling shook the foundations of both political and media systems. Developments that took place in most liberal democracies after the Second World War—like rapid technological progress, a rising level of education and spending potential, mass tourism, and a growth of the tertiary sector with its expanding new middle class—had a special effect on the precarious balance along the religious dividing lines of Dutch society. Amplified by these structural changes, religion lost its unifying and integrating function. The associations, organizations, and political parties became less segmented and more pluralist: The pillars lost their flocks.

During the 1960s loyalty within the pillars and obedience to the political elite came under pressure and affected electoral stability; the floating voter appeared on the electoral scene. Docility gave way to an ever stronger call for participation at the base of society. With the benefit of hindsight one can wonder whether the changes in Dutch political culture were as dramatic as they seemed at the time (cf. Lijphart, 1989; van Praag, 1992). In spite of changes in the rules of the game (openness and controversy instead of secrecy and compromise became the new creeds), the politics of accommodation did not undergo as complete a metamorphosis as is often supposed.

The Netherlands is still a consensus democracy, and the party political structure has been only relatively affected. There still is a multiparty system, with an electoral system based on an extreme kind of proportional representation; the threshold for new parties is very low (0.67% of the votes is needed for a seat in Parliament). The system has always been one of minority parties; at elections all are confident that no single party will gain an independent majority. At the same time, this softens the tone of the campaign, because the day after the elections the laborious consultations prior to forming a coalition cabinet begin.

Two significant changes in the party system did, however, take place. First, there appeared a political movement aimed more at renewing the concept of democracy and breaking through the stalemate of Dutch political culture: D66 (Democrats '66). Emphasizing pragmatism, they aimed at more electoral influence and entered the political arena after market research had established their viability. They immediately made use of modern campaign methods and what later came to be known as political marketing. An advertising agency rewrote part of their manifesto pamphlet and stylized the 1967 election campaign. The television performance of the leading candidate helped to build the image of a fast, young, dynamic party. D66 had its ups and downs but is still very much present in the 1990s.

Second, at the end of the 1970s, the three major denominational parties (the Catholic KVP, the Calvinist ARP, and the Reformed CHU) formed a new Christian Democratic party, CDA, after having lost much of their support: from 56% in 1948, to 50% in 1963, to only 32% in 1977. Since that year (when they came second after the PvdA), in each of the following four elections, the Christian Democrats came out first.

The Changing Political Broadcasting System

Many of the developments of the 1960s were triggered by television, but at the same time the medium was affected by the de-pillarization and decline of religious disposition, too, leading to a decline in self-evident membership. Although the political parties now had to search for floating voters, the broadcast media had to aim for new consumers. Traditional supporters, who followed the creed of their religious or ideological background when subscribing to a broadcasting corporation, could no longer be counted on.

The uncertainty of the party elites regarding a changed political culture was mercilessly shown by the young and dynamic medium with which the old party politicians were not yet familiar. Until the mid-1960s there was only one channel on Dutch television, with each traditional broadcasting organization having its own evening to broadcast current affairs programs, shows, and the like—everything with its own Catholic, Protestant, or Socialist flavor. But with people watching every night, television broke through the isolation of the pillars and opened the window to show how the other half lived.

The new Broadcasting Act of 1969 introduced advertising by means of a separate noncommercial foundation (STER), which broadcast blocks of advertisements outside the actual programs. Commercial broadcasting companies were not allowed, but the closed system was opened up to newcomers like TROS and VOO, public broadcasters aiming at a more general audience. Their entertainment focus—also in current affairs programs—was very successful, but at the same time, according to Daalder (1974, p. 64), they reduced politics to sheer incidents and played to negative feelings within the electorate vis-à-vis politics. With the growing competition over members necessary for the allocation of broadcasting time, the other companies gradually followed this more commercial kind of programming, which was soon to be called *verTROSsing*, after its originator. Objectivity, human interest, and the personalization of political reality took over from the partisan stand customary in broadcasting until then.

In spite of this development, at election time the internal competition between the broadcasting corporations meant they all wanted prominent candidates on their programs. Above all, they still operated to a large extent as platforms for the parties in the respective pillars. The news might be impartial, basing its selection more on news values, but there were still informal ties between parties and broadcasting organizations. So, in the current affairs programs of the respective organizations one would often find the politician of that creed. A Labour leader could still be quite sure of prime-time coverage with the VARA at election time, and as a KRO publication put it in 1975: "A broadcasting corporation which calls itself Catholic must have very strong reasons for publicly criticizing a political party which calls itself Catholic" (Brants, 1985, p. 112).

Changes in the political culture prompted political parties to modernize their election campaigns. The PvdA, which had been conducting regular surveys of voters since 1960, was the first to start a campaign along modern lines in 1967: It had a more centralized campaign organization; one leading candidate, as opposed to three in 1963; and a strategy clearly directed toward the media. The activities of advertising agencies were no longer limited to executive tasks, but now also included planning the campaign (van Praag, 1991). Even more media-centered was D66 that year; its campaign was loosely organized, with the help of party members with advertising experience. The party's media success was due to its young party leader and the novelty at the otherwise stale political front.

The other parties were soon to follow, but as a sort of carryover from the politics of accommodation, campaigns (including party political broadcasts) were only mildly attacking in style and certainly not aggressive. All major parties were aware of the postelection necessity of forming a government, which prompted a certain caution in what one accused a potential coalition partner of. Also—rightly or wrongly, and certainly not supported by any research—an aggressive campaign style was considered "American" (and everyone seemed to know what that adjective meant) and counterproductive in Dutch political culture.

With the floating voter and the party changer estimated at some 30% of the total electorate, increasingly research was used by CDA, PvdA, and VVD in locating electoral target groups. Other parties, including D66, having only limited campaign budgets, had to depend on research published by the media. The emphasis in research was on intended electoral behavior, the salience of issues, and the popularity of leading candidates. Campaign feedback surveys were considered too expensive and too risky to build a strategy on.

Part of the modernization of the election campaign was a hesitant introduction, between 1967 and the mid-1980s, of more affective aspects: the style and image of party and candidate, more generally the nonpolitical "radiation." In the light of increasing research and campaign professionalization, it is, however, remarkable that the parties had no clear influence model. They began to realize that image is important but did not get much further than a simple argumentation model: When people do not vote for us, we did not get our message across (van Praag & Brants, 1991).

In the political spot the focus was even more cognitive. This was also true with D66, which experimented with style forms. The content (if the limited availability allows for generalizations) depended partly on the time of broadcasting. Spots at election time had a more propagandistic function, propagating the party's manifesto issues and its slogan. In the period between elections, they were more informative, carrying views on issues of the moment. Interviews by journalists were sometimes used to overcome the credibility problem most party political broadcasts have with viewers, but often the TV-journalist could still be associated with the party's pillar.

As part of a modernized election campaign, all through the 1970s and 1980s the political spot occupied only a marginal position. Only a small percentage of the total campaign budget was spent on these broadcasts, and even if they had had more money, STER did not allow advertisements with a political content. The spot's lack of importance, not in the least in the eyes of campaign managers and politicians, was confirmed by audience ratings. From 26% in 1968, the average rating dropped to 21% by the mid 1970s and, more dramatically, to 6% in the mid-1980s. That one in five viewers still watched these spots in the 1970s was mainly due to their placement between the news and a feature film.

The extra party political broadcasts at elections were even worse off. During the elections of 1971 and 1972 they attracted only 5% of the viewers, and at the 1981 elections viewers had dropped to 3.5%. The explanation for this lack of interest at election time could be that there were not only the parliamentary parties with their spots but also another 20 miniparties, and most of the spots were scheduled outside prime time.

The Current Politics of Uncertainty

The changes in political culture and communication in the 1960s were considered dramatic and drastic at the time. Certainly, things changed, but politics in the Netherlands remained consensual, electoral broadcasting was still characterized by informal links between parties and organizations, and the political spot kept on muttering on the sidelines of political communication. The new and the near might make the strongest impression, but the changes since the end of the 1980s are indeed more fundamental with regard to political campaigning in general and political communication in particular.

The present political culture is marked by what has been called "a growing gap between citizens and politics." Three developments are often mentioned as proof. In the first place, the gap is seen in the changing image of and interest in politics. All political parties have seen a steady decline in membership; since the 1950s it has shrunk from 15% to 4% of the electorate. In recent elections turnout has decreased, too. A survey in seven major cities after the 1990 local elections—in which, for instance, Amsterdam saw a drop of 10% in turnout as compared to the 1986 elections—showed that one in five respondents had a negative image of and was cynical about local government and civil servants, had little trust or interest in politics, saw no difference between parties, did not know local politicians, and in no way participated in politics (Onderzoeksgroep Lokale Democratie, 1991).

In a longitudinal study of political efficacy between 1972 and 1989, van der Eijk, Pennings, and Wille (1992) found that only 40% of the national electorate was satisfied with government. They did not find, however, any significant change in political mistrust or cynicism over the years, an experience not shared by politicians. According to a newspaper survey in 1992, 81% of MPs think there is a growing gap between politics and citizens (NRC Handelsblad, 3-14-1992).

In the second place, the gap is reflected in the success of right-wing extremism. In the local elections of 1990 two extremist parties (CD and CP'86) attracted almost 7% of the electorate in Amsterdam, Rotterdam, and The Hague; and an opinion poll in 1992 showed a large electoral potential for the racist opinions of these parties. Both not only advocate anti-migrant sentiments and clear aversion against asylum seekers but also articulate political cynicism themselves while embracing those with a growing distaste for genuine politics.

The third development affecting the citizen-politics relation has been labeled alternatively the crisis in the interventionist state, the end of ideology, and even the end of history altogether. It points to the disappearance of communism, the difficult ideological position many West European social democratic parties find themselves in, and the relative success of liberalism. On the whole, it refers to the decline of ideologies aiming at change and building on notions such as welfare and solidarity, in favor of a more Thatcherite "survival-of-the-fittest" discourse. A political-psychological description would point to an individualistic trend in society, away from social values, and a decrease in traditional party politics.

The result of this development might well be twofold: uncertainty within the electorate about (or even lack of interest in) their own ideological position, and no more consensus about the positioning of political parties within the electoral space. Party identification on the basis of political knowledge and the determining role of the traditional Left-Right dimension in electoral behavior (cf. van der Eijk & Niemöller, 1983) will then lose their importance, and affective image factors will come to the forefront.

Politics might be in a state of flux and uncertainty; the broadcasting system is in turmoil. By the beginning of the 1980s, the high degree of cabling in the Netherlands (85%) enabled broadcasting of both terrestrial (public) and satellite (commercial) foreign stations. This did not upset the viewing habits of the audience, however; more than three quarters of the population stuck to Dutch channels. The introduction in

TABLE 9.1 Audience Ratings of the Public Channels

	86/87	*87/88*	*88/89*	*89/90*	*90/91*
Heavy information	7	6	4	3	4
Current affairs	14	15	9	7	7
News	18	12	8	7	7
Light information	13	10	7	4	5

SOURCE: NOS-KLO 1992 (18.00-24.00 hours), NOS Department of Audience Research.

1989 of the Luxembourg-based, but Dutch-language and Netherlands-aimed, RTL4 did change all this.

In a short period the audience ratings of the three public channels fell to 55%, and RTL4 gained 30% of the market. With RTL5, which was launched in 1993 to attract a young, more affluent audience, the public channels fell back to around 50%. The total time people spend in front of "the Box" rose from 114 to 145 minutes per day in that same period, but it was only the RTL stations that profited from this increase.

In order to compete, and partly under pressure from the Minister of Culture, the public channels have reacted in two ways.[4] First, they are combining strength in coproductions and in coordinating their programming efforts. From a pillarized system, with nine different organizations sharing three channels but each having their own (religiously or secularly colored) programs, public broadcasting in the Netherlands now is becoming a channel system, with the traditional pillars gradually losing their identity. For the main political parties this might well mean that they will lose their self-evident link with those broadcasters and therefore their easy access to political communication at election time.

Second, "heavy" informative programs—which are practically absent on both RTLs—are increasingly scheduled outside prime time; but in "light" information (e.g., a growing number of talk shows in which the interviewer seems more important than the interviewee or the subject) the presentation of politics as infotainment is paramount. What little political content there is, is treated in a personalized and human interest style. To make things worse for political communicators, audiences are avoiding programs traditionally containing political information (see Table 9.1). The electorate is not only floating, it is now zapping, too, which seems to confirm Holtz-Bacha's (1990) hypothesis of an increasing "entertainment-slalom" in dual broadcasting systems (p. 82).

A scattered audience, zapping away from political content that is often scheduled outside prime time anyway, and a loss of traditional access to the public channels are turning elections into a campaigner's nightmare. The answer to this dilemma is mainly sought in the field of free publicity, where news programs are still considered the primary means of political communication. RTL News is not dissimilar to that of the public channels, but the 1994 elections will be the first test case for party political access and RTL's style, factuality, and impartiality in covering the campaign. At the same time, the political parties show a growing interest in light informative programs, like talk shows and high audience entertainment shows. Current affairs programs, often scheduled outside prime time, seem to lose their importance for campaign managers.

Increased Attention to Political Spots

Hesitantly, the spotlight is falling on paid (political spots on commercial channels) and pseudo-paid publicity (party political broadcasts on the public channels). About half the campaign budget of political parties used to go to newspaper advertising. For the 1994 elections, three of the four main parties planned to buy time on the commercial RTL channels. Conspicuously absent is D66, which in the 1960s was one of the first to use advertising agencies in its campaigns. Lack of money and doubt about cost-effectiveness have made the Democrats decide against commercial spots, but there is also a genuine distaste for the commercialization of politics.

However, the kind of spot one would expect on a commercial channel was already introduced on the public channels during the elections of 1989. Until that year, each political party (participating in all 18 electoral districts) was twice allocated 10 minutes of TV time, at prime time and around midnight, during a period of 3 to 4 weeks before elections. This system was changed for the 1989 elections. Each party was allowed 2 minutes twice and 5 minutes three times, which made the first two, at least in length, somewhat comparable to a "real" spot.

The style and format did indeed change, as compared to the spots at the previous election in 1986 and those of the 1970s.[5] This is first of all noted in the faster pace of the spot. The number of shots, changes of pictures per minute, has risen from just under two to more than nine shots per minute (Figure 9.1). The increase is particularly due to the CDA party, which on the whole has advanced most in modernizing the spot. Together with PvdA, they also made most use in 1989 of cinema-

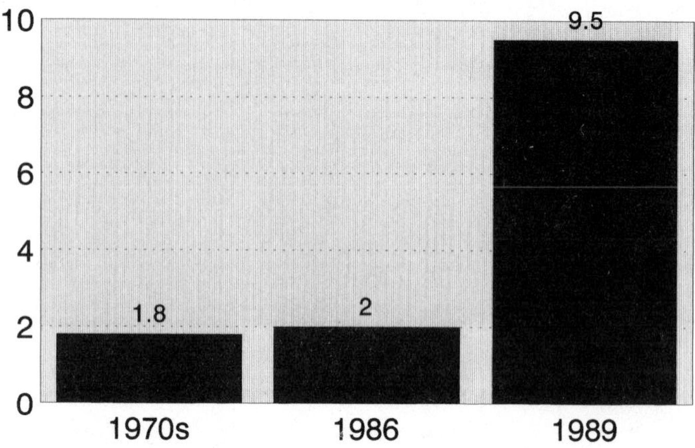

Figure 9.1. Number of Shots per Minute

tographic means, such as dramatic contrasts in color, picture, and sound. D66, on the other hand, not only opposed the shortening of time but also had the least modern spot.

In two other, related aspects there was also a change, although more gradual: the use of music and text (Figure 9.2). Marketing strategists claim that images are more effective than texts when the public has a low level of involvement (Floor & Van Raaij, 1989, p. 232). In the 1970s the spoken word was still dominant, but verbal statements now form less than two thirds of the spot, and music has gone up to 19%. Again, it is CDA that has advanced most. In its 1989 spots of both 2 and 5 minutes, almost three quarters consisted of music. A 3-minute spot, which it produced to build the image of its new party leader in 1993, had only music, slow-motion pictures, lots of "sphere," and no text at all.

On the whole one can say that there is a shift in most spots over the years from explication to association, from a more cognitive to a more affective content. Building the image of the party leader as competent, knowledgeable, trustworthy, and hardworking, but also sympathetic and honest, has become more important than explaining the party's program and its stand on specific issues. With PvdA and to a lesser degree with CDA, the social attitude of the leader is also emphasized.

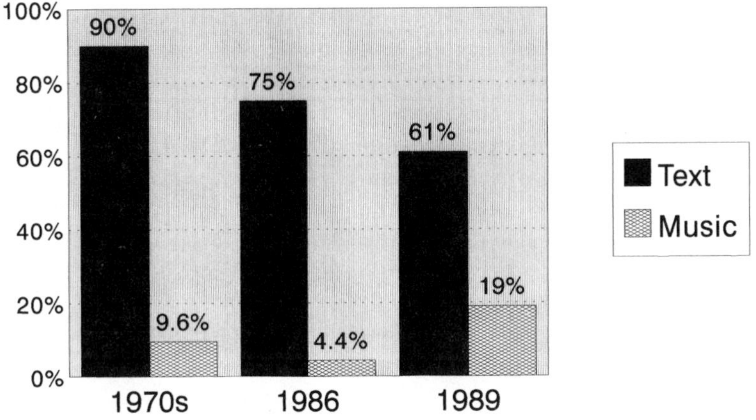

Figure 9.2. Text and Music in Political Spots

The Uncertainty of the Future for Political Spots

The introduction of the modern spot during the 1989 elections does not mean that party political broadcasts will automatically get a more prominent position in election campaigns, although since 1993 all spots are 3 minutes long. First of all, the television audience is too scattered over a vast array of channels and therefore too small, but also too little interested in politically informative programs, to focus a campaign on, let alone a target group strategy. The average rating of the election spots in 1989 was 4.3%, ranging from a mere 0.8% to a surprising 16.3%. Out of 83 broadcasts no more than 11 reached an audience of 10% or more, all on what was the most popular channel, after the news and before a show.

There has been a dramatic fall in viewership since 1965, and party campaigners still wonder where it will end. But even with an audience of 10%, one is never sure whether the public does not use the spot as a relaxing interval between more popular programs. No research has been done by any party on whatever effect spots might have, which shows not only the parties' lack of interest in the phenomenon but also their inability to evaluate its usefulness. Research is gradually occupying a more important place in campaigns, but the money is mostly spent on locating the floating voter, his or her motivations, and the affective qualities of the party leader. Campaign effects are seldom measured.

Second, a good spot is expensive, and political parties scarcely have money, certainly not now that their membership is falling. Apart from production costs, a 30-second spot at prime time on RTL4 in 1993 cost around Dfl 30,000. For regular 3-minute party political broadcasts on the public channels (24 per year from 1994 on) parties get Dfl 4600 per broadcast, and for the total of 20 minutes that they get during the 3 weeks running up to an election, government pays out Dfl 31,000 per party.[6] The in-house production of the CDA spot in 1989 was only a few thousand guilders, but the PvdA paid out Dfl 750,000 (50% of its campaign budget) for its spot, which was produced by Saatchi & Saatchi and directed by a well-known Dutch feature film director.

Compared to those of other European countries, the campaign budgets of political parties in the Netherlands are among the lowest and have scarcely risen over the years.[7] In 1989 CDA had a budget of Dfl 1.42 million, PvdA 1.34, VVD 1.03, and D66 only 0.56. With the exception of the PvdA in 1989, spots occupy between 1% and 8% of the total campaign budgets. Although it is not forbidden by law, sponsoring by industry is not done in the Netherlands.

However, even if parties were to skip all their newspaper and magazine advertisements, which now account for half of the campaign budget, it would still be virtually impossible to buy regular airtime on the commercial channels, and campaign managers know that just one showing will not do, that continual repetition of a spot is necessary to have some sort of impact. With this in mind, the position of the party spot in Dutch political communication remains blank, and its future bleak.

Notes

1. The empirical research presented here on the modernization of the spot in the Netherlands was done with the help of Bernadette Houdijk and Marion van Luneburg.

2. In the first years of audience ratings, political preference was not asked. Even in later years, when it was, the variable was never used in cross-tabulations. This only shows the lack of interest in the phenomenon of party political broadcasts.

3. The NOS research department changed the composition of people interviewed over time. In the 1960s it was those 15 years and older, whereby 1% stands for 90,000 people. In the 1970s until 1988 it stood for 12 years on up (1% = 100,000). At the moment there

are two scores: from 6 years and from 13 years up. In the audience ratings used for party political broadcasts from 1988, 1% stands for 133,000 people 6 years and older.

4. There is also a financial strategy, but this is less relevant with regard to political communication.

5. For reasons of availability, only a sample of four spots of the four main parties was analyzed, and for 1986 and 1989 it was two spots each. In the latter two elections usually only one or two spots were shown anyway.

6. At the time this text was finalized, it was not certain how the 20 minutes per party would be divided for the May 1994 elections.

7. Per voter, Dutch parties spent 0.17 British pounds in 1989. For other countries this was: Italy (1987) 0.66, Denmark (1988) 0.68, United Kingdom (1987) 0.70, Sweden (1988) 1.33, and Germany (1987) 3.90 (Katz & Mair, 1992).

References

Boef, C. (1971). Politiek op de televisie [Politics on television]. *Acta Politica*, Jrg. *VI*, 92-107.

Brants, K. (1985). Broadcasting and politics in the Netherlands: From pillar to post. In R. Kuhn (Ed.), *Broadcasting and politics in Western Europe* (pp. 104-122). London: Frank Cass.

Daalder, H. (1974). *Politisering en lijdelijkheid in de Nederlandse politiek* [Politicization and passivity in Dutch politics]. Assen: Van Gorcum.

Floor, K., & van Raaij, F. (1989). *Marketing-communicatie strategie* [Marketing-communication strategy]. Leiden: Stenfert Kroese.

Holtz-Bacha, C. (1990). Videomalaise revisited: Media exposure and political alienation in West Germany. *European Journal of Communication, 5*, 73-85.

Katz, R. S., & Mair, P. (Eds.). (1992). *Party organisations in Western democracies 1960-1990: A data handbook.* London.

Lijphart, A. (1968). *The politics of accommodation: Pluralism and democracy in the Netherlands.* Berkeley: University of California Press.

Lijphart, A. (1989). From the politics of accommodation to adversarial politics in the Netherlands: A reassessment. In H. Daalder & G. A. Irwin (Eds.), *Politics in the Netherlands. How much change?* (pp. 139-153). London: Frank Cass.

Manschot, B., Niemantsverdriet, H., & Noldus, T. (1968). TV-uitzendingen van politieke partijen [TV broadcasting of political parties]. In *Massamedia en Politiek. 24 Essays ter nagedachtenis aan prof.mr. L.G.A. Schlichting* [Mass media and politics: 24 essays in remembrance of Prof. Mr. L.G.A. Schlichting] (pp. 81-95). Utrecht: Amboboeken.

Onderzoeksgroep Lokale Democratie. (1991). *Lokale democratie en bestuurlijke vernieuwing in Amsterdam* [Local democracy and administrative renewal in Amsterdam]. Delft: Eburon.

van der Eijk, C., & Niemöller. (1983). *Electoral change in The Netherlands.* Amsterdam: CT-Press.

van der Eijk, C., Pennings, P., & Wille, A. (1992). Politieke betrokkenheid—Is de burger afgehaakt? [Political bewilderment—Does anybody care about the citizen?] In

J.J.M. Holsteyn & G. A. Irwin (Eds.), *De Nederlandse kiezer 1989* [The Dutch voter 1989] (pp. 3-32). Amsterdam: Steinmetzarchief/Swidoc/Skon.

van Praag, P., Jr. (1991). *Strategie en illusie. Elf jaar intern debat in de PvdA (1966-1977)* [Strategy and illusion: Eleven years of internal debate within the PvdA]. Amsterdam: Het Spinhuis.

van Praag, P., Jr. (1992). The Netherlands: The 1989 campaign. In S. Bowler & D. M. Farrell (Eds.), *Electoral strategies and political marketing* (pp. 144-163). London: Macmillan.

van Praag, P., Jr., & Brants, K. (1991). Politieke campagnes [Political campaigns]. In B. Klandermans & E. Seydel (Eds.), *Overtuigen en activeren* [Persuasion and activation] (pp. 102-120). Assen: Van Gorcum.

10. The North European Exception

Political Advertising on TV in Finland

TOM MORING

In 1990 Finland was the first country in the Scandinavian region to allow political advertising on radio waves over nationwide terrestrial television. Thus Finland is a special case in comparison with most countries in Northern Europe.[1] In Norway and Denmark, political ads are still forbidden through national regulations if they are carried independently by radio waves or cable networks. In Sweden, domestic distribution is also prohibited; however, Swedish political parties or candidates could get around the restrictions by purchasing time on direct satellite broadcasts.

Before the 1990 parliamentary election in Denmark, the London-based TV 3, broadcasting by satellite over Scandinavia, offered the Danish parties the opportunity to air political ads, but the Danish parties agreed not to accept the offer. In Norway, TV 3 itself has kept to the restrictions on political advertising. In Sweden, however, the moderate right-wing party (Moderaterna) aired some spots over TV 3 in the 1991 election, and it has been followed by the Liberal party. The regulations are somewhat less categorical in Sweden than in Denmark and Norway; in Sweden, legislation permits political parties to allow political ads on domestic channels. Although that is unlikely to happen, political television ads distributed by satellite are expected to appear in increased numbers in the next Swedish election.

In Finland, political ads have never been banned from cable TV. However, the audience ratings of domestic cable programs averaged less than 3% of the total audience in the early 1990s, not a large enough audience to trigger more than marginal investments in TV slots until ads were also allowed on the nationwide domestic commercial programs.

The Finnish Semi-Commercial Broadcasting System

Finland differs from its Nordic neighbors in that its commercial TV has long-standing traditions, whereas in the other Scandinavian countries, commercial television on radio waves over terrestrial networks is a newcomer of the 1990s. In Finland a public service company (the Finnish Broadcasting Company, Yle) and a commercial company (MTV) have been operating side by side since the early days of television. Yle is publicly owned, and its major income is derived from license fees, with its second biggest source of income the channel rent paid by MTV.

MTV is a private television company, the sole commercial TV company in Finland with nationwide distribution, as Yle does not sell advertising time. Until 1993 MTV mainly operated on time slots that it bought from Yle on the two nationwide channels, broadcasting not only ads but also programs. Thus until 1993 the two channels carried a mixed menu of Yle's and MTV's programs.

In the late 1980s a third channel was established as a joint venture between Yle, MTV, and the Finnish electronics industry. Soon after that, MTV bought the majority of the shares of TV 3. The transmitting system of TV 3, however, remained in Yle's hands, and the channel still operated on Yle's license to broadcast. In 1993, when Yle had built the network of TV 3 to cover the whole country, MTV moved all its programs to the new channel and changed its name to MTV 3. Later the same year, the Finnish government allowed MTV 3 its own license to broadcast; however, there remained an obligation to contribute to the financing of the public service company.

Until 1993 the gatekeeper with power to allow political ads was the Administrative Council of Yle. The decision to allow MTV to air political TV ads was originally made in 1990. Had the decision been immediately carried out, the first nationwide TV campaign would have been the parliamentary election in March 1991. For economic reasons the Finnish political parties agreed to postpone putting the reform into force until some months after the parliamentary election. During the 1991 campaign, only a few spots (mainly using "bulletin board" graphic techniques) were seen on cable television.

The first actual Finnish political advertising campaign on television was during the 1992 local elections. At that time, the commercial company MTV still operated on all three domestic channels. On TV 1 and TV 2, MTV purchased time from Yle, and also had full command of TV 3, which at that time reached only two thirds of the Finnish population.

The 1992 local election campaign is the focal point of this chapter.[2] The nature of this campaign could be described as something of a pilot study for the parties, in preparation for the much more telegenic presidential campaign in 1994.

Changes in Finnish Electoral TV in the Early 1990s

The changes in the Finnish campaigns in the early 1990s have not only concerned the introduction of political TV advertisements but also cover a whole range of changes in electoral television as well as political practice. All these changes seem to influence the Finnish political system in the same "Americanized" direction. Therefore, the total process must be briefly described to provide a context for the political TV spot campaign in 1992.

There is a strong tradition in Europe of strictly regulating electoral television. In many countries there is a TV and radio "quarantine," prohibiting candidates from appearing in programs close to the elections, with the exception of special strictly regulated election programs, which can be free time slots allotted to parties according to strict rules. There can also be debates in which the parties are allowed fixed amounts of time to make their presentations and answer questions. Scandinavian countries also have special journalistic party interviews in which (usually two) journalists do a (usually quite critical) directly broadcast interview with a party representative (Esaiasson & Moring, 1993).

These principles also guided Finnish electoral television until the early 1990s. The formal equal rights for each party to appear on public service TV during the campaign were strictly followed; the party interviews were equally long, independent of the size of the party; and commercial television in Finland was not expected to carry campaign programs.

Gradually, these principles started to erode. By the beginning of the 1980s, the amount of time allotted each party in Finnish party debates was allowed to diverge, to the benefit of the bigger parties. In the latter part of the 1980s the TV and radio quarantine was gradually lifted, starting with news and current affairs programs.

In the early years of the 1990s, the Finnish television campaign culture changed dramatically. In the campaign before the 1991 parliamentary election, commercial MTV aired its own party leader debate for the first time. On TV 3, MTV aired political entertainment programs on which party representatives appeared on the screen discreetly in the nude, within the moral code of Finnish sauna culture. Among these party representatives were actual candidates running for seats, who appeared on this entertainment show close to the election (Moring & Himmelstein, 1993).

The publicly owned broadcasting company (Yle), in its current affairs programs, introduced more vivid reporting about the campaign, thus opening the way for more competitive journalism. Party leader duels were introduced, but with only the largest parties included.

In the local election campaign in 1992, the development took a step further: Political TV spots were introduced on nationwide television. The appearance of political leaders on entertainment programs (quiz programs, kitchen shows, and so on) proliferated. The commercial MTV had not one TV debate, but two.

The public service broadcasting company, Yle, in its turn strengthened journalistic competition at the expense of equality among the parties. Yle limited the number of parties allowed to appear in the debates to those represented in Parliament. Of the 17 parties who took part in the debates in 1991, only 9 were allowed to appear in the campaign programs of 1992. The order of appearance in party interviews, which had earlier been decided by lottery, was now decided by journalistic considerations. Furthermore, party leaders from the two government parties were presented in (critical) social reporting programs close to the election. The two programs, presenting four party leaders in debates before the elections in 1991, were in 1992 reduced to one program presenting two party leaders, the prime minister and the leader of the biggest opposition party.

All of these changes followed in the same direction taken a year earlier, away from strictly regulated electoral television toward a system that would open up political representation to commercial as well as journalistic competition. This development has continued in the early phases of the campaign leading up to the Finnish presidential elections in 1994, which already bear clear resemblances to the "talk show democracy" that developed in the United States in the presidential campaign in 1992 (Dennis et al., 1993).

A Shift Toward Popular Democracy

Some of the ground rules for electoral politics in Finnish society were changing simultaneously with the changes in electoral television. Like that of other Scandinavian democracies, the Finnish political system has traditionally been a multiparty system, based on five parties: a moderate right-wing party, a liberal party, a center party (with agrarian traditions), a social democratic party, and a radical Left. Gradually, three of the Finnish parties (the moderately right-wing National Coalition party, the Centre party, and the Social Democratic party) grew to dominate the political scene. As the support for these three parties varied between 15% and 25%, the support for the other parties fell to around 10% of the votes or less. The Liberal party became almost nonexistent, and an environmentalist party, the Green Union, started growing.

Political structures in Finland have, however, been less flexible than in its Scandinavian neighbor countries, as the parliamentary rules in Finland have favored broad coalitions (Jansson, 1992). Because of rules requiring a qualified (two-thirds) majority for important parts of new legislation to be accepted by the parliament, the parties were led to seek broad government coalitions. From the late 1960s to the late 1980s, the Finnish political rule was consensual in its nature, a development also supported by the powerful labor market corporations. When the demand for a qualified majority was changed in the early 1990s, the stiffness of the system was reduced, and the parliamentary character of Finnish decision making was strengthened.

From 1987 onward the Finnish political scene changed. The consensual features weakened, and the division between government and opposition grew more important. This development started as an unusual government coalition was formed, a "blue-red" government that bridged the National Coalition party and the Social Democratic party, and left the Centre party in opposition.

TABLE 10.1 Major Finnish Parties and Their Support in the 1991 Parliamentary and 1992 Local Election

Party/English Abbreviation (Name in Finnish)	*% of Vote in 1991*	*% of Vote in 1992*
Centre Party, CP (Suomen Keskusta)	24.8	19.2
Christian League, CL (Suomen Kristillinen Liitto)	3.0	3.2
Green Union, GU (Vihreä Liitto r.p., VL)	6.8	6.9
Left-Wing Alliance, LWA (Vasemmistoliitto)	10.1	11.7
Liberal Peoples Party, LPP (Liberaalinen Kansanpuolue)	0.8	1.0
National Coalition Party, NCP (Kansallinen Kokoomus)	19.3	19.0
Rural Party, RP (Suomen Maaseudun Puolue)	4.8	2.4
Social Democratic Party, SDP (Suomen Sosialidemokraattinen Puolue)	22.1	27.1
Swedish People's Party, SPP (Svenska Folkpartiet)	5.5	5.0
Other parties and political movements	1.9	4.5

In the following parliamentary election in 1991, the Centre party increased its share of the votes by more than 7%, which for the Finnish could be called a landslide (see Table 10.1 for the election results in 1991 and 1992). After the election a new bourgeois government was formed by the Centre party and the National Coalition party, now leaving the Social Democratic party in opposition. In the local elections only 18 months later, the SDP gained 5% compared with the results in the parliamentary election. The Centre party lost almost all it had gained in 1991.

The parliamentary nature of Finnish politics has also developed in other ways. The position of the Finnish government was strengthened in the internal power balance with the president, who can no longer change the composition of the government or dismiss the parliament without an expressed initiative from the prime minister.

Thus there have been changes both in political practice and in the fundamental rules by which the political system works. Furthermore, these changes all work in the same direction: to make Finnish political life more parliamentary in nature. As has been seen since the early 1970s in Sweden, this development seems to favor the opposition at the cost of the government coalition.

Because the Finnish electoral system is based on a choice of individual candidates, changes of the above-mentioned nature could be expected to lead to individualized election campaigns. In Finnish parliamentary elections the total vote for the candidates of each party (or electoral alliance of parties) determines how many representatives the party or alliance gets from each electoral district.[3] The number of votes given to the individual candidates then decides which candidate is elected. The same applies to local elections, the difference being that in local elections the electoral district is the local constituency (*commune*). To be elected, candidates have to defeat their competitors within the party by getting more personal votes, so this type of proportional system brings a strong incentive for individual candidates to have their own campaigns.[4]

The individual nature of elections is especially clear in the presidential elections. Today, the system is based on direct popular elections, in a maximum two rounds. Earlier, however, Finnish presidential elections were indirect. Voters elected an electoral assembly, which in turn elected the president. Because of the Finnish multiparty system and a political culture in which electors did not have to reveal their second choice, parties were quite influential in this system.

The system for electing the president was partly reformed in 1988, and it was totally changed before the 1994 elections. The new system resembles the French system for presidential elections: If no candidate gets an absolute majority (50%) of the votes in the first round, there will be a second round 3 weeks later, between the two most successful candidates from the first round.

The direct elections immediately led to an American-style nomination rally. The major parties were pressed to nominate their candidates through pre-elections. The pre-elections in 1994 led to a change of candidate in two of the three biggest parties (the Social Democratic party and the National Coalition party) as the voters in the pre-elections overthrew the original plans of the party core.

The changes in the system for presidential elections are dramatic, when compared to the former relatively autonomous and within-the-elite status of the Finnish political leadership (Luebbert, 1986; Moring,

1989). These changes could be seen as the most important new features in Finnish electoral democracy and party life.

The Rules for Political Advertising on TV

As mentioned above, the decision to allow political advertising on MTV was originally made by the politically composed administrative council of the Finnish Broadcasting Company (Yle) in 1990. Earlier regulations had not allowed political ads on the network owned by Yle; however, according to the decision (Oy Yleisradio Ab, 1990):

1. MTV was allowed to sell advertising time for political advertising to registered parties.
2. Political advertisements could contain comparative and criticizing elements. Advertisements built on negative assessments of single persons were, however, prohibited.
3. Political advertisements were not allowed to contain any other advertising content.

Political ads were also obligated to follow the general principles for advertising practiced by MTV and international rules for advertising. The rules contain no restrictions limiting the amount of commercial political presentation. Any party is allowed to purchase as much time as it can afford.

The rules restricted political advertising to registered parties. In the 1994 presidential election, this became a problem. According to the nomination system, popular movements may nominate a candidate by collecting 20,000 names to support the nomination. As several such candidates were nominated, the rules were changed to also allow the supporters of these candidates to purchase advertising time.

By the time of the presidential elections in 1994, the media environment in Finland had changed. As was noticed above, MTV then operated on a separate channel, with its own license to broadcast. Thus the new regulation of political advertising had actually become an internal affair for the commercial company itself. It did, however, not change the other restrictions in the original decision regulating political advertising. Thus negative campaigning against individual persons on television was still prohibited in the presidential elections in 1994, as well as advertising that mixed political and other commercial messages.

Political Advertising in Finland

In general, political advertising before elections has been dominated by newspaper ads. This corresponds with the general distribution of advertisement investments in Finnish mass media. According to figures published by Finnish Gallup-Media, 65% of all advertisement investments in mass media in 1992 were in newspaper ads and ads in free sheets. The investments in ads aired on national television (MTV) were 18%, on cable television 0.5%, and on local radio 5%. Advertisement investments in weeklies and magazines amounted to 10%.

Due to the recession in the Finnish economy the total investments in mass media advertisement decreased by 20% in 2 years, from 4800 million Finnish marks (FIM) in 1990 to 3850 million FIM in 1992. In this process, the relative share of investments in newspaper and free sheet ads decreased by 3.5%, and the investments in television ads increased by 4.5%.

The figures describing advertisement investments in mass media do not include investments in directly distributed advertisements, and the relative share of such advertising has been gradually increasing. In 1991 investments in direct advertising were at the same level as the investments in advertising through magazines (about 420 million FIM).

Looking at the political advertising, it is evident that most of the advertising consists of candidate ads in the newspapers. There are no exact figures available for the relative share of political ads with respect to different types of media in 1992. It is, however, quite obvious that the newspapers kept their leading position in political advertising at a candidate level. The only field of political advertising in which television was able to challenge the leading position of the newspapers was in the competition for party ads.

It has already been noted that the television advertisement campaign in 1992 could best be seen as a preparation for the 1994 presidential elections. Although the parties had sufficient time to prepare for their first television ads, not all large parties found it worth the costs to use ads in the actual campaign. On the other hand, the upcoming presidential election increased the interest in trying the new medium.

The interest of the political parties in the new medium varied. One of the three big parties aired only one spot in the preliminary phase of the campaign, whereas the two others used a considerable share of their campaign resources for political advertising on TV. Those parties airing political ads in 1992 used 40% of the party campaign budget to purchase television time. As was noted above, candidate ads were not very common in the 1992 local elections.

Because of the individual nature of the voting in Finnish elections, described above, most of the newspaper advertisements focus on individual candidates. In the parliamentary election in 1991, almost 90% of the newspaper ads focused on candidates, and only slightly more than 10% on party.

Candidate ads have also dominated in political radio advertising. Advertisements on local commercial radio stations have been allowed since 1985; but because nationwide commercial radio broadcasting is not allowed in Finland, radio advertising is limited to local advertising. This can, however, be expanded because many local stations allow chained purchase of marketing time. By purchasing time from the chain office, advertisers get their ad aired on all the stations belonging to this chain.

The parties as well as the candidates also produce directly distributed leaflets and, from a fixed date before the election, parties are allowed equal space on billboards. Since 1991 some local authorities have also allowed commercial political outdoor advertising.

Although new competing forms of political marketing are entering the scene, the dominant role of the press in political advertising in the 1991 and 1992 elections was clearly visible in the election survey research.[5] When people were asked where they got information for their voting decision, they cited newspapers and, among ads, newspaper ads (Table 10.2).

Although the small number of respondents in 1992, together with possible panel effects due to research techniques (see Note 5), make the results less reliable, some conclusions from the surveys could be suggested. It is reasonable to expect that the local nature of the election in 1992 explains the generally lower level of importance given to all types of media in 1992, compared to 1991. This would also explain a higher level of importance given to discussions with friends and colleagues. Interestingly, however, party meetings were not considered more important in 1992 than in 1991. The findings would indicate that the nature of Finnish elections at all levels is mediaized.

There are reasons to be quite cautious when interpreting voter survey data based on self-perception of the respondents. It could be expected that people tend to give less importance to sources of influence that they believe are partial, and perhaps propagandistic. This could be seen in the difference between how people responded when they first were asked if political ads on TV affected them, and then were asked if they

TABLE 10.2 The Importance of Different Sources of Information in the Finnish 1991 Parliamentary Elections and the 1992 Local Elections

Relative share of respondents saying the source had influence on their decision how to vote (%):

Type of Media	*Year* *1991*	*1992*
Newspaper articles	49%	20%
TV news/current affairs	41%	19%
Public service TV debate	21%	13%
Radio programs	31%	10%
Political newspaper advertisements	23%	10%
Political TV advertisements	*	4%
Political local radio advertisements	10%	5%
Other political advertisements	11%	7%
Party meetings	5%	5%
Discussions (friends and colleagues)	10%	14%
Number of cases	1,326	558

* This question was not asked in 1991, as national TV did not air political advertisements on television.

thought political ads affected other persons who shared their political views. Only 5% thought that political TV ads had at least some effect on their own decision, whereas 32% of the respondents thought that other people were affected by political TV ads. This finding is in line with the findings of Cohen and Davis (1991).

It should also be kept in mind that the local nature of the 1992 elections did not provide the best context for a TV campaign. Because the country is divided into about 450 communes, most of the local constituencies in Finland are very small. The voters elect the members to the local councils. In most parts of Finland, except for the bigger cities in the southern and western parts of the country, the constituencies are too small to make even regionalized television advertising cost-effective.

Observations From the First Commercial Political TV Campaign

The pilot-study character of the 1992 political advertising campaign on TV could be seen in how the spots were produced. The parties were very careful, in the design of their first commercial TV campaign, not

TABLE 10.3 Number of Political Spots and Number of Contacts (in millions) by Party in the 1992 Finnish Local Election

Party	*Spots*	*Contacts (million)*
National Coalition Party	16	43
Social Democratic Party	7	20
Left-Wing Alliance	4	22
Swedish People's Party	2	*
Green Union	1	*
Total	30	85

NOTES: The number of contacts has been calculated on the basis of estimates of the audience figures for the programs to which the spots were attached (see Note 8).
* Spots aired within smaller regions only. Contact estimates not available.

to scare off voters; as a result, the messages were broad in design, which made them vague, sometimes even diffuse.

Political campaigns designed this way do not provide good research material to study possible campaign effects, especially if the volume of the campaign is rather modest. It does, however, provide an opportunity to study other features of general importance to the political campaign. A main focal point of the research project carried out in Finland in 1992 concerned the diffusion of political information to different groups of voters, allowing for both measurement of people's exposure to different types of political messages during the campaign and an estimation of the extent to which political ads on television expand the political audience.

In 1992 a total of 30 political spots were produced for national television (see Table 10.3). The length of the spots varied from 10 to 25 seconds, the mean being 16.2 seconds. Compared to spots in political campaigns in the United States, the Finnish spots were quite short (spots in the United States usually vary between 30 seconds and 1 minute). The Finnish political spots were also shorter than the average length of advertising spots on Finnish television (22 seconds).

The total campaign investments made by the major Finnish parties in 1992 were 6.5 million FIM.[6] The total investments for political spots on the nationwide television channel were 1.8 million FIM, which was 28% of the total campaign investments of the major parties. As the Centre party (and most of the small parties) did not purchase television time during the actual TV campaign in 1992, those five parties that decided to air ads in the campaign used an average of 40% of their campaign budget on political spots. In 1992 the political parties were allowed to purchase time at a reduced price. This "introductory offer" was given to all parties equally.[7]

The National Coalition party invested twice as much as any other party in its television campaign. The party produced more than twice as many spots as the Social Democratic party and four times as many as the Left-Wing Alliance. The number of audience contacts bought by the National Coalition party was twice as high as the contacts bought by the two other parties.

According to the voter survey, the campaign of the National Coalition party seems to have reached most of the audience. Three out of four viewers who remember having seen political spots on television remember having seen this party's spots. The two other parties were far behind. Somewhat more than half of the audience mentioned having seen ads aired by the Social Democratic party, but only one third mentioned having seen ads by the Left-Wing Alliance.

In total, however, the political spots seem to have expanded the audience of political television significantly. According to Finnish audience research, based on an audience meter system,[8] traditional political programs presenting the parties and their political platforms reached only about 60% of the audience in 1992. According to the voter survey, this figure grows to 65% if we also consider reading about party politics in newspapers and following news stories about parties on television newscasts. A majority of the 35% who claimed they were ignoring information about party politics in the media were, however, reached by political spots on television (Table 10.4).

The pattern of exposure to political spots is discriminatory with respect to certain socio-demographic background variables. All groups were exposed to political TV spots; however, the variation occurred when looking at which groups were exposed to TV spots only and which groups were exposed to a broader menu of political programs.

Among those exposed only to TV spots, there was a relatively larger share of women, young people, and people with low income. In this group, the relative share of people in leading positions was low. Among those exposed to a full menu, there was a relatively larger share of old people, which corresponds to the general finding that television viewing in Finland increases with age.

Although a cumulative pattern in exposure to political information from different sources can be detected, it is not an easy task to draw conclusions about what this means to political knowledge in different

TABLE 10.4 Exposure to Different Types of Information About Political Parties in Finland in the 1992 Local Election Campaign

	Those Who Followed Political Information About Parties on TV or in Newspapers	*Those Who Did Not Follow Political Information About Parties on TV or in Newspapers*	*Total*
Those who did not remember having seen political TV spots	18%	14%	32%
Those who remembered having seen political TV spots	47%	21%	68%
Total	65%	35%	100%

NOTE: The figures are derived from a series of four panel surveys; in each survey the number of cases varied from 567 to 610.

social groups, because the effects of these differences in exposure on political knowledge are not given once and for all. In their classic study, Patterson and McClure (1976) claim that in certain conditions political spots on television may increase political knowledge, especially among people who know very little about politics and who are not exposed to other sources of political information.

It is evident that the content of the political spots is relevant with respect to what effect the spots have on people's political knowledge. In the campaign studied by Patterson and McClure (the race between Richard Nixon and George McGovern in 1972), 42% of the spots included issue communications, and 41% of the spots were about 5 minutes long. This length spot is not typical for American political campaigns, and though spots in the United States often include some issue information, it is often not very specific (see, e.g., Joslyn, 1984, p. 43; Kern, 1989).

As described later, the first spots in Finland in 1992 differed, to their disadvantage, from the American spots on both measures. The Finnish spots were not only short but also usually rather uninformative. Many spots were produced to create general "good feelings" in connection with the party image, a kind of image advertising that, as in the United States, has been found to go together with a lack of specific issue information (Kaid & Johnston, 1991).

TABLE 10.5 Attitudes Within the Finnish Electorate Toward Political Advertising on Television 2 Weeks Before the 1992 Election

Attitudes Toward TV Spots	*TV Spots Promoting Party (n = 680)*	*TV Spots Promoting Candidate (n = 680)*
Positive	9%	8%
More positive than negative	29%	21%
More negative than positive	30%	32%
Negative	25%	30%
Do not know	7%	9%

SOURCE: Finnish Gallup (1992); Moring and Himmelstein (1993).

The audience reactions to the political spots in Finland were mixed. There was little enthusiasm but no signs of strong rejection. It is, however, clear that spots promoting a party are more often accepted than spots promoting single candidates (Table 10.5).

When comparing the attitudes of supporters of different parties to political spots, the biggest differences were found in grade of rejection or acceptance. In all parties, somewhat more of the supporters were negative than positive in their attitudes toward political spots presenting parties. There was, however, a difference among parties in how polarized their supporters were. Among the supporters of the right-wing National Coalition party, the unconditioned "positive" group was twice as big as in any other party. Among the supporters of the Left-Wing Alliance and the Green Union, the unconditioned "negative" group was clearly bigger than in the other parties (Table 10.6).

Although more people were against than in favor of political ads on TV, the ads did not seem to be a reason for people not to vote. The turnout in the Finnish local elections in 1992 was 70%. This was a slight increase in comparison to the last local election in 1988, but in a Scandinavian comparison, the turnout is rather low. When asked if political TV spots were influential on people's decision not to vote, only 1 out of 100 respondents (1%) claimed that political ads had this effect to at least some extent. Almost no respondents claimed that political TV spots had a decisive impact on their decision not to vote. The most frequent reason for people not to vote was, however, a general distrust in politics and politicians (according to 81% of the nonvoters, this affected their decision not to vote at least to some extent). The second

TABLE 10.6 Attitudes Toward Political Ads Among the Supporters of the Five Largest Finnish Parties

	NCP (*n* = 97)	*CP* (*n* = 70)	*SDP* (*n* = 116)	*GU* (*n* = 75)	*LWA* (*n* = 19)
Positive	22%	10%	11%	1%	11%
More positive than negative	24%	31%	35%	37%	29%
More negative than positive	29%	22%	36%	23%	15%
Negative	21%	25%	14%	38%	41%
Do not know	5%	13%	4%	–	4%

NOTE: NCP = moderate right-wing party, CP = center party, SDP = Social Democratic party, GU = environmentalist party, LWA = radical Left.
SOURCE: Moring and Himmelstein (1993, p. 114).

most frequent reason for abstention was the difficulty in finding a suitable candidate to vote for (64%).

When asked about the content of the political advertisements on television in 1992, the general response was that the ads were image-oriented rather than informative, and positive in approach rather than negative. Questions concerning orientation and approach were posed both 2 weeks before the election and in the postelection study. According to the results in both rounds, about 60% of those who said they had seen ads on TV perceived the ads as being image-oriented rather than informative. About 14% perceived the ads as being informative. Somewhat more than 20% could not tell.

The same relation could be found in how the approach of the ads was perceived. Again, 60% perceived the approach to be positive, that is, that the political ads on TV presented the positive side of the parties and candidates, rather than criticizing other parties or candidates. Only 15% of the respondents who had seen ads perceived them as being negative. And again, somewhat more than 20% could not tell.

Something for Everybody— The Strategy of the 1992 TV Spots

The findings describing how people perceived the orientation and approach of the political advertisements on television in 1992 correspond to a qualitative content analysis of the actual spots (Moring &

Himmelstein, 1993). The most striking feature was the lack of a conceptual center in most of the spots. Together with rather simplistic aesthetics ("radio with pictures"), this created an image of a static and defensive campaign. To give a more concrete picture of the TV campaign, the verbal rhetoric of some of the spots and the broadcasting strategies of the bigger parties using political spots is presented in more detail.

THE NATIONAL COALITION PARTY SPOTS

The spots of the National Coalition party were the most numerous. They were aired during the last 4 weeks of the campaign but concentrated on the last 2 weeks. Only 25% of the audience contacts purchased (see note 8) were aired before the last 2 weeks of the campaign. The TV campaign was most active the week before the election, when 45% of the audience contacts were purchased. The remaining 30% were purchased the last week (election was on a Sunday).

More than half of the NCP spots were aired in connection with fiction and entertainment programs. Another third of the spots were aired in connection with news and current affairs programs.

Three of the 16 spots produced by NCP were talking-head images of party representatives. Three spots developed a "nightmare theme," to arouse people to vote. Only 1 (the only actual attack ad in the campaign) was more specifically content-oriented. The verbal rhetoric of these 7 spots is described below in somewhat more detail.

Of the remaining spots, 1 was a humorous spot targeted to young voters, urging them to vote. The remaining 8 spots were candidate presentations, with only a limited local distribution and generally low audience ratings.

The spots in the first group were all a talking-head type. Two of them built on statements of the party chairman. The issue content was embedded in the different surroundings (a city site in the first spot, a lake landscape in the second) and in the clothes (conservative black suit in the first spot, trousers and khaki vest in the second). In both spots, the actual message remained vague. In the city spot, the chairman said: "Did you know that local communities are getting more independent? In the future, more and more of the community matters will be decided within the community itself. The state doesn't interfere with everything any more. Therefore, it's important that in the community elections you decide who decides." The second spot spun around an environment theme: "Do you want to have pleasant and secure surroundings? These things are more and more decided in your local community because the community is getting more independence. Therefore, it's important that you decide who decides."

The third talking-head spot presented a young female candidate from a small city, talking in a schoolyard: "It always pays to be an optimist. It pays to study, to found a family, and to try to start a company. And it's always worth voting, especially now. There are differences between those who make decisions. Therefore, it's important that you decide who decides."

The three "nightmare spots" were short (12-second) series of black-and-white pictures, the first from an empty Russian bread store, the second of a Swedish young man (skinhead) in a riot, and the third from an oil catastrophe. All three spots presented the same text on the screen: "The one who sleeps may wake up to a nightmare." This text was followed by a new text, "You decide who decides. The independent people. National Coalition Party."

The National Coalition party attack spot was a last-minute product, based on a promise given to the voters by the party chairman in the party leader debate only 2 days before the election. Here, the NCP party leader attacked the other big government party and the biggest opposition party for employing a tax increase strategy, whereas the NCP would stand as a guarantee that a recently decided increase in taxation is to be considered a loan: "SDP and the Centre Party have suggested a return to the old tax rates which would take thousands of marks from your pockets. Instead of that, NCP only accepted a loan, and this was decided because a tax is a tax and a loan is a loan. A loan means it is paid back to the penny."

THE SOCIAL DEMOCRATIC PARTY SPOTS

The Social Democratic Party divided its advertising campaign on television into three rounds. One series of spots was aired in the spring 1992, half a year before the election. In these spots, the SDP presented ordinary people criticizing the government. In the actual campaign, the SDP produced five spots with a nationwide distribution. Three of them were aired mainly on the morning television show of the Finnish commercial TV company MTV, in a relatively early phase of the campaign. The spots on morning television reach an audience skewed toward elderly viewers.

In terms of timing, the SDP strategy was opposite the timing of NCP. Almost one fifth of the audience contacts (19%) were purchased during the first campaign week, 4 weeks from the election. During the next week, another third of the campaign was on the air (30%). Two weeks from the election there was almost a pause; only 10% of the campaign was on the air. During the election week, SDP aired 42% of the campaign spots, in terms of audience contacts. Finnish voters may cast their vote through post offices during a time period starting 2.5 weeks before the election and ending half a week before the election day. The SDP campaign party clearly tried to activate older voters to support the party in the phase of advanced election. The election week campaign again was targeted to reach a younger and more mobile vote.

Half of the SDP contacts were placed in connection with fiction and entertainment programs; one third were in connection with morning TV shows; less than one fifth were connected to news and current affairs programs.

In the early spots 4 weeks before the election, the SDP presented three candidates in their "natural surroundings" (a young man sporting and with his family, a woman in her work, and an elderly pensioner conducting an amateur orchestra). A fourth spot was simply an invitation to party meetings for women around the country.

In a late phase of the campaign, however, the SDP introduced one somewhat more sophisticated spot, presenting a general critique against the government and calling for the last-minute vote. In an analysis of all the 1992 political TV spots, this spot was found to be the whole campaign's most sophisticated spot in imaging (Moring & Himmelstein, 1993, p. 123). This spot is described in somewhat more detail below.

The spot operates through some strong Finnish condensation symbols, starting with the wartime hero, later Finnish president C.G. Mannerheim, the national flag, a worker throwing a tool box, the law book, a lawyer and a businessman, and a young boy sitting alone. All of these images construct the story of the Finnish crisis: "Finland. 75 years. 400,000 out of work. The end of the road for the entrepreneur. Welfare falling apart. Do you let everything go? Or do you vote for Finland to rise? Vote." The last word is directly addressed to the camera by a young woman.

Although the visual image of this spot was the most creative of all (Moring & Himmelstein, 1993, p. 124), it still did not avoid certain

problems typical of the whole television campaign. It was conceptually heterogeneous and broad in spectrum. Thus the spot did not focus on any specific group of potential voters who might be urged to make a last-minute decision.

THE LEFT-WING ALLIANCE SPOTS

The campaign of the Left-Wing Alliance was concentrated in the last 3 weeks before the election. During its first campaign week, LWA aired 23% of its audience contacts, during the second 18%, and during the last week 59%. The party clearly was after a last-minute protest vote.

Also, the choice of context of the TV slots purchased suggests that LWA was out to attract new groups of voters, rather than to activate the traditional working-class vote. Almost the entire TV spot campaign (80% of the audience contacts) was aired in connection with entertainment and fiction programs. The remaining one fifth of the campaign (20%) was aired in connection with news. Unlike the other parties, LWA did not purchase television time in the morning hours.

The lack of focus was also evident in the spots of the Left-Wing Alliance. The main spot was obviously designed to target a broad leftist and environmentally minded audience outside the traditional working-class core of party support. The spot started dramatically: "Record unemployment and bank crisis." Then it turned into an emphatic song: "Where is the country that gives the jobs, that loves the children, that protects the environment, and offers you tomorrow? The answer's on the left." This spot was wallpapered with a series of pictures, including symbols of corrupt capitalism (piles of money falling), portraits of family happiness with pictures of people in different ages, countryside nostalgia, and machines and people in construction work and industrial work.

In the two shorter nationwide spots, the Left-Wing Alliance gave somewhat more pointed statements to defend Finnish welfare. Both these spots were variants of talking-heads television. One of the spots presented the party chairman stating: "This country was built through work. More important than saving the banks is saving Finnish welfare. That's a fact." The other presented one of the vice-chairs (a young woman) saying: "Every fourth young person is without a job. Hasn't this clowning around gone far enough? Obviously you should do something about it." The last lines in both ads alluded to favorite expressions

Spending for Political Spots in U.S. Elections

One key to understanding how television advertising works in political campaigns is to follow the money—the spending totals and the spending patterns. In the United States television is a merchandiser/persuader. Surely television informs and educates; surely it entertains and provides escapist fare; but more important, because advertising pays the major toll for television, it is the advertisements that are the stars of commercial television. In American presidential campaigns the real stars are the ads.

In 1992, three presidential candidates, Clinton, Bush, and Perot, contested the election, spending more than was ever spent before—$133 million on television advertising (Devlin, 1993, p. 272). Both Clinton and Bush received $56.2 million in federal funds, and an additional $10.3 million in federal funds from their parties. Each campaign spent a total of $66.5 million.

The Bush campaign spent approximately $49 million, about three quarters of all its money, on television advertising. Bush spent approximately $38.5 million (Kelly, 1992) of his Bush/Quayle funds and the full $10.3 million (Cooper, 1992) of Republican National Committee funds on television advertising through jointly sponsored ads. The Clinton campaign spent approximately $44 million, or two thirds of its money, on television advertising, approximately $35 million of his own campaign funds (Greer, 1992). The Democratic National Committee spent an additional $9 million (Greer, 1993), mainly on generic ads targeted at segments of the electorate, such as college-age or under-30 voters. Perot spent approximately $60 million (Martin, 1992) of his own money on his campaign. Slightly less than $40 million (O'Brien, 1992), or two thirds of his campaign money, was spent on television advertising. In 1988 Bush spent two thirds of his $54.4 million on advertising, and Dukakis spent slightly more than half of his money on TV ads.

To put some historic perspective on these figures, it is useful to compare the 1952 and 1992 presidential television spending. Wood (1985) estimated that Eisenhower's 1952 television spending may have reached as high as $6 million when all television time buying (national, state, and local) was factored in. Using the base year of 1982/1984 and factoring in inflation, Eisenhower's $6 million would equal around $32 million 1992 dollars. So his TV spending was less than the average $44 million spent by three candidates in 1992—but not that much less. Examined another way, in 1980 Reagan spent a total of $13 million on television ads. Eisenhower actually outspent Reagan, $32 million to $22 million in terms of 1992 dollars. However in 1980, when an additional $7 million spent by the Republican National Committee, and unavailable to candidates prior to 1980, is factored in, Reagan actually outspent Eisenhower, $34 million to $32 million in terms of 1992 dollars. The big story is that candidates always spent a lot on television advertising; current candidates now spend up to 75% of all of their total budgets on television advertising.

In U.S. campaigns, a lot of advertising money is also spent to help gain the nomination for the presidency. For example, the 1992 New Hampshire primary election had a $552,000 overall limit on expenditures. Most of the seven major candidates spent that limit on advertising alone. In fact, by beaming ads from Boston, Massachusetts; Portland, Maine; and Burlington, Vermont; in addition to Manchester, New Hampshire; "several candidates spent almost double (Clinton $950,000) or triple (Buchanan $1.4 million) the limit on television advertising alone just to finish second" (Devlin, 1994, p. 82). New Hampshire was bombarded with ads. In New Hampshire all major and minor Republican and Democratic candidates spent around $5.2 million on television advertising to achieve 348,000 votes, or approximately $15 per vote. That is a huge investment in primary campaign television advertising dollars per vote. In 1992 Clinton spent $950,000 on television in New Hampshire and achieved 41,522 votes, spending almost $23 per vote. In the New York primary, thought to be much more driven by paid media, Clinton spent just $555,000 on ads and achieved 421,000 votes, spending $1 per vote.

Length of Ads

In the United States political commercials come in various time frames. They come in half-hour speeches (1952 Stevenson) or biographies (1972 McGovern, 1992 Perot) and half-hour or 1-hour and longer election eve programs (1968 Humphrey, 1976 Carter). Historically, few except partisans were thought to watch these longer programs. "Only one in twenty adults bothered to watch the typical 30 minute broadcast during 1972" (Patterson & McClure, 1976, p. 121). However, Perot in 1992 disproved the theory that only partisans watch by getting close to 30 million viewers to watch his most-watched, repeated half-hour program, "Problems."

Ads come in mini programs or 4-minute, 20-second segments between regularly scheduled programs (1992 Bush). In the 1972 and 1976 campaigns around 40% of all campaign advertising was in these longer formats. Carter's ad creator, Jerry Rafshoon, preferred 5-minute spots because "it was the only vehicle short of personally introducing Jimmy Carter to 113 million Americans that would reveal the depth of my candidate" (Devlin, 1977, p. 243). Even today this time frame is used because it is sold at program rates rather than spot commercial rates, often making it cheaper than several network ads.

Most commonly, commercials come in 60-second and especially 30-second segments and sometimes 2-minute segments purchased primarily in local markets. Ninety-seven percent of all Clinton's 1992 time buys were for 30-second commercials. Campaigns in the 1980s and 1990s rely on 30-second ads.

During the first 20 years of presidential ads, the 60-second spot was the dominant time frame; in the 1970s the 4-minute, 20-second spot was dominant; even Reagan in 1980 had almost 30% of his spots in this length. During the 1980s the 30-second spot became dominant. This is not surprising, because both product and political commercial research have shown that the longer spot lengths do not always offer an advantage in message recall (Devlin, 1986, p. 32).

Political advertisers have increasingly emphasized the use of the 30-second spot in relation to the 60-second or 4-minute, 20-second spot. In 1980, 55% of all Reagan spots were 30-second spots. In 1984 all of Mondale's general election spots were 30-second spots, and in 1992, 97% of Clinton's spots were 30-second spots. There are glitches; for example, Perot in 1992 used primarily 60-second spots and Clinton used several 15-second spots. "But stations are set up to sell time and viewers are prepared to view commercials in 30-second units" (Devlin, 1986, p. 33).

Regulations Related to U.S. Political Spots

Federal laws allow for, facilitate, and have loopholes that encourage circumvention of advertising laws in federal elections. "The Federal Communications Act of 1934 as amended requires broadcasters to sell equal time to all legally qualified candidates for federal office" (Kaid, 1981, p. 252). The key word is "sell," not "give," equal time. U.S. law mandates only limited and reasonable access. It gives legally qualified federal candidates the right to purchase reasonable amounts of time for campaign purposes once their campaigns have commenced. Opportunities for purchased time must be available at the lowest rate charged to other nonpolitical advertisers. Stations that sell time to one candidate are required to sell time opportunities to all other legally qualified candidates. All ads must carry a disclaimer, indicating which candidate, party, political action committee, or individual paid for the ad.

Equal time does not mean one candidate must have as many commercials as the opponent. Equal time means equal opportunity—if a candidate has the money to buy comparable time. And equal time does not pertain to a station's coverage of bona fide news events, such as speeches or debates, or news reports on their news broadcasts.

The Federal Communication Commission has ruled that broadcasters cannot censor political commercials the way they can product ads. In 1980 a minor candidate for president, Barry Commoner, was allowed to use a radio commercial that included the word "bullshit." Similarly, no control can be placed over objectional pictures, as exemplified when a congressional candidate used graphic pictures of aborted fetuses in a series of ads. FCC rules allow for the use of offensive language and pictures if the candidate chooses to use them.

After 20 years of commercial television usage, Congress passed regulations pertaining to political advertising and presidential elections. The Federal Election Campaign Act of 1971 (FECA) and its amendments in 1974 and 1976 established equal federal financing of presidential elections and the federal subsidy of presidential primary elections. The act set ceilings on what candidates could spend on television advertising and forced public disclosure of campaign contributions. The ceilings—roughly 60% of total budgets—have been dropped, but reality has established de facto ceilings of two thirds to three fourths of all campaign funds for TV.

The revenue section of the acts established an income tax check-off to allow taxpayers to designate $1 of their taxes to finance presidential elections. Over the history of this act, on average, only 20% to 30% of the taxpayers have authorized this voluntary check-off.

In 1976 the Supreme Court, in *Buckley v. Valeo,* upheld public financing but struck down the limits political action committees may spend if they remain independent from the presidential campaigns of candidates. The Court also allowed for unlimited spending by individuals. So in 1992 Perot was free to spend an unlimited amount of his personal money as long as he did not accept federal financing.

Campaign spending limits are set for both the primary and general election campaigns. To qualify for a federal subsidy in the primary campaign, a candidate must raise $5,000 in contributions in 20 states, in amounts of $250 or less. This has been easily done by all serious presidential contenders since 1976. To encourage smaller contributors while still raising adequate money, all primary campaign contributions of $250 or less are matched from the government fund. However, amendments to the FECA in 1979 introduced the loophole of "soft money." Soft money is unlimited contributions an individual can make to state and local parties, which can then spend the money in direct support of a candidate's election. From a 1974 base of $10 million in primaries and $20 million in the general election, plus a cost of living escalator, federal financing limits have grown in 1992 to $28.2 million in the primary and $56.5 in the general election.

Types of Spot Ads in U.S. Elections

Ads are meant to bring voters issue information, and most important, to help create an image impression of the candidate for the viewer. TV ads bring voters issue information—an average of five times as much information about a candidate's positions on an issue as a 60-second snippet on the evening news (Patterson & McClure, 1976). Most recent campaigns produce and play about 25 to 35 ads, with a dozen or so of these ads being the real workhorses of the campaign. Some presidential campaigns, for example, 1976 Ford, 1980 Carter, and 1988 Dukakis, produced and played too many ads, dissipating their overall effectiveness.

The more important goal of ads is to help create an image impression of the candidate for the viewer. Ads seek to foster a feeling in the viewer about the personal qualities of the candidate—qualities such as communicativeness, leadership, expertise, or trustworthiness.

No better ad exists to help explain the interplay of issues with image than the talking-head ad. Talking-head ads—ads that show the candidate talking directly to the viewer—are one of the most frequently used ad types in presidential advertising. These ads have been used by all candidates, from Eisenhower in 1952 to Clinton in 1992.

Talking-head ads focus on issues or substance, but most important, help create an image or feeling about the candidate. They join verbal copy (words) and vocal delivery (pitch or rate) with the visual (picture and setting) to help explain a candidate's position on an issue (crime or defense) while also creating an image impression (leadership or likability) with the viewer. For example, in 1960 Kennedy would talk about "Medicare" and Nixon would talk about "civil rights." Both used 60 seconds of copy to help explain their positions on these important issues. However, the setting and the way in which the camera captured both speakers were very different. Nixon was more formal, in a dark suit. He was sitting at an angle, at a desk with his hands clasped. The camera was not in close, but Nixon's face was highlighted with complimentary lighting, possibly to compensate for the light suit and darker face that were captured by the camera during his famous first debate with Kennedy. Kennedy's ad was much more informal. His gestures and voice were more conversational. The camera came in closer, to foster intimacy between the viewer and candidate. There were family pictures on the walls, to give the viewer additional viewer information. Both candidates talked about the issues, but each candidate conveyed an image of communicativeness—Kennedy more casual and likable, yet committed; Nixon more serious, more formal, more concerned.

Research by Patterson and McClure (1976) found that a candidate can develop a more favorable image through issue-oriented spots, like those that seek to convince the voter that the candidate has positions—but most important, that he has the character to handle the difficult problems of the presidency. Research indicates that the best way to make a positive impression on the voter is to use issues as a vehicle or tool to effect a positive image. The purpose of most talking-head spots is to focus on an issue and use the candidate communicatively to convey an impression that he is committed to the issue, but most important, to convey the impression that he can handle the job of president:

> Talking head ads are the ultimate Rorschach tests of political advertising . . . a candidate's speaking to television viewers is a test of voters' feeling more than it is a way to convey issue message. The candidate is the primary message in a talking head ad. The real star of the Clinton "Plan" ad was not the plan, it was Clinton. (Devlin, 1993, p. 286)

When I play talking-head ads for my students they always come away with an image impression—why they like the candidate or remember how he was pictured. They seldom remember the copy—his issue positions stated during the ad. The vocal and the visual supersedes the verbal.

There are other types of ads that have been heavily used in presidential campaigns, such as person-in-the street ads (1960 Nixon, 1968 Humphrey, 1976 Ford, 1980 Carter, 1992 Bush); documentary ads (1952

Eisenhower, 1960 Nixon, 1964 Johnson, 1968 Nixon, 1972 McGovern and Nixon, 1976 Carter and Ford, 1980 Reagan and Carter, 1984 Mondale and Reagan, 1988 Bush, and 1992 Clinton, Bush, and Perot); testimonial ads (1960 Kennedy and Nixon, 1964 Goldwater, 1968 Humphrey, 1976 Ford, 1980 Carter); and negative attack ads by all candidates except Nixon in 1960 and Carter in 1976.

Person-in-the-street ads have real people saying nice things about one candidate and/or nasty things about the opponent, and in 1992, half of the anti-Clinton ads used by Bush were ads of this type. These ads are:

> [E]xcellent reinforcing tools but they are seldom persuasive tools. Too often the impression of undecided voters upon seeing these ads is "you can get somebody to say anything about anybody." Because these ads do use real people saying real things many ad makers use them. They think they have a quality of believability. (Devlin, 1986, p. 31)

Documentary ads are biographical ads, or ads that show the leadership accomplishments of the candidate. No candidate emphasized documentary ads more than Ronald Reagan in 1980. Reagan's ad makers wanted to play down the perception of Reagan as an actor and play up the perception of Reagan as an effective governor, so 40% of all of their 1980 ads were documentaries, using either a 4-minute, 20-second or a 60-second version of the Reagan "record" to accentuate his accomplishments as governor of the seventh-largest "country in the world." In 1988 George Bush used footage of his being rescued by a U.S. submarine after being shot down in combat during World War II to document his being a bona fide war hero. The Man from Hope, Arkansas, Bill Clinton, used a piece of documentary footage worth millions. Pictures of a teenage Clinton shaking President Kennedy's hand at the White House were used again and again to link Clinton with the Kennedy legacy. In a 60-second primary campaign biographical documentary called "Hope," the Kennedy meeting was shown, using one cut that lasted 5 seconds. During the general election campaign in a documentary called "Journey," the Kennedy footage had expanded to 22 seconds of the 60-second ad. The general election ad accentuated the meeting by having Clinton and not an announcer do the voice-over. There were three full-color cuts of Clinton reminiscing on camera, and four cuts of the Kennedy meeting in black-and-white, with the camera zooming in on the famous handshake and using slow-motion to accentuate it. What better way to link one respected president with another soon-to-be president than with this potent piece of documentary footage!

Documentaries allow for music to be used to maximize the mood of the piece. Some documentaries are labeled "shiver spots" because they strive to send a shiver up the spine of the viewer by linking dramatic pictures, dynamic words, and inspirational music; for example, Lee Greenwood singing "God Bless the USA" in the 1984 Reagan documentaries, or a 1972 spot titled "Russia," with Nixon laying a wreath on the monument to Russians who lost their lives during the siege of Leningrad as he recited words from the diary of "Tanya," a young girl who lost her entire family.

Testimonial ads have prominent politicians or movie stars speaking on behalf of a candidate (1956 Stevenson, 1960 Kennedy and Nixon, 1964 Goldwater, 1968 Humphrey, 1972 Nixon, 1976 Carter and Ford, 1980 Carter). In 1960 an Eisenhower "testimonial" was even used by Kennedy to show that Nixon was less experienced than he claimed. Eisenhower, when asked at a press conference to name one thing that Nixon had suggested or contributed in 8 years as vice president, answered: "If you give me a week, I might think of one." In 1980 Carter used a fireside endorsement by Ted Kennedy, and Reagan used ads showing footage of Kennedy wailing out in opposition to Carter during their 1980 primary battle. The Kennedy in the Reagan ads was more believable than the Kennedy in the Carter ads. Often the endorser used in a testimonial has to be more prominent than the candidate; for example, Henry Fonda or Eleanor Roosevelt in 1960 Kennedy endorsement ads. In 1992, none of the three candidates used testimonial ads—an indication that this type of ad may be out of style.

The most memorable presidential television ads are creative idea spots—production spots that seek to create a negative image of the opposition. Ads like the 1964 anti-Goldwater spot, with the East Coast being sawed off and dropping into the sea, or the 1968 anti-Nixon spot of the word "Agnew" appearing on the screen, while accompanied by nothing but laughter, are prominent ads that stand out in viewers' memories. These prominent negative ads are exemplified by a 1972 anti-McGovern spot, showing his face turning around like a weathervane to indicate changing positions; or the 1988 anti-Dukakis spot, picturing a foul Boston harbor and stating: "Now Michael Dukakis says he wants to do for America what he's done for Massachusetts. America can't afford that risk"; or the 1992 ad, with George Bush promising "Read my lips," while graphics and an announcer tick off how he has gone back on his word. Darrell West makes an appropriate distinction between typical ads and prominent ads. West found that, starting in 1964, "advertising turned more negative. Fifty percent of the prominent ads in 1964 and 60 percent of the prominent ads in 1968 were negative" (West, 1993, p. 47). Negative advertising is so important in presidential campaigning that it deserves extensive and separate analysis.

Negative Ads in American Politics

Television ads help voters to vote for or against either candidate. In reality there are five ways to vote: "voting for or against either of the party nominees or not voting at all" (Sabato, 1981, p. 324). In many presidential races, for example, Goldwater in 1964 or McGovern in 1972, the negative motivations to vote against a candidate were high. In fact, in 1988 a Peter Hart poll taken during the 1988 presidential race found that more people voted against Dukakis or Bush than voted for them (Hart, 1988). Citing doubts about the other pair as the single largest reason for their vote, 50% of those polled had doubts about Dukakis and Bentsen, and 44% had doubts about Bush and Quayle. Only 39% and 34%, respectively, indicated that they voted for Bush/Quayle or Dukakis/Bentsen because they "liked them and thought they were a good choice" (Devlin, 1989, pp. 406-407). In 1988 people voted against Bush because he chose Quayle as his vice president, and Dukakis reinforced this Bush vulnerability in one of Dukakis's few good ads—"Oval Office." In 1988 people voted against Dukakis because they perceived him to be weak on penalties for criminals, a point potently emphasized in a Bush anti-Dukakis ad, "Revolving Door." Negative ads highlight negative perception. Currently it is not always the most liked candidate, but more the least disliked candidate who wins an election. As Reagan pollster Vincent Breglio explained: "It has become vital in campaigns today that you not only present all of the reasons why people ought to vote for you but you also have an obligation to present the reasons why they should not vote for the opponent. Hence, the negative campaign, or the attack strategy becomes an essential part of any campaign operation" (Devlin, 1986, p. 23).

So essential had negative advertising become that by 1992, both Clinton's and Bush's ad coordinators admitted that half of their ad buys were for negative ads. In 1992 a 50/50 positive to negative ad use ratio "was a new high in negative advertising by two presidential candidates" (Devlin, 1993, p. 287).

According to Republican consultant Roger Stone, "Voters will tell you in focus groups that they don't like negative ads, but they retain the information so much better than the positive ones. The point is, people like dirty laundry. Why do tabloids sell?" ("Negative Advertising," 1986, p. 104). In their excellent book on negative advertising, Johnson-Cartee and Copeland (1991) conclude, "whereas people may say they hate negative political spots, they learn from them and are persuaded by them" (p. 11). Negative political advertising, they say, is used "because it works" (p. 30).

There are many reasons for the dominance of negative ads in presidential campaigns. First, negative ads are memorable—more memorable than positive ads. This is because "people process negative information more deeply than positive information," according to pollster Ed Nellman (Taylor, 1986, p. A7).

Second, negative ads move the numbers. Candidates see surges in polling numbers and increases in negative numbers regarding opponents. Tracking polling is increasingly used to monitor effectiveness and to cut down on boomerang effects. In the old days, candidates put on or took off ads on the instinctive judgments of the creator and campaign managers. Now expensive and sophisticated polling and focus group research can monitor the effectiveness or the ineffectiveness of negative advertising better than it used to. Doug Bailey, ad creator for Ford in 1976, observed: "I know no matter how good the positive spot is, I can't move people with the positive spot as easily as I can move people with the negative spot" (Bailey, 1988). Ian Weinschel, ad creator for Buchanan in 1992, observed:

> When I ran commercials that let George Bush talk about himself and then showed what he said was untrue, our numbers climbed. When I took commercials that said, "I am Pat Buchanan and here is my seven point plan" our numbers fell. . . . We tracked every night and the only time our numbers would start falling is when I ran positive ads in any quantity. (Weinschel, 1992)

According to John Nugent, "positive appeals confirm your support, negative appeals tend to convert the undecided" (Nugent, 1987, p. 49).

Third, negative ads are newsworthy. Negative ads get additional free coverage in newspaper stories and television news that positive ads do not get. As Bush's media adviser Roger Ailes disclosed, "There are three things that the media are interested in: pictures, mistakes, and attacks. . . . If you need coverage, you attack, and you will get coverage" (Runkel, 1989, p. 136). Ailes went on to explain, "You get a 30 or 40 percent bump out of [an ad] by getting on the news. You get more viewers, you get credibility, you get it in a framework" (West, 1993,

p. 14). The infamous 1988 Willie Horton ad was only played on a few stations in several Southern states, yet NBC News played it in its entirety on the evening network news and allowed millions to see what all the fuss was about. In 1992 ad watches in prominent newspapers and on CNN and CBS were set up to counteract the "double bang for a buck" effect of the unadulterated reinforcement of negative ads through newspaper and television coverage.

Fourth, negative ads are more creative and ingenious than positive ads. They play, and people want to see them again. Whether they are direct attack ads, like Nixon used against McGovern in 1972, or comparison ads, like Reagan used against Mondale in 1984, or whether they are innuendo ads, like the Daisy Girl ad of 1964, negative ads are often creative production commercials that evoke viewers' feelings or bring to viewers negative information in an interesting, provocative way.

Fifth, some negative ads are humorous. Humor in commercial advertising has been found to be very effective. Ads that use humor sell products and get Clio Awards. Generally, the only humorous ads in politics are the negative ads. As Buchanan's ad maker in 1992, Ian Weinschel, disclosed, "Laughter is a disarming thing making negatives more powerful" (Weinschel, 1992). Too many positive ads have a talking-head, or a person-in-the-street testimonial, or a documentary that soon fades into forgetfulness—not so with standout negative ads like the 1992 Buchanan or Clinton "Read My Lips" ads.

Negative ads often become the synecdoches—the small part that stands for the whole—of the campaign. The Willie Horton ad of 1988 was hardly shown, the Daisy Girl ad of 1964 was shown only once, the Bear ad of 1984 was heavily tested and held back—yet each of these ads emerges in those golden hits of the oldies, replayed over and over again on television news about campaigns. Through this replaying, they become the synecdoches of the campaign.

Kaid and Johnston (1991), in a comprehensive study of negative and positive advertising in past presidential campaigns from 1960 to 1988, counted and categorized the ads created. They could not document the crucial variable of whether and how often an ad was played; however, they found all campaigns from 1960 through 1988 were 72% positive and 29% negative. Campaigns went from a negative low of 7% (Kennedy/Nixon in 1960) to a negative high of 40% (Johnson/Goldwater in 1964).

In 1992 Clinton used negative ads. Sixty-three percent of his 30 ads used during 1992 were negative. Bush produced 24 ads—56% of them were negative. "Having both candidates produce more negative than positive ads and especially having presidential candidates air a 50/50 ratio of positive/negative ads is a high watermark in negative ad emphasis in a presidential campaign" (Devlin, 1993, p. 288).

Doug Bailey (1988), media creator for Ford in 1976 and now editor of *Hotline,* astutely observed several changes in negative advertising:

> It used to be twelve years ago, before you ran a negative ad, you worried a bit because you knew you were going to pay a price. The question was always whether the pluses would outweigh the minuses. Now I have learned there is no price to pay for negative advertising as long as you stay within the boundaries of good taste. There have been two major changes. Once it used to be that if there was one thing that wasn't true in an ad it destroyed the whole credibility of the ad. Press and public reaction would force you to pull it off the air. Now we have gone the other way. Innuendo and accusation are built on one accuracy—if one statement is true, almost anything else you say in an ad must also be true. The "Tank" and "Furlough" ads of 1988 are good examples. Second, it used to be the public was so skeptical of negative advertising that they tended not to believe it. Now they are so conditioned and accepting of negative advertising that they tend to believe it if it is not answered . . . that is pretty scary.

Effect of Ads

Political television ads are memorable. Both Atkin and his colleagues (Atkin, Bowen, Nayman, & Sheinkopf, 1973) and Swanson (1973) found about 75% of the people they studied recalled seeing political ads. O'Shaughnessy found that almost 80% of television viewers can recall political ads, but only 20% can recall product commercials (O'Shaughnessy, 1990, p. 61).

However, Tony Schwartz argues that recall of specific ads (their visuals, actor dialogue, or announcer copy) is an inappropriate way to measure the impact of political ads. Recall testing "is of little value, primarily because it is directed toward what a viewer remembers in relation to a commercial, not how people are affected by a commercial message" (Schwartz, 1973, p. 68). Schwartz, who has created ads for several presidential campaigns, concluded, "I do not care what number of people remember or get the message. I am concerned with how people are affected" (Schwartz, 1973, p. 69).

Research on how people are affected—how their votes are affected—has more importance but is harder to measure. The impact of political advertising is harder to measure, because in a campaign so much is happening simultaneously—speeches, debates, media coverage, events attacks by the opposition, advertising—that it is hard to measure the impact of a single and isolated phenomenon like an ad, or even an entire ad campaign.

In 1952 Eisenhower sought to influence about 3% of voters through his advertizing blitz. In 1972 Patterson and McClure researched the effectiveness of political ads and found that only 18% of voters were late deciders. In 1972 many people had made up their minds; yet even in this landslide win for Nixon, many were still late deciders. The ads of the 1972 campaign were found to have influenced "roughly three percent of the total electorate" (Patterson & McClure, 1976, p. 135). In 1972 there was a 23% spread between Nixon and McGovern in the final tally. Therefore, a 3% impact with a 23% spread is not much of an impact. But in the 1976 campaign there was only a 2% disparity between Ford and Carter in the final tally. If the 1976 ads affected 3% of the electorate toward primarily one candidate, "the effectiveness or the ineffectiveness of ads might become crucial" (Devlin, 1986, p. 23). Certainly, it is not clear what overall effects the ads have. Realistically, the effectiveness of ads must be relegated to the "limited effects" model analyzing political communication phenomena such as conventions, debates, or advertising—their effects are marginal, at best.

In many campaigns, ads certainly reinforce decided and committed voters, just as debates in 1984 or 1992 primarily reinforced voters (Friedenberg, 1990, p. 207). Atkin and his colleagues found that ads favoring a preferable candidate strengthened the commitment of 31% of the voters favoring that candidate and weakened only 4% (Atkin et al., 1973). Some ads also sharpened the support of some partisans and weakened that of others. Thus a preferred candidate's ads are generally viewed positively and reinforce partisans, and ads for the opposition are viewed negatively and also tend to reinforce partisans (Devlin, 1978, p. 9).

Conclusion

Examination of the thousands of political television advertisements used from 1952 through 1992 disclose some important insights. The following are worth noting:

1. Good foundation spots are as important today as they were in 1952, when Eisenhower's anchor spot, "The Man from Abilene," was shown

over and over. In 1984 Reagan used the unneeded millions left over from his easy primary campaign to film foundation footage used during his general election campaign. His lush ads emphasized "Reagan's vision of America with people at work, buying homes, getting married, children playing, parades, flags waving, and the Statue of Liberty being restored" (Devlin, 1987, p. 28). The quality of Reagan's foundation ads was unprecedented in presidential advertising. In 1988 Bush used several early ads focusing on him as a family man, a world leader, a "man with a mission," and a good communicator. In 1992 Bush moved away from solid foundation ads, and his ad coordinator admitted, "a fundamental mistake was in not building a foundation like we did in 1984 and 1988" (Devlin, 1993, p. 278). An anchor spot that is so good it can be played from the beginning to the end of a campaign is an indication of a successful advertising strategy.

2. A few rather than many spots are the mark of a good television advertising campaign. Rather than 1 to 2 hours of 30-second, 60-second, and 4-minute, 20-second spots, the best presidential campaigns air no more than two dozen spots, with about a dozen becoming the prominent core spots. Too many spots dissipate a campaign. Yet, because of the multiple creative talents available during a campaign, there is a tendency to feel as did Doug Bailey, who coordinated the 1976 Ford's ads, that "it's dumb to produce good advertising that never runs. And therefore, since you have a number of good ads that never run you sort of run them all rather than trying to make one point. . . . I do think we made a mistake, not in producing as much, but in showing as much as we did" (Devlin, 1977, p. 246). Clinton in 1992 used 30 ads during the 1992 campaign, but about half of his 19 negative ads were targeted to single states or regions. Clinton used fewer than two dozen ads as the real workhorses of his advertising campaign.

3. A good television advertising campaign needs a few memorable spots. These memorable spots reinforce the creative themes that become the synecdoches of the campaign. In my articles that chronicle advertising over the past six presidential campaigns, I have always tried to pinpoint the best ad or ads that could represent the entire ad campaign. Usually this is a fairly easy task, because only a few rather than many spots stand out. Starting in 1972, when McGovern's "Vets" spot focused on the riveting interview he had with Vietnam paraplegics, and Nixon's "Russia" spot used words from Tanya's diary during the Leningrad scene to emphasize the emotional unity between Russians and Americans, there have always been a few memorable spots that not only played well during the campaign but also hold up well over time.

Sometimes these memorable spots are emotional "shiver" spots. Other times they are humorous negative ads. But in any good campaign there are really only a half dozen good ads that stand out, like Clinton's 1992 "Hope" ad, or Buchanan's "Read Our Lips" ad during the primaries, or Clinton's "How Are You Doing?" 15-second ad during the general election. This memorable ad opens with a closeup of George Bush's mouth saying, "Read my lips." An announcer says "Remember!" at the same time this word is also displayed in text. Then Bush is shown saying, "You will be better off four years from now than you are today." Then the announcer concludes, "Well, it's four years later. How are you doing?" Nothing has the power of a succinct idea conveyed through a memorable ad.

4. Image and issue ads are both important in presidential campaigns. Many scholars seek to separate image ads from issue ads. I make no distinction, because issue ads really do create image impressions on the part of the viewer, and image ads can convey substantive information. Ads do many things—convey substance and brief stands on issues, convey accomplishments and the candidate's record, and convey personal qualities such as warmth or communicativeness. Because the best television ads are emotional ads, political ads that convey in an emotional way stands on issues, or accomplishments, or personal qualities are often the best political ads. However, it is ironic but true that often the best way to help create or convey an image is to use a talking-head ad that shows the candidate's stand on an issue—but most important, does so in an intimate and communicative way.

5. A good presidential television campaign uses good negative ads as well as positive ads. In 1988 Dukakis lost because he failed to use good negative ads. Instead, Dukakis allowed Bush to define him, rather than he defining Bush. "The 1988 election was won or lost because it became a referendum on Mike Dukakis" (Devlin, 1989, p. 408). The crucial Dukakis mistake was not that he did not respond sooner to the Bush negative ads, "it was that he did not initially want to use negative ads, later grudgingly used them, and then had very few good ones. He needed to define the Bush vulnerabilities. He did not do it well" (Devlin, 1989, p. 406). In 1972 Charles Guggenheim, McGovern's ad maker, did not believe in the use of negative spots because "we believe in advocacy. Let someone else do the name calling. We don't want the campaign to degenerate into a pissing match" (Devlin, 1973-1974, p. 23). Although Nixon was vulnerable and many disliked him, Guggenheim did not emphasize these vulnerabilities. Instead he allowed the Nixon campaign to air unanswered devastating "Democrats for Nixon" spots,

exposing McGovern's vulnerability on defense and welfare and on changing his mind, concluding: "Last year, this year, the question is: what about next year?" In 1992 Clinton was not only effective in using response ads to answer his vulnerabilities, he was also extremely effective in using George Bush's words and promises against him in a way that was not perceived as overtly negative by viewers. In 1992 Clinton made it a referendum on George Bush; Bush did not make it a referendum on Clinton. Any good television ad coordinator tries to make an election a referendum on the other guy. All this brings me back to my opening, which emphasized that the candidate whose ads best define himself or herself, as well as the other candidate, wins.

References

Atkin, C., Bowen, L., Nayman, O. B., & Sheinkopf, K. G. (1973). Quality versus quantity in televised political ads. *Public Opinion Quarterly, 37*, 209-224.

Bailey, D. (1988, November 30). Interview with Douglass Bailey, editor of *Hotline*.

Cooper, B. (1992, November 20). Interview with B. Jay Cooper, director of communications, Republican National Committee.

Devlin, L. P. (1973-1974). Contrasts in presidential campaign commercials of 1972. *Journal of Broadcasting, 18*, 17-26.

Devlin, L. P. (1977). Contrasts in presidential commercials of 1976. *Central States Speech Journal, 28*, 238-249.

Devlin, L. P. (1978, March). *The effectiveness of television political commercials*. Paper presented at the Eastern Communication Association Convention, Boston.

Devlin, L. P. (1986). An analysis of presidential television commercials, 1952-1984. In L. L. Kaid, D. Nimmo, & K. R. Sanders (Eds.), *New perspectives on political advertising* (pp. 21-54). Carbondale: Southern Illinois University Press.

Devlin, L. P. (1987). Contrasts in presidential campaign commercials of 1984. *Political Communication Review, 12*, 25-55.

Devlin, L. P. (1989). Contrasts in presidential campaign commercials of 1988. *American Behavioral Scientist, 32*, 389-414.

Devlin, L. P. (1993). Contrasts in presidential campaign commercials of 1992. *American Behavioral Scientist, 37*, 272-290.

Devlin, L. P. (1994). Television advertising in the 1992 New Hampshire presidential primary election. *Political Communication, 11*, 81-99.

Friedenberg, R. V. (Ed.). (1990). *Rhetorical studies of national political debates*. New York: Praeger.

Greer, F. (1992, December 18, 28). Interviews with Frank Greer, president of Clinton's 1992 Great American Media.

Greer, F. (1993, January 25). Interview with Frank Greer, president of Clinton's 1992 Great American Media.

Hart, P. (1988). *Chicago Tribune* poll of 5 key states. Washington, DC: Peter D. Hart Research Associates.
Johnson-Cartee, K. S., & Copeland, G. A. (1991). *Negative political advertising*. Hillsdale, NJ: Lawrence Erlbaum.
Kaid, L. L. (1981). Political advertising. In D. D. Nimmo & K. R. Sanders (Eds.), *Handbook of political communication* (pp. 249-272). Beverly Hills, CA: Sage.
Kaid, L. L., & Johnston, A. (1991). Negative versus positive television advertising in U.S. presidential campaigns, 1960-1988. *Journal of Communication, 41*, 53-64.
Kelly, G. (1992, November 7). Interview with Geoff Kelly, director of production for Bush's 1992 November Company.
Kern, M. (1989). *30-second politics*. New York: Praeger.
Martin, M. (1992, December 2). Interview with Murphy Martin, interviewer for Perot's 1992 270 Group.
Negative advertising pro and con. (1986, November 10). *Advertising Age*, p. 104.
Nugent, J. (1987). Positively negative. *Campaigns and Elections, 7*, 47-49.
O'Brien, H. (1992, December 2). Interview with Hugh O'Brien, media director for Perot's 1992 270 Group.
O'Shaughnessy, N. (1990). *The phenomenon of political marketing*. New York: St. Martin's Press.
Patterson, T. E., & McClure, R. D. (1976). *The unseeing eye*. New York: G. P. Putnam.
Runkel, D. R. (Ed.). (1989). *Campaign for president: The managers look at '88*. Dover, MA: Auburn House.
Sabato, L. (1981). *The rise of political consultants*. New York: Basic Books.
Schwartz, T. (1973). *The responsive chord*. New York: Anchor Books.
Swanson, D. (1973). Political information, influence and judgment in the 1972 presidential campaign. *Quarterly Journal of Speech, 59*, 130-142.
Taylor, P. (1986, October 5). Negative ads becoming powerful political force. *Washington Post*, pp. A1, A6-A7.
Weinschel, I. (1992, April 9 & June 4). Interviews with Ian Weinschel, media creator for the Buchanan campaign.
West, D. M. (1993). *Air wars*. Washington, DC: Congressional Quarterly Press.
Wood, S. C. (1985, May). *Television's first political spot ad campaign: Eisenhower answers America*. Paper presented at the meeting of the International Communication Association, Honolulu, Hawaii.
Wood, S. C. (1990). Television's first political spot ad campaign: Eisenhower answers America. *Presidential Studies Quarterly, 20*, 265-283.

12. Political Advertising Across Cultures

Comparing Content, Styles, and Effects

LYNDA LEE KAID

CHRISTINA HOLTZ-BACHA

In every democratic system political candidates and parties face the fundamental problem of how they can communicate with, and incidentally persuade, voters to accept their leadership. Televised political advertising has become important to many democratic systems because it provides a solution to this problem that also has the advantage of being under the direct control of the party/candidate. Unlike news coverage or debate formats, the party/candidate determines the content and style of televised political advertising messages and can, therefore, have an opportunity to affect the outcome or the effect of the message.

Despite this fundamental advantage to political advertising, the role of such messages varies across democratic systems. As demonstrated in other chapters in this book, media, cultural, and political system differences often determine the role that televised political advertising can play in any given democracy. The differences also make it difficult to compare and contrast the role of advertising across cultures; it is far less challenging to say simply that the differences are so overwhelming that no comparison is possible. The research reported here rejects that premise and attempts to provide a comparison across Western democracies of the content, style, and effects of modern political television commercials.

The American Model

Among Western democracies, there is no question when it comes to political television advertising that the United States has done it first, most, and, arguably, best. Political television spots have played a role in U.S. presidential elections since 1952, when Eisenhower adopted this format in his first campaign. Since that time, the use of spot advertising has grown to the point that television advertising is now used in almost every primary and general election campaign for every major political office in the United States, from president down to school board elections in local communities. The commercial nature of the U.S. media system has virtually guaranteed political candidates unlimited access, controlled only by the financial resources necessary to purchase television time.

Other democratic systems have been said to adopt American principles of political television advertising, but most have been limited by the nature of the media system/political system interface. Public media systems have dominated Western democracies until the past decade. Such systems did not allow parties and candidates to purchase time, but rather provided "free" time for political party messages to be broadcast. The governmental/media system decided how much time would be given to a party or candidate and when the message would be broadcast. Only the proliferation of private broadcasting in recent years has opened the possibility for more availability of purchased time for political advertising, and the exact parameters of such systems are still evolving in most countries.

Research on Political Broadcast Content and Effects

Because of the pervasiveness of the political television spot in American campaigns, there has been much more research on the content and effects of political commercials in the United States than in other democratic systems. However, the past two decades have seen an increased interest in research on the political broadcasts in other countries. Most of the research across all democracies falls into two categories, content/style research and effects research.

CONTENT AND STYLE OF POLITICAL TELEVISION ADVERTISING

Although some researchers have provided historical/critical overviews (Diamond & Bates, 1984; Jamieson, 1992) of political spot content in American campaigns, few scholars have offered comprehensive or systematic descriptions. Joslyn's (1980) seminal work on spot content, although limited by a small convenience sample, established that the dominant content of American political spots has been issue content. The issue content was not particularly specific or policy-oriented, but it made up the major content of the spots analyzed. Other researchers have confirmed this emphasis on issue information in television spots at all campaign levels in the United States (Kaid & Davidson, 1986; Kaid & Johnston, 1991; Kern, 1989; Shyles, 1983).

Other research in U.S. spot content has considered the specific issue and image characteristics conveyed in spots (Kaid & Davidson, 1986; Shyles, 1984a). Several researchers have also identified the visual characteristics of spots and how these might relate to issue and image content (Shyles, 1984b) and to candidate political positions, such as incumbent/challenger status (Wadsworth & Kaid, 1987). A considerable amount of work has also been done on the concept of "videostyle," the verbal, nonverbal, and production characteristics that define how a candidate presents himself/herself to voters through political spot advertising (Kaid & Davidson, 1986; Kaid, Tedesco, Chanslor, & Roper, 1993, 1994; Wadsworth & Kaid, 1987).

Much less is known about the content and style of political party/candidate broadcasts in other countries. Johnson and Elebash (1986) have identified a similarly strong issue content in British PEBs from the 1983 general election. Similar findings validate the importance of issue content in political broadcasts in France (Johnston, 1991). In Germany, long-term analyses also show that issue content has dominated spots (Klein, 1992), except in 1990 (Holtz-Bacha & Kaid, 1993; Holtz-Bacha, Kaid, & Johnston, 1994).

EFFECTS OF POLITICAL TELEVISION ADVERTISING

In the United States considerable research has been focused on what effects the spots actually have in election campaigns. Early researchers verified that political spots do, in fact, have cognitive, affective, and behavioral effects on voters (Kaid, 1981). Atkin and his colleagues determined that political spots could overcome selective exposure, thus guaranteeing that nonsupporters, as well as supporters, were exposed to a candidate's message (Atkin, Bowen, Nayman, & Sheinkopf, 1973).

Both survey research and experimental studies in the United States have yielded strong support for the effectiveness of political spots. One of the earliest effects verified by researchers was the ability of ads to communicate issue information to voters. Patterson and McClure (1976) used survey research to show that voters learned substantially more issue content from spots than from television news in the 1972 presidential campaign. Researchers in experimental studies have also demonstrated that spots can have strong effects on a candidate's image (Basil, Schooler, & Reeves, 1991; Cundy, 1986; Kaid, Leland, & Whitney, 1992; Kaid & Sanders, 1978) and on vote intent (Basil et al., 1991; Kaid & Sanders, 1978).

The special case of negative advertising has also occupied American effects researchers. Garramone has shown that negative ads can affect sponsor and opponent images and vote intentions (Garramone, 1984, 1985; Garramone & Smith, 1984). Kaid & Boydston (1987) demonstrated that negative ads can hurt a candidate's image, even with natural supporters and partisans.

In other democratic systems, very little research has addressed effects of political party/candidate advertising on voters. As Scammell and Semetko point out earlier in this book (Chapter 3), research in Britain has indicated that in earlier years party election broadcasts did affect voter knowledge levels (Blumler & McQuail, 1968) and may have some effects on undecided or low-interest voters. Other countries have been slow to take notice of the impact of such broadcasts. Recently, however, the authors have demonstrated that exposure to television party broadcasts can affect images of French prime minister candidates (Kaid, 1991) and German chancellor candidates, at least for respondents in the former East Germany (Kaid & Holtz-Bacha, 1993).

Measurement Approach Across Cultures

The purpose of this chapter is to make some comparison of political television advertising across cultures, examining content, style, and effects. The bases of this comparison are content analytic and experimental studies conducted in election campaigns from 1988 through 1992.

CONTENT ANALYSIS STUDIES

The content analytic procedures were applied to a sample of spots from six countries: the United States[1] (1992 presidential election), France[2] (1988 presidential campaign), Germany (1990 national election), Italy[3] (1992 national election), Britain[4] (1992 general election), and Israel[5] (1992 national election). The number of spots from each country varied; the samples were composed as follows:

United States—81 spots from Bush and Dukakis
France—20 spots, 10 each for Mitterrand and Chirac
Germany—38 spots from all parties allocated TV time
Italy—sample of 41 spots from various parties
Israel—sample of 60 spots from Labour and Likud Parties[6]
Britain—8 broadcasts from Labour and Conservative parties

The categories developed for the content analysis followed the procedures set forth in prior studies of videostyle (Kaid & Johnston, 1991; Kaid et al., 1993, 1994; Wadsworth & Kaid, 1987). Verbal content categories included image versus issue content of the ads, types of appeals used in ads (emotional, logical, ethical), negative versus positive focus of the ad, specific candidate qualities stressed in the spot, and types of strategies (incumbent versus challenger strategies, identified by Trent & Friedenberg, 1983). Nonverbal categories focused on setting of the ad, speaker in the ad, and presence of other nonverbal cues such as music. The television production technique categories encompassed production styles of the spots (cinema verité, documentary, head-on, and the like). The content analysis was done by trained student coders; in the case of foreign ads, by native speakers of the language. Intercoder reliabilities were calculated using the formula suggested by Holsti (North, Holsti, Zaninovich, & Zinnes, 1963) and averaged +.86 across all categories for all samples.

EXPERIMENTAL STUDIES

Data from experimental studies exist for only four of the above countries:[7] France (1988 presidential election), Italy (1992 national election), Germany (1990 national election), and the United States

(1988 presidential election). In each case the data were gathered using student samples and a before-after experimental test design. Respondents were given pretest instruments to measure their attitudes toward candidates/parties; they were shown samples of spots from the campaign; and then a posttest instrument was administered to measure attitudes and effects after exposure to the spots.

The specific sample sizes for each country study are included in the tables and discussion that follow. The questionnaires used in the pretest and posttest experiments for all studies were virtually identical and were translated from the original English version into French, German, and Italian by native speakers. A major component of the questionnaires was a semantic differential scale designed to measure candidate image. This scale consisted of 12 bipolar adjectives[8] and achieved acceptable reliability coefficients, even when transferred across languages.[9]

Comparison of Content and Styles of Spots

One of the most common elements of spots across the six countries analyzed here is that the majority of ads concentrate on issues, rather than images of candidates or parties.[10] As Table 12.1 indicates, issues are the dominant content of spots in the United States (61%), in France (100%), in Italy (71%), and in Britain (88%). The split is 50/50 in Israel; only 1990 German spots concentrate less on issues (26%) than on image or combination content.

A few differences are apparent when examining the specific party/candidate emphasis within each individual country. For instance, although the Israel split is 50/50 overall, the Labour party concentrated 59% of its spots on issues, and Likud emphasized images in 58% of its spots.

It is also clear from Table 12.1 that another commonality across countries is the positive focus of the ads. In all six countries the dominant focus of the ads was positive, ranging from 85% of the ads in Italy to 58% in Israel. Although the United States, Israel, and Germany had somewhat higher percentages of negative ads than did France, Italy, and Britain, the dominant approach was still positive.

Again, there are a few differences when individual parties or candidates within a country are considered. In the United States, Dukakis sponsored more negative spots than did Bush. In Israel, 48% of the

TABLE 12.1 Content and Appeals of Broadcasts

	United States *81*	*France* *20*	*Germany* *38*	*Italy* *41*	*Britain* *8*	*Israel* *60*
Emphasis of the ad						
issues	61%	100%	26%	71%	88%	50%
image	39%	0	57%	29%	12%	50%
combination	0	0	16%	0	0	0
Focus of ad						
positive	63%	75%	68%	85%	75%	58%
negative	37%	25%	32%	15%	25%	42%
Dominant type of appeal						
logical	33%	80%	16%	15%	50%	25%
emotional	36%	10%	53%	54%	38%	40%
source credibility	31%	10%	24%	31%	12%	35%
combination	0	0	8%	0	0	0
Political party emphasized in ad	9%	5%	13%	7%	38%	7%

Labour party's spots were negative. In Italy, the challenging parties (those not in power at the time of the election) used a much higher percentage of negative ads than the overall totals would indicate.

Another interesting comparison is in the number of spots with content focused primarily on the political party in each country. In no country was the party the focus of even half of the spots. In France only one spot emphasized political party over issue, image, or interest group concerns (5%). In Italy and Israel (7%), the United States (9%), and Germany (13%), the percentages were also small. The largest percentage of party dominated spots was in Britain, where three of the eight spots analyzed (38%) focused on the party. This trend may provide some evidence that spots are contributing to a declining emphasis on parties in democratic systems, resulting in a more personalized campaign system.

There is more divergence among countries when the type of appeal is considered, however. Spots were categorized according to whether the dominant type of appeal or proof offered in the ad was logical, emotional, or ethical, corresponding to Aristotle's original distinctions between logos, pathos, and ethos. The French spots were the most likely to use logical proof, relying on this form of persuasion in 80% of ads. In British spots, logical reasoning was also more common than other types of proof and was used in 50% of the British broadcasts. Other countries found emotional proof to be more attractive. Emotional proof was dominant in the Italian spots (54%), German spots (53%), Israeli spots (40%), and American spots (36%). However, the Israeli and American spots showed more balance among the three types of proof. British spots also used some emotional proof (38%), a good example being the "Jennifer's Ear" spot described earlier by Scammell and Semetko in Chapter 3.

INCUMBENT AND CHALLENGER STRATEGIES

Research on American political spots has identified patterns of strategies attributable to candidates running as incumbents and as challengers. This research utilizes these strategies to assess whether such strategies have any consistency across cultures, applying the categories derived from the work of Trent and Friedenberg (1983).

Tables 12.2 and 12.3 indicate that there are, indeed, some consistencies in these strategies across cultures. Looking first at incumbents, only

Italian spots fail to utilize the traditional incumbent strategies with any regularity. The most consistent strategies used across countries for incumbents were emphasizing accomplishments and stressing the competency of the government office occupied. However, some marked differences also occur. German and French spots never rely on surrogates to speak for candidates. British and Italian incumbents never use the symbolic trappings of their offices.

Incumbents also borrowed a few traditional challenger strategies. In every country (although less so in the United States) incumbents were eager to emphasize optimism for the future. French, German, and Italian spots were particularly eager to do this, in many cases concentrating on hopes for economic growth as the EC union develops. Most incumbents also found it prudent to speak to traditional values; Italy was the exception here.

Challengers, however, were even more consistent in their display of traditional challenger stances in their spots, as Table 12.3 indicates. Challengers consistently called for change, took the offensive on issues, and attacked the record of the opponent in their spots. Challengers, too, generally stressed optimism for the future. A major exception here was Germany, where only 20% of challenger spots conveyed such positivity, due partly to concerns about the economic situation, particularly in light of German unification concerns.

A few challengers also adopted incumbent strategies, but patterns were not as consistent here. German challengers were eager to wrap themselves in the symbolic trappings of the government (60%). The French challenger Chirac was able to stress competency and the office (70%) and to emphasize accomplishments (50%) because he, too, was an incumbent of sorts (being the prime minister while running for president).

Another aspect of the content of the spots across cultures is the question of whether the leaders and parties emphasize similar traits or image qualities in their spots. All of the spots were coded for the presence or absence of a series of image traits, displayed for incumbents and challengers in Tables 12.2 and 12.3. Again, there are some remarkable similarities in the characteristics that political leaders attempt to portray in their advertising across cultures. Almost every candidate/party is eager to stress competency and performance/success in its advertising. Both incumbents and challengers also emphasize toughness and strength (except for British incumbent broadcasts). Stressing warmth and compassion was important to most, but less so for American

TABLE 12.2 Image Content and Strategies Used by Incumbents

	United States 37	*France* 10	*Germany** 6	*Italy* 17	*Britain* 4	*Israel* 33
Incumbent strategies						
use of symbolic trappings	41%	30%	100%	0	0	36%
presidency stands for legitimacy	49%	80%	60%	6%	0	55%
competency and the office	81%	100%	80%	11%	50%	76%
charisma and the office	16%	46%	60%	0	25%	36%
consulting with world leaders	32%	36%	40%	6%	50%	24%
using endorsements by leaders	0	0	20%	0	0	18%
emphasizing accomplishments	54%	70%	80%	18%	25%	88%
above-the-trenches posture	32%	100%	80%	0	0	18%
depending on surrogates to speak	68%	0	0	6%	25%	82%
Challenger strategies						
calling for changes	0	0	0	47%	0	30%
emphasizing optimism for future	38%	100%	80%	88%	50%	49%
speaking to traditional values	62%	100%	40%	12%	75%	49%
representing center of party	27%	30%	20%	41%	25%	55%
taking the offensive on issues	30%	0	0	0	50%	45%
attacking record of opponent	35%	0	0	0	50%	58%
Characteristics						
honesty/integrity	60%	36%	40%	0	50%	52%
toughness/strength	65%	73%	60%	35%	0	64%
warmth/compassion	22%	64%	40%	53%	50%	27%
competency	87%	100%	60%	77%	25%	88%
performance/success	78%	100%	80%	18%	75%	82%
aggressiveness	16%	50%	0	29%	0	39%
activeness	19%	82%	60%	82%	25%	67%

* For purposes of this category, only the spots of the largest German parties were used.

TABLE 12.3 Image Content and Strategies Used by Challengers

	United States 41	*France* 10	*Germany** 5	*Italy* 24	*Britain* 4	*Israel* 27
Incumbent strategies						
use of symbolic trappings	14%	20%	60%	0	0	26%
presidency stands for legitimacy	18%	20%	0	0	0	52%
competency and the office	48%	70%	40%	0	25%	52%
charisma and the office	23%	20%	40%	0	0	48%
consulting with world leaders	0	10%	0	0	0	11%
using endorsements by leaders	16%	0	0	4%	25%	11%
emphasizing accomplishments	27%	50%	0	4%	0	4%
above-the-trenches posture	2%	0	0	0	0	44%
depending on surrogates to speak	66%	0	60%	16%	75%	56%
Challenger strategies						
calling for changes	75%	70%	100%	88%	100%	100%
emphasizing optimism for future	68%	80%	20%	42%	75%	63%
speaking to traditional values	43%	60%	0	13%	75%	33%
representing center of party	30%	40%	40%	79%	25%	58%
taking the offensive on issues	43%	50%	80%	42%	50%	44%
attacking record of opponent	64%	50%	40%	25%	25%	55%
Characteristics						
honesty/integrity	61%	20%	80%	38%	25%	78%
toughness/strength	59%	90%	60%	50%	25%	59%
warmth/compassion	39%	40%	60%	17%	50%	56%
competency	57%	100%	60%	33%	75%	78%
performance/success	46%	80%	40%	0	25%	22%
aggressiveness	59%	80%	40%	63%	0	19%
activeness	68%	100%	40%	25%	50%	59%

* For purposes of this category, only the spots of the largest German parties were used.

and Israeli incumbents and for Italian challengers. In the midst of all the similarities, two divergences stand out. German incumbents are very careful not to display aggressiveness, because of postwar and cultural concerns about the historical implications of this trait. It is perhaps ironic, in light of the subsequent scandals in Italy, that no Italian incumbents and only about one third of Italian challengers saw a need to stress honesty/integrity in their ads.

NONVERBAL AND PRODUCTION ASPECTS OF SPOTS

One of the most interesting nonverbal aspects of spots is the subtlety conveyed by whether the candidate himself/herself is the speaker in the spot. As Table 12.4 shows, French and German candidates are the most likely to be the dominant speaker in their spots, but even then the candidate is the main speaker at most only 50% of the time (France). British broadcasts trail all others in this regard, with the party spokesperson being the main speaker only 12% of the time. However, even the United States, Israel, and Italy do not reach the one-third point in this regard.

The setting of a spot is also an important nonverbal indicator. Formality is a major distinction in settings, and in this sense there are major differences among the six countries compared. French settings are very formal (95%), as are more than half the Israeli settings (55%). The American (17%), British (12%), and Italian (9%) spots use formal settings much less frequently. These countries have adopted more informal settings for their commercials and generally use either informal settings or combination settings. The French tendency toward formal settings is partly explained by the more stringent controls on the content of French ads, mentioned earlier in Chapters 2 and 4.

Production techniques also indicate some differences among countries. Again, France is more constrained in the production options by system regulations. Consequently, most French ads are either head-on production (25%) or a combination of techniques (75%). This latter category was probably dominant in French production because of the new tendency in 1988 to use preproduced clips as part of French productions. These innovative aspects of 1988 French spots, used particularly by Mitterrand, employed fast-paced music and quick cuts to heighten the drama and visual interest of the spots. However, by law, these clips could occupy only a small percentage of the total spot time.

TABLE 12.4 Nonverbal and Television Production Aspects of Spots

	United States *81*	*France* *20*	*Germany* *38*	*Italy* *41*	*Britain* *8*	*Israel* *60*
Setting						
formal	17%	95%	37%	9%	12%	55%
informal	43%	5%	13%	37%	24%	13%
combination	18%	0	32%	27%	64%	3%
not applicable	22%	0	18%	27%	0	29%
Candidate is dominant speaker	32%	50%	40%	27%	12%	27%
Production technique						
cinema verité	27%	0	5%	34%	25%	3%
slides w/print, movement, voice-over	9%	0	11%	7%	0	2%
head-on	20%	25%	42%	15%	0	62%
animation and special production	1%	0	8%	17%	0	3%
combination	43%	75%	34%	27%	75%	31%

Thus most French spots used a combination of preproduced clips and head-on or interview formats. Interestingly, the format named for French production techniques (cinema verité) was not dominant in any French spots, but it was widely used by the Italians (34%) and Americans (27%). The head-on technique was dominant in Germany (42%) and in Israel (62%). In Germany, the majority of the spots using this technique were those from the smaller parties (not the CDU/CSU or SPD parties) whose approach in the ads was the more traditional, talking-head oriented.

Another point of interest related to production techniques has been the increasing use of special-effects video techniques in spots. The use of special sounds and music is one aspect of this trend. In some countries, for instance, music was used in 100% of all political advertising productions (Israel and Britain). The United States led in the use of special-effects techniques, with frequent use of computer graphics, superimpositions, and slow- and stop-motion techniques. British ads also capitalized on such techniques, using slow motion, montages, superimpositions, and computer graphics in several broadcasts. The French broadcasts were also notable for their use of such techniques, primarily, as mentioned above, in the preproduced clips contained within the spots. Several of these French segments were actually more like American MTV (Music-Television) productions than political spots.

Effects of Political Advertising Across Countries

The comparisons on effects of political advertising involve the four countries (1988 United States, 1992 Italy, 1988 France, and 1990 Germany) in which similar experiments were conducted. The primary concern was with the extent to which exposure to a sample of spots from the campaign would affect the image ratings of each candidate, and the extent to which emotional responses to the ads might relate to the image scores.

EFFECTS ON IMAGES OF POLITICAL LEADERS

In comparing the pretest and posttest image scores for each leader in each country, the 12 items (7-point scale) on the semantic differential were summed. In Table 12.5, these mean scores are compared before and after viewing the ads in each country. One of the first things that is

TABLE 12.5 Effects of Political Advertising Exposure on Candidate Images

	Pretest	*Posttest*
United States 1988		
(n = 43)		
Bush	58.54	61.40*
Dukakis	48.98	48.63
France 1988		
(n = 55)		
Chirac	41.95	40.25*
Mitterrand	58.82	58.98
Germany 1990		
West Germany		
(n = 98)		
Kohl	43.54	43.73
Lafontaine	53.37	54.91
East Germany		
(n = 73)		
Kohl	43.84	44.21
Lafontaine	56.71	57.94*
Italy 1992		
(n = 53)		
Martinazzoli (DC)	44.85	43.13*
Occhetto (PDS)	46.33	46.33

* indicates t-test between pretest and posttest score is significant at $p \leq .05$.

clear is that political advertising exposure can significantly affect a leader's image rating. In every country, this is true for one of the candidates. In two cases (Bush in the United States in 1988, and Lafontaine among East Germans in 1990) the direction of the change is positive. After seeing the spots, the respondents rated the leader higher. The opposite is true for candidates Martinazzoli in Italy in 1992, and Chirac in France in 1988. After the viewing of their television portrayals, their images declined.

It is also interesting to note how similar the absolute scores are for the political leaders across countries. With a maximum possible score of 84, all of the scores cluster between 40 and 61. Bush, Mitterrand, and Lafontaine all have scores well above the midpoint, with Bush's posttest score being the highest, at 61.40. The lower absolute scores of the Italian leaders are undoubtedly due to the breaking political scandals in effect at the time of the experiment in Italy, although the pretest/posttest design helps insulate the experimental effects from that problem.

EMOTIONAL REACTIONS TO POLITICAL ADVERTISING

In the U.S. research, one concern with political advertising has been the accusation that the ads, particularly image ads, are designed to engage viewer emotions, instead of viewer rationality and reasoning. Examination of the results in Table 12.6 suggest that this concern should not be limited to the United States. Respondents were asked how much each of a series of emotions was aroused by the advertisements, and these levels of emotion were then correlated with the posttest image scores of the political leaders. These results clearly indicate that a candidate's image is related to the emotional responses elicited by ad viewing.

These findings are extremely consistent across countries. For instance, the more *optimistic* an ad made the viewer feel, the higher the image rating for seven of the eight candidates (only Martinazzoli in Italy is an exception). The amount of *confidence* generated is also a strong emotional connector to image. The more confidence the ads generated, the higher the rating for Bush, Dukakis, Chirac, Mitterrand, Occhetto, and Lafontaine. A significant relationship also existed for Kohl, but in a negative direction. *Security* was also strongly related to image for most of the political leaders (Martinazzoli and Kohl again being the exceptions). The generation of *excitement* was a positive force for Dukakis, Bush, Mitterrand, Occhetto, and Kohl.

Results for several other emotions were more mixed. Low levels of *boredom* seemed to raise image ratings (a negative relationship) for all candidates except Chirac and Lafontaine. Dukakis, Bush, and Mitterrand benefited from low fear levels. *Patriotism* helped both U.S. and both French candidates, as well as Kohl, but made little difference for Italian candidates or Lafontaine.

Conclusion

These comparisons among several Western European democratic systems of the content, style, and effects of exposure to televised

TABLE 12.6 Correlations of Emotional Responses With Candidate Image

	United States		*France*		*Italy*		*Germany (West)*	
	Dukakis	*Bush*	*Chirac*	*Mitterrand*	*Martinazzoli*	*Occhetto*	*Kohl*	*Lafontaine*
Optimistic	.56*	.58*	.38*	.51*	.28	.54*	.41*	.35*
Confident	.72*	.63*	.22*	.59*	.24	.54*	–.44*	.30*
Anxious	–.01	.20	–.21	–.33*	–.45*	–.21	–.42*	.08
Excited	.30*	.60*	–.12	.22*	.19	.41*	.31*	–.11
Secure	.63*	.71*	.46*	.61*	.12	.60*	–.14	.28*
Fearful	–.66*	–.55*	–.07	–.39*	–.27	–.13	–.12	–.14
Bored	–.56*	–.41*	–.17	–.51*	–.37*	–.55*	–.24*	–.18
Patriotic	.41*	.58*	.44*	.48*	.02	.16	–.21*	.09
Concerned	–.19	–.18	–.35*	–.65*	–.24	.10	–.51*	.44*

* indicates Pearson correlation between emotion and posttest image score is significant at $p \leq .05$.

political advertising show some striking similarities across cultures. Although there are admitted differences in media and political system variables in these countries, as detailed in other chapters in this book, the form and effect of their controlled broadcast messages have many similarities. Although there are many individual differences, the trends are important to note:

1. Most countries concentrate the content of their ads on issues.
2. The political broadcasts across countries are overwhelmingly positive, not negative in their focus.
3. Despite the emphasis on issues and positivity, most leaders and parties rely on emotional, rather than logical, proof to make their points. France and Britain are the exceptions here.
4. Both challengers and incumbents show similarities in the strategies they adopt to convey their messages. This trend is strongest for challengers who adopt traditional challenger strategies, such as calling for change, taking the offensive on issues, and attacking opponents. Challengers and incumbents across countries also show some, but not uniform, similarity in the types of image characteristics they attempt to convey in their messages (competence, toughness/strength).
5. The greatest differences among the ads may be in the production and nonverbal aspects. France, in particular, is constrained by regulations on format. Despite the differences, new technologies are increasing the variety of production styles. In these six countries from 1988 to 1992, documentary formats were definitely out of style, and simple talking-head productions were used primarily by minor parties whose finances probably did not allow for more exotic production techniques.
6. In terms of effects, it is clear that political advertising exposure can have a significant effect on candidate images, sometimes positive and sometimes negative.
7. The emotions aroused by political advertising exposure correlate with image ratings of candidates, indicating strong payoffs for candidates who can succeed in striking the proper resonance with voter emotions.

The research reported here is admittedly limited by many factors. The spots' formats and lengths are not the same in each country; the timing of the experiments was not always ideal, nor was the use of student subjects necessarily completely representative of the general population. However, this is the first attempt to bring together any comparable data on these countries; the results warrant further research.

One area that might be pursued is further determination of the effects of advertising exposure. Experimental and survey work could help isolate more detailed effects. For instance, the experimental work completed in Germany, France, and the United States has indicated that in France and the United States viewers are much more likely to recall *image* characteristics of candidates than *issue* stances after viewing ads (Kaid, 1991). In Germany the opposite was true in 1990 (Kaid & Holtz-Bacha, 1993). Results from Italy have not yet been analyzed. Further research might attempt to tie exposure to voting patterns as well.

Finally, this research needs to be replicated in subsequent elections in the countries already studied and expanded to additional political systems and settings. This would be helpful, not only for the other countries outlined in this book but also for newly developing democratic systems in Eastern and Central Europe. Asian systems are also beginning to use political advertising, and comparisons with those systems might also be useful.

Gurevitch and Blumler's (1990) caution that one cannot simply import identical methods and approaches across cultures is well taken. However, if media and political system differences are accounted for, there may be something to be learned from the application of similar, if not identical, approaches across a large number of cases.

Notes

1. The spot sample was provided by the Political Commercial Archive at the University of Oklahoma.

2. The authors wish to thank Jacques Gerstlé for his assistance in obtaining these ads and Anne Johnston for her work on the content analysis of the materials (Johnston, 1991; see also Johnston & Gerstlé in Chapter 4).

3. The authors appreciate the assistance of Gianpietro Mazzoleni and Cindy Roper for the provision and content analysis of the Italian spots (see also Chapter 6).

4. The authors thank Holli Semetko for assistance in obtaining the 1992 British ads and John Tedesco for his assistance in the content analysis process.

5. The authors acknowledge the assistance of Akiba Cohen for providing copies of the Israeli ads, and a special thanks is given to Keely Cormier for the content analysis work on these ads.

6. The particular spots used here were part of a larger sample of 246 spots used during the 1992 Israeli campaign by all parties. These particular spots were part of a sample of spots that used Russian-language subtitles to appeal to the new subpopulation in Israel. Except for a small percentage of spots that specifically addressed Russian immigrant

problems, these spots did not seem to differ from other 1992 campaign spots in the total sample (Cormier, 1993).

7. The United States data were gathered just prior to the November 1988 election, using students from the University of Oklahoma; and the German data were gathered just prior to the December 1990 national election, using student samples from Munich, Hannover, and Leipzig. Both the French data gathered at the University of Paris I-Sorbonne (Spring 1989) and the Italian data from the University of Salerno (Spring 1993) were gathered after the actual elections had taken place in those countries. However, the purpose of the studies was to examine the effects of the exposure to the television spots, and the presence of the pretest helped to control for any problems created by the scheduling of the experiments. The authors want to thank Holli Semetko, Klaus Schoenbach, Jacques Gerstlé, Gianpietro Mazzoleni, and Cindy Roper for their assistance in collecting the experimental data.

8. The bipolar adjective pairs making up the semantic differential are qualified-unqualified, sophisticated-unsophisticated, honest-dishonest, believable-unbelievable, successful-unsuccessful, attractive-unattractive, friendly-unfriendly, sincere-insincere, calm-excitable, aggressive-unaggressive, strong-weak, and active-inactive.

9. Cronbach's alpha levels for the 12-item semantic differential scale on pretest/posttest measures were: United States (.90/.92 for Bush and .86/.91 for Dukakis), France (.86/.91 for Chirac and .85/.88 for Mitterrand), Germany (.49/.59 for Kohl and .68/.75 for Lafontaine), and Italy (.67/.76 for DC party candidate and .77/.84 for the PDS candidate).

10. The definition of issue and image used here is the same as that used in many other studies (Kaid & Johnston, 1991; Kaid & Sanders, 1978). Issue ads concentrate on a candidate's or party's concern for or position on policy or public concerns, such as foreign policy, taxes, and so on. Image ads, on the other hand, display a candidate's personal qualities or qualifications, such as honesty, compassion, and so on.

References

Atkin, C., Bowen, L., Nayman, O. B., & Sheinkopf, K. G. (1973). Quality versus quantity in televised political ads. *Public Opinion Quarterly, 40*, 209-224.

Basil, M., Schooler, C., & Reeves, B. (1991). Positive and negative political advertising: Effectiveness of ads and perceptions of candidates. In F. Biocaa (Ed.), *Television and political advertising: Vol. 1. Psychological processes* (pp. 245-262). Hillsdale, NJ: Lawrence Erlbaum.

Blumler, J. G., & McQuail, D. (1968). *Television in politics*. London: Faber and Faber.

Cormier, K. Q. (1993). *Alluring and informing the Russian immigrants: A content analysis of the 1992 Israeli political campaign commercials*. Master's thesis, the University of Oklahoma.

Cundy, D. T. (1986). Political commercials and candidate image: The effect can be substantial. In L. L. Kaid, D. Nimmo, & K. R. Sanders (Eds.), *New perspectives on political advertising* (pp. 210-234). Carbondale: Southern Illinois University Press.

Diamond, E., & Bates, S. (1984). *The spot: The rise of political advertising on television*. Cambridge: MIT Press.

Garramone, G. M. (1984). Voter responses to negative political ads. *Journalism Quarterly, 61*, 250-259.

Garramone, G. M. (1985). Effects of negative political advertising: The roles of sponsor and rebuttal. *Journal of Broadcasting and Electronic Media, 29*, 147-159.

Garramone, G. M., & Smith, S. J. (1984). Reactions to political advertising: Clarifying sponsor effects. *Journalism Quarterly, 61*, 771-775.

Gurevitch, M., & Blumler, J. G. (1990). Comparative research: The extending frontier. In D. Swanson & D. Nimmo (Eds.), *New directions in political communication: A sourcebook* (pp. 305-325). Newbury Park, CA: Sage.

Holtz-Bacha, C., & Kaid, L. L. (1993). *Die Massenmedien im Wahlkampf* [The mass media during election campaigns]. Opladen: Westdeutscher Verlag.

Holtz-Bacha, C., Kaid, L. L., & Johnston, A. (1994). Political television advertising in Western democracies: A comparison of campaign broadcasts in the U.S., Germany, and France. *Political Communication, 11*, 67-80.

Jamieson, K. H. (1992). *Packaging the presidency: A history and criticism of presidential advertising* (2nd ed.). New York: Oxford University Press.

Johnson, K. S., & Elebash, C. (1986). The contagion from the right: The Americanization of British political advertising. In L. L. Kaid, D. Nimmo, & K. R. Sanders (Eds.), *New perspectives on political advertising* (pp. 293-313). Carbondale: Southern Illinois University Press.

Johnston, A. (1991). Political broadcasts: An analysis of form, content, and style in presidential communications. In L. L. Kaid, J. Gerstlé, & K. R. Sanders (Eds.), *Mediated politics in two cultures: Presidential campaigning in the United States and France* (pp. 59-72). New York: Praeger.

Joslyn, R. A. (1980). The content of political spot ads. *Journalism Quarterly, 57*, 92-98.

Kaid, L. L. (1981). Political advertising. In D. D. Nimmo & K. R. Sanders (Eds.), *Handbook of political communication* (pp. 249-271). Beverly Hills, CA: Sage.

Kaid, L. L. (1991). The effects of television broadcasts on perceptions of political candidates in the United States and France. In L. L. Kaid, J. Gerstlé, & K. R. Sanders (Eds.), *Mediated politics in two cultures: Presidential campaigning in the United States and France* (pp. 247-260). New York: Praeger.

Kaid, L. L., & Boydston, J. (1987). An experimental study of the effectiveness of negative political advertisements. *Communication Quarterly, 35*, 193-201.

Kaid, L. L., & Davidson, J. (1986). Elements of videostyle: Candidate presentation through television advertising. In L. L. Kaid, D. Nimmo, & K. R. Sanders (Eds.), *New perspectives on political advertising* (pp. 184-209). Carbondale: Southern Illinois University Press.

Kaid, L. L., & Holtz-Bacha, C. (1993). Audience reactions to televised political programs: An experimental study of the 1990 German national election. *European Journal of Communication, 8*, 77-99.

Kaid, L. L., & Johnston, A. (1991). Negative versus positive advertising in U.S. presidential campaigns, 1960-1988. *Journal of Communication, 41*, 53-64.

Kaid, L. L., Leland, C., & Whitney, S. (1992). The impact of televised political ads: Evoking viewer responses in the 1988 presidential campaign. *Southern Communication Journal, 57*, 285-295.

Kaid, L. L., & Sanders, K. R. (1978). Political television commercials: An experimental study of type and length. *Communication Research, 5*, 57-70.

Kaid, L. L., Tedesco, J., Chanslor, M., & Roper, C. (1993). Clinton's videostyle: A study of the verbal, nonverbal, and video production techniques in campaign advertising. *Journal of Communication Studies, 12*(1), 11-20.

Kaid, L. L., Tedesco, J., Chanslor, M., & Roper, C. (1994, April). *Videostyle in the 1992 campaign: Presidential presentation through televised political spots.* Paper presented at the Midwest Political Science Association Convention, Chicago.

Kern, M. (1989). *30-second politics: Political advertising in the eighties.* New York: Praeger.

Klein, T. (1992). *Zum Wandel des Kommunikationsstils in Wahlwerbespots von 1972 bis 1990.* Unpublished manuscript. Diplomarbeit Universität Erlangen-Nürnberg.

North, R. C., Holsti, O., Zaninovich, M. G., & Zinnes, D. A. (1963). *Content analysis: A handbook with applications for the study of international crisis.* Evanston, IL: Northwestern University Press.

Patterson, T. E., & McClure, R. D. (1976). *The unseeing eye.* New York: G. P. Putnam.

Shyles, L. C. (1983). Defining the issues of a presidential election from televised political spot advertisements. *Journal of Broadcasting, 27*, 333-343.

Shyles, L. C. (1984a). Defining "images" of presidential candidates from televised political spot advertisements. *Political Behavior, 6*, 171-181.

Shyles, L. C. (1984b). The relationship of images, issues, and presentational methods in televised political spot advertisements for 1980's American presidential primaries. *Journal of Broadcasting, 28*, 405-421.

Trent, J. S., & Friedenberg, R. V. (1983). *Political campaign communication.* New York: Praeger.

Wadsworth, A. J., & Kaid, L. L. (1987, May). *Incumbent and challenger styles in presidential advertising.* Paper presented at the International Communication Association Convention, Chicago.

Index

About the Contributors

Kees Brants is Assistant Professor at the Department of Communication of the University of Amsterdam. He is a member of the Euromedia Research Group and has published extensively on media policy, political communication, and right-wing extremism.

Akiba A. Cohen received his Ph.D. from Michigan State University in 1973. He is the Danny Arnold Professor of Communications at the Hebrew University of Jerusalem. He served as the Director of the Smart Family Foundation Communication Institute at the Hebrew University from 1986 to 1990, and as chair of its Department of Communication and Journalism from 1990 to 1993. His major area of interest is comparative media research on television news. He has published several books in this area and is currently working on a new volume, to be published in 1995, titled *Eurovision and the Globalization of TV News*. He is the current president of the International Communication Association.

L. Patrick Devlin received his Ph.D. from Wayne State University. He is Professor of Communication at the University of Rhode Island. He is an archivist and analyst of presidential campaign television commercials. Every 4 years since 1972, he has written a definitive article which describes, analyzes, and evaluates the presidential television ads used during the campaign. He is the author of the books *Contemporary Political Speaking* (1971) and *Political Persuasion in Presidential*

Campaigns (1987) and has published numerous articles and chapters in books on political communication.

Jacques Gerstlé is Professor of Political Science at the University of Versailles. He also teaches political communication in the Department of Political Science at the University of Paris I (Sorbonne) and in the Institut Français de Presse. In addition to articles in French and international publications, focusing on electoral campaigns, political communication, and political theory, he is the author of *Le Langage des Socialistes* and *Lexique/Sociologie Politique*. He is coauthor of *Giscard d'Estaing/Mitterrand: 54,774 Mots pour Convaincre* and *Democratie Cathodique: L'Élection Présidentielle de 1981 et la Télévision*.

Christina Holtz-Bacha has studied mass communication, political science, and sociology in Münster/Germany where she also received her Ph.D. She is now Professor in Mass Communications at the Ruhr-Universität in Bochum. Before she went to Bochum in 1991, she taught at the University of Munich for 10 years. She also was a visiting professor at the University of Minnesota in Minneapolis in 1986. She is an editor of a book series on *Women and Mass Media* and coedits the German journal *Publizistik*. Her articles on political communication, journalism, and on gender-related topics in communication are published in numerous books and journals.

Anne Johnston is Associate Professor in the School of Journalism and Mass Communication at the University of North Carolina, Chapel Hill. She has written chapters on the use of mass communication directed at children and on recent trends in political communication research. She has coauthored chapters on content analysis, political advertising, and political themes in music videos.

Lynda Lee Kaid is Professor of Communication at the University of Oklahoma, where she also serves as the Director of the Political Communication Center and supervises the Political Commercial Archive. Her research specialties include political advertising and news coverage of political events. A Fulbright Scholar, she has also done work on political television in several Western European countries. She has coauthored/coedited 12 books, including *Political Campaign Communication: A Bibliography and Guide to the Literature*, *New Perspectives on Political Advertising*, *Mediated Politics in Two Cultures*, and *Politi-*

cal Communication Yearbook 1984, and numerous journal articles and book chapters on various aspects of political communication. Her research efforts have been supported by substantial federal grants from the U.S. Department of Education and the National Science Foundation. She is a former president of the Political Communication Division of the International Communication Association and has served in major leadership roles in the Speech Communication Association and the American Political Science Association.

Gianpietro Mazzoleni is Professor of Sociology of Communication at the University of Salerno, corresponding editor of the *European Journal of Communication*, and member of the Euromedia Research Group. His research interests are in the domains of political communication, media systems, media policies, and journalism. His most recent book is *Comunicazione e Potere* (Communication and Power) (Liguori, Naples, 1992).

Tom Moring is the Director of the Swedish Radio Programmes at the Finnish Broadcasting Company (Yle). Until 1993 he was an Associate Professor in Communication and Journalism at the University of Helsinki. He is a Doctor of Political Science and has published books and articles about political elite action in the democratic process, media, and political campaigns. In his latest book (*Politics in the Nude. A Political Campaign Culture in Transition in the Age of Television*, published in Finnish in 1993, written together with Hal Himmelstein), he analyzes the Finnish political television campaign culture, with a special focus on the first political advertisement campaign on television.

Cynthia S. Roper is Assistant Professor in the Department of Communication at Abilene Christian University. She has coauthored articles and book chapters on political debates, media coverage, and political advertising. Her current work deals with cross-cultural comparisons of content and effects of political advertising in the United States and Italy.

Margaret Scammell lectures in politics and communications studies at the University of Liverpool. She has published widely in the area of British election news coverage and party advertising and is the author of *Designer Politics* (forthcoming), which examines the use and impact of political marketing in Britain.

Holli A. Semetko is Associate Professor of Television/Radio/Film and Political Science at the S. I. Newhouse School of Public Communications and the Maxwell School of Citizenship and Public Affairs at Syracuse University. She completed her Ph.D. at The London School of Economics and Political Science; her dissertation was awarded the Samuel H. Beer Prize. She was a research fellow at the Joan Shorenstein Barone Center on the Press, Politics and Public Policy, at the Kennedy School of Government, at Harvard University in Spring 1994. She is coauthor of *The Formation of Campaign Agendas: A Comparative Analysis of Party and Media Roles in Recent American and British Elections* and *Germany's "Unity" Election: Voters and the Media in 1990*. She is currently writing *Campaigning on Television: News and Elections in Comparative Perspective*. She has also authored and coauthored numerous articles and book chapters on the U.S. and European news media elections, and on public opinion.

Karen Siune, a Doctor of Political Science, is a Professor of Political Science at the University of Aarhus, Denmark. She has studied party political use of broadcasting at national and European elections, and she has published several books and articles on election campaigns. Her most recent studies are about Danish referenda related to European integration. In addition, she studies European media politics as a member of the Euromedia Research Group.

Gadi Wolfsfeld is a Senior Lecturer at the Hebrew University of Jerusalem, with a joint appointment in the Department of Political Science and Communication. His research interests are focused in the field of political communication, and especially on the role of the news media in political conflicts. His most recent publication is a monograph published by the Joan Shorenstein Barone Center of the Kennedy School at Harvard University and is titled *The Role of the News Media in Unequal Political Conflicts: From the Intifada to the Gulf War and Back Again*.